Enterprise Information Management: The Next Generation of Enterprise Software

Mark J. Barrenechea
Tom Jenkins

ACKNOWLEDGEMENTS

This book is dedicated to the staff, partners, and customers of OpenText Corporation and its subsidiaries. This book is possible due to their combined efforts, innovation, and collective vision.

We would like to thank the staff, users, and partners of OpenText Corporation for their contributions to this book.

Special thanks go to writer and editor Rebecca Graves, editor Elizabeth Chestney-Hanson, and the following contributors:

Adam Howatson, Xavier Chaillot, Kevin Cochrane, Marten Den Haring, Kimberly Edwards, Lynn Elwood, Liz Kofsky, Agnes Kolkiewicz, Ankur Laroia, Debra Lavoy, Stephen Ludlow, Marci Maddox, Muhi Majzoub, John Price, Lubor Ptacek, Jason Weir, Gary Weiss, Brian Wick, Neil Wilson, Daniela Santarossa, Erin Schwab, Melissa Noto, Adam Binaut, Jeff Cowan, Keith Sauve, Craig Reidel, and Joe Dwyer.

We would also like to thank program managers Eric Bencina and Greg Beckman, as well as the contributors to the EIM white paper series. Their efforts and significant contributions made this book possible.

Specific resources are accredited in the Bibliography.

CONTENTS

Barrenechea, Mark J.

Jenkins, Tom

Enterprise Information Management: The Next Generation of Enterprise Software

First Printing, November 2013
Printed in Canada

First Edition

ISBN

ISBN 978-0-9936047-0-6

$29.00 U.S.

Published by

Open Text Corporation

275 Frank Tompa Drive

Waterloo, Ontario, Canada

N2L 0A1

(519) 888-7111

info@opentext.com

www.opentext.com

FOREWORD

The role of the CIO is evolving. This is, in part, because technologies that CIOs and IT executives commandeer are evolving—some faster than the enterprise can keep up with. The focus of the CIO has shifted from concerns about infrastructure, performance, cost reduction, risk control, and adoption to requirements for security, governance, virtualization, integration, the consumerization of IT, growth, competitive advantage, and innovation.

The responsibilities of the CIO hinge on mastering a multi-faceted and rich technology infrastructure that's greatest disrupters are cloud computing, consumerization, and mobile technologies. Today's CIO is required to deliver value at individual, departmental, and enterprise levels. This reaches beyond the firewall to an ability to create and capitalize on opportunity to implement technology solutions that build competitive advantage. In today's global economy, technology plays a pivotal role in helping organizations stand out in a crowded marketplace.

Technologies like social media and the way it is consumed (the consumerization of IT) are impacting the tech buying process. Increases in budget have been designated to areas of mobility, analytics, security, and collaboration. These areas align around enterprise content—content that must be created, shared, transformed, analyzed, and protected. Doing all of this well helps differentiate an organization from its competitors. Data and analytics, for example, add insight to improve business decisions and uncover new opportunities for business transformation.

Over the last 30 years, CIOs have been focused on automating processes and transactions for structured information with Enterprise Resource Planning (ERP). This book contends that CIOs will spend the next 30 years focused on automating processes and transactions for unstructured information with Enterprise Information Management (EIM).

Unstructured information is today's oil. Being able to capture, preserve, manage, and build information-oriented applications on this information is the next frontier of competitive business.

This book describes how EIM is the key—the force multiplier—that will help organizations unlock the untapped value of their information to realize true competitive advantage.

The core sets of technologies for Enterprise Content Management (ECM), Business Process Management (BPM), Customer Experience Management (CEM), Information Exchange, and Discovery form a comprehensive platform for Enterprise Information Management.

ECM directs information flows effortlessly from capture through archiving and disposition for more secure and consistent governance policies across any type of content in the enterprise.

BPM technologies empower employees, customers, and partners with smart processes applications and information to accelerate processes and build agile enterprises.

CEM solutions help organizations deliver exceptional experiences in response to market feedback and opportunities, accelerating time to market.

Information Exchange solutions empower people to accelerate and control how information is delivered—increasing the security and reliability of sensitive or complex communications.

Discovery applications derive value from growing volumes of content trapped in silos across an organization to help the enterprise transition from query to insight to action.

As an approach, a strategy, and an integrated suite, EIM optimizes the information flows that formulate the foundation of an organization's commercial operations. Enterprise Information Management unlocks the potential for superior quality and performance, reduced regulatory cost and risk, optimally efficient business processes, more engaging social and personalized experiences, and effective online commerce and information exchange—on premise, in the cloud, and on mobile devices.

Mark J. Barrenechea
President & CEO, OpenText Corporation

INTRODUCTION

When information workers are given the ability to connect, they create value by increasing each other's knowledge and decision-making ability. When exchanges like this are captured they become an enterprise resource that can be used to create value for all employees and impact the entire business.

In an increasingly social and mobile world, the means by which information can be shared are practically everywhere. While this proliferation in media means that there are more ways than ever to capture information and turn it into knowledge, it also means potential information silos, information loss, and information leaks. Within the enterprise setting, most companies today recognize this problem. They understand that unmanaged information creates chaos and that information silos pose a threat. According to a report by CMS Wire[1], 60 percent of companies cite "content chaos" as being the main driver behind deploying an ECM strategy. Despite that, most technology deployments do not address all islands of information. When that happens, organizations face gaps in compliance, process inefficiencies, and increased maintenance costs. Furthermore, as volumes of data increase so do the number and size of silos, which, in turn, adds to information chaos. For enterprises to realize value and turn information into a competitive advantage, those islands need to be addressed, managed, and controlled.

The efficient management of information can re-invigorate existing technology investments and increase user experience and retention thereby driving revenue without great increases in expense. As unstructured information becomes further digitized and connected throughout an organization, managing and analyzing that information becomes a critical competitive factor for organizations. For that to happen, information needs to be accessed across the enterprise, across its applications—be it Enterprise Resource Planning (ERP), Customer Relationship Management, or email—and across its information silos; it needs to be captured, possibly digitized, connected, exchanged, and processed; and it needs to be managed through records management and classification policies and metadata extraction. When organizations understand their information flows and build an information management strategy around that framework, they are best positioned to not only realize the best ROI but also to derive significant competitive advantage gained through efficient use of existing intellectual capital.

To those familiar with Porter's value chains, this may sound like a familiar scenario. Value chain enablement has formed the foundation of the enterprise computing industry and specifically ERP. But where ERP is focused on structured information, a whopping 90 percent is unstructured. To drive value from that 90 percent of unstructured information,

[1] David Roe, *"State of the ECM Industry 2010: Enterprises Still Battling Content Chaos"*, CMS Wire (May 2010), http://www.cmswire.com/cms/enterprise-cms/state-of-the-ecm-industry-2010-enterprises-still-battling-content-chaos-007576.php (accessed 6 Nov. 2012).

CHAPTER 1

ENTERPRISE INFORMATION MANAGEMENT

EIM: The Evolution of Information Management

"As of 2012, about 2.5 exabytes of data are created each day, and that number is doubling every 40 months or so. More data crosses the internet every second than were stored in the entire internet just 20 years ago." [3]

Information, in some form or another, has always been available to us, but never before has there been so much within our grasp, in so many different forms, and coming at us with such speed. The way we've been managing our enterprise information for 30 years is no longer sufficient. A new generation of information management is upon us, and it's not going away.

Information is only useful to us if we can understand it, and to understand it, we have to have access to it, put it in context, and compare it to what we already know. The way we make use of it is up to us, but the more information we have on which to base a decision, the better the decision. Andrew McAfee, a principal research scientist at MIT's Center for Digital Business, made a controversial statement about how most organizations have been relying on the HiPPO, the Highest Paid Person's Opinion, for direction regarding this influx of information.[4] That worked for some and didn't work for others, but regardless where you're sitting, with so much information today coming at us much faster and in different ways, we need to start basing decisions on hard data, not just intuition.

---

[3] Andrew McAfee and Erik Brynjolfsson, *"Big Data: The Management Revolution"*, Harvard Business Review (2012), *http://hbr.org/2012/10/big-data-the-management-revolution/ar/pr* (accessed 5 Nov. 2012).
[4] Andrew McAfee, *"Big Data, Bright Future"*, on24.com (2012), *http://event.on24.com/view/presentation/flash/EventConsoleNG.html* (accessed 5 Nov. 2012).

ERP is not enough

For the past 30 years, CIOs have focused on automating and improving processes related to structured information, such as contracts, customer data, transactional data, or project data. Their goal has been to collect this information and push it to the right people to have it analyzed and processed—and they have had to make this happen as quickly as possible for the organization to remain competitive. To manage this, CIOs have depended on Enterprise Resource Planning (ERP).

Gartner® Inc. defines ERP as "the ability to deliver an integrated suite of business applications. ERP tools share a common process and data model, covering broad and deep operational end-to-end processes, such as those found in finance, HR, distribution, manufacturing, service, and the supply chain."[5] Basically, ERP helps organizations find the answers to two important questions within their structured data: what happened and why did it happen?

However, there has always been information out there that ERP has not been able to capture. We call it unstructured information, and it has been growing exponentially for many years. Today, it is widely believed to represent about 80 percent[6] of available data-data we could be using to make smarter business decisions.

Unstructured information is the conversation around the structured information, such as email, business documents (word, pdf, fax documents), collaborative communications, social media, and audio, video, and graphical files, and within that unstructured data, we can find answers to some new questions: what is happening at this minute, what is likely to happen, and which events could affect the future? We need to ask these questions because if we don't, we'll be left behind and eventually out of business. We need to manage all the information we can get our hands on as quickly and as accurately as possible so that we can make the best business decisions possible. And, like the industry experts say[7], this isn't going away. Unstructured information is going to get bigger and faster and more powerful, and we need to be ready.

The deep web

Here is a staggering statistic: the public web, with more than eight billion pages, encompasses only four percent of the world's data—an incredibly small amount of information. The rest is behind firewalls, inside our organizations; this is called "the deep web". To the average internet user, it's unfathomable to believe that the ubiquitous consumer sites like Google® and Facebook® represent only a diminutive fraction of the sea of data stored in modern systems. It seems impossible that anything could be bigger than Google, but this dichotomy is a stark

---

[5] Gartner Inc., *"Enterprise Resource Planning (ERP)"*, IT Glossary, Gartner.com, *http://www.gartner.com/it-glossary/enterprise-resource-planning-erp/* (accessed 2 Dec. 2012).
[6] CNME, *"Big Data Deserves IT's Attention"*, CNME Online (Aug. 2012), *http://www.cnmeonline.com/insight/big-data-deserves-its-attention/* (accessed 18 Jan. 2012).
[7] Andrew McAfee, *"Big Data, Bright Future"*, on24.com (2012), *http://event.on24.com/view/presentation/flash/EventConsoleNG.html* (accessed 5 Nov. 2012).

reality. And accommodating these large, unstructured datasets and tending to their business requirements for compliance, access control and permissions, auditability, finability, and reusability is no mean feat.

Imagine if Google had to check the permissions of every user who issued a search against every web page or asset it had ever indexed to determine if that user could access data and view a specific set of results—all of which would be completed in real time, simultaneously tracking and auditing that user's activities against these data sets. Each user would have a specific view of the dataset, receiving results unique to their access and their relationship to every object it contained. It almost seems impossible—we would need something that captures, manages, and capitalizes on these intricate and amorphous mountains of unstructured information.

In the Google example above, the varying complexities of managing data for public and private consumption make it clear that managing the datasets of the deep web far is more complicated than those of the public internet. With 96 percent of available information behind a firewall, secure and locked inside a digital corporate vault, it's like it's floating beneath the surface like an iceberg—an iceberg so large that it's measured in zettabytes.

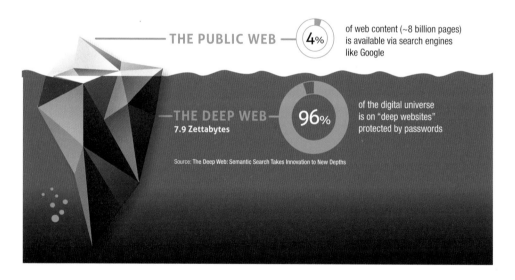

The deep web[8]

---

[8] Invention Machine, *"The Deep Web: Semantic Search Takes Innovation to New Depths"*, Goldfire Blog, *InventionMachine.com*, *http://invention-machine.com/the-Invention-Machine-Blog/bid/79363/The-Deep-Web-Semantic-Search-Takes-Innovation-to-New-Depths* (accessed 5 Oct. 2012).

The deep web is what companies run their business on every day. It's the archived supplier invoice, the contract repository, the Business Process Management (BPM) system that runs your operations, the PowerPoints® from your presentations, and every email you have ever sent on the job. In short, the unstructured data is the business. Banish this information and you banish the company. This information has untapped wealth and value that's only beginning to be understood.

Unstructured data requires more than ECM

Unstructured information has always existed in various formats, and we've been using Enterprise Content Management (ECM) solutions to get the most out of this data for about 15 years, but things have been changing. Quickly. We are outgrowing what ECM, on its own, can do for us. According to Gartner, ECM was designed "to create, store, distribute, discover, archive, and manage unstructured content (such as scanned documents, email, reports, medical images, and office documents), and ultimately analyze usage to enable organizations to deliver relevant content to users where and when they need it".[9] We certainly still need ECM to capture and manage all of this content, but with the advancements of social media, the various types of new files, and the unprecedented speed at which this information is being created, it takes new-generation solutions to capture today's unstructured data. "You're dealing with a huge amount of data, so you need a different set of tools and you need a different set of skills to make use of that world," states McAfee.[10]

The new tools exist today within something the industry calls Enterprise Information Management (EIM). Coupled with a solid business strategy designed to handle the increased speed with which information is arriving on our doorstep, the vast array of social media content, more and more compliance and security risks, and specific filtering needs to decipher the helpful information from the misleading or incorrect, EIM brings with it a new generation of information management. And this is all very good news. First of all, we can build on what we have already created with ERP and ECM, and secondly, this ocean of information that is coming our way offers incredible and never-before-seen opportunity for the enterprise—if we are prepared for it.

---

[9] Gartner Inc.,"*Enterprise Content Management (ECM)*", IT Glossary, Gartner.com, *http://www.gartner.com/it-glossary/enterprise-content-management-ecm/* (accessed 2 Oct. 2012).
[10] Andrew McAfee, "*Big Data, Bright Future*", *http://event.on24.com/view/presentation/flash/EventConsoleNG.html* (accessed 5 Nov. 2012).

VP, Strategic Marketing, OpenText

…On systems of record and systems of engagement

For the last couple of years, the terms "systems of record" and "systems of engagement" have been used regularly throughout the industry. The systems of record are the traditional solutions, such as ECM, that enterprises rely on to manage their critical information. The systems of engagement are those hip, new applications that are mostly focused on customer and employee engagement and experience—these put a lot of emphasis on the user adoption, mobility, social collaboration, and cloud deployment.

But the more I think about it, the more I'm convinced that this distinction is wrong. When I look at the current landscape, the traditional enterprise applications have all taken on the aspects of systems of engagement. Pretty much every application has a mobile story, and most enterprise software vendors have added social capabilities to their software and launched their cloud initiatives. In fact, I am not sure that there are many viable, "pure-play" systems of engagement left out there. Even the vendors who started in the systems-of-engagement world are rushing to add some systems-of-record features like a repository, security, and governance in an attempt to look more like real enterprise software.

In reality, there aren't two separate worlds: there are no systems of record over here and systems of engagement over there. What was referred to as systems of engagement are now the capabilities that have greatly improved the traditional enterprise applications. When done right, they can significantly augment the usability and adoption rates of enterprise software. But they are not a separate market. They are simply features. There is only one type of enterprise software today: Enterprise Information Management.

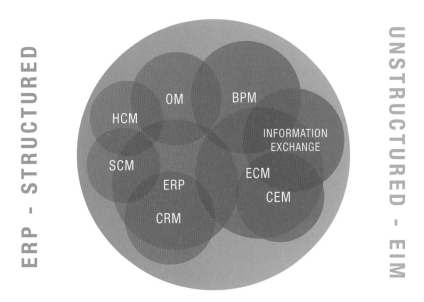

Enterprise information should be connected

To further explore the value inherent in unstructured information, consider your employees. An employee is potentially represented as a row or set of rows in an ERP database. That same employee is likely associated with hundreds or thousands of documents: expense information, receipts, correspondence, contracts, and myriad unstructured data.

Consider your organization's assets. An asset is also potentially a row or set of rows in an ERP database. But this asset could be an airplane, a train, a fleet, an energy plant, a pump, or a complex piece of equipment. Each of these items have hundreds of thousands of documents associated with them, from acquisition information, quality reports, maintenance, operation manuals, incident reports, all the way through to disposal records.

Alongside traditional content, document, and records management, the social interactions and information exchanges, business processes, and a vast array of other communicative data types combine with unstructured artifacts to form the full view of an enterprise's digital thread.

A combination of both structured and unstructured information formulates the deep web. These are the data types that few leverage but many collect. Imagine if we could tie our corporate memory to the communicative and unstructured data, which accompany its creation and utilization throughout its existence.

We envisage a future where this information is easily and seamlessly discovered, captured, managed, governed, secured, leveraged, and transformed into great value using information-based applications.

We call this discipline Enterprise Information Management (EIM). EIM data is by its nature unstructured and follows the required EIM functional technologies of Enterprise Content Management (ECM), Business Process Management (BPM), Customer Experience Management (CEM), Information Exchange, and Discovery.

EIM can be deployed on its own to capture, manage, and store enterprise information. It also integrates with ERP and additional information management systems to provide a "single version of the truth" for the enterprise. The closer and tighter the connections between EIM and ERP data, the more value can be extracted from it to lower costs for IT and reduce the risk of mismanaged information for the business.

You may have heard different definitions of EIM. We define it as "the discipline of discovering, managing, extracting value from, and building applications on top of unstructured enterprise information in order to maximize the value of this information, while minimizing its risks." The value is clear: new thinking and technologies will help us get the most out of our enterprise information.

Big data is not new

"Data deluge" and the promise of "big data" are increasingly featured in the news. It's as if the media just discovered big data, but big data is not new. The Global 5000 have been working with extremely large data sets for decades, applying agents to scour the mountains of information contained within their repositories to better understand their customers through demographic and purchasing identities, the way they transact with the company, and how they influence other buyers in their peer group. In fact, this is the original big data.

What's new is the technology base that allows us to understand big data sets. These technologies allow big data sets to fit into non-mechanical memory, leverage more powerful processors and grid configurations, and have operations work 100 times or even 1,000 times faster than was traditionally possible. This means that our big data sets are usable, and we can extract massive amounts of value from them—from demographic behavior and optimal product positioning recommendations to buyer propensity models and geographical market uptake patterns.

While many modern business intelligence capabilities are backward-looking, the promise of big data is the ability to make predictions based on it. Information can be viewed and analyzed, trends can be understood, and correlations can be plotted. The promise of big data is forward-looking. The challenge, of course, is finding the "diamonds in the rough". Content volume is doubling more rapidly than ever. Even more challenging than this are the automated tools that are creating new content without any human intervention, whatsoever. This system-generated data can easily put us awash in information that isn't vital to business operations. This is why the capacity to manage unstructured content in a central, authoritative EIM system is so critical.

Unstructured information has its challenges

Unstructured data has a lot of challenges, not unlike the challenges of structured information in the early days of ERP. The most prevalent challenges of unstructured information include (1) the fragmentation of information and processes, (2) the three "Vs" of information: variety, volume, and velocity, (3) security, and (4) governance.

These top four challenges, if left unsolved, can result in organizations that are slow to create change, projects that are harder to automate, increased tunnel vision among internal organizations and the silo effect, the introduction of business risk, and a higher cost of operations for IT.

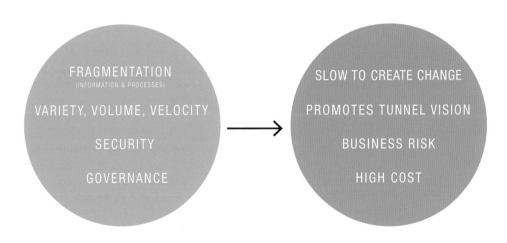

The consequences of mismanaged unstructured information

1. Fragmentation: data and processes

In the early days of ERP, there were hundreds of software providers, many bespoke systems, and in some cases, non-automated business functions. This created a large-scale fragmentation of processes and data. If a process is not automated, data and processes are fragmented. If processes and data live in different systems, data and processes are fragmented.

The better the process, the better the data; the better the data, the better the process—it's a basic, cyclical improvement. Over many years and many versions of the software, enterprise-wide systems created standard process models: Campaign to Quote, Quote to Order, Order to Cash, Procure to Pay. The fragmentation of unstructured information creates barriers for processes, leaves data stranded, unused, and at rest. Data at rest is data at risk. Fragmentation also promotes organizational tunnel vision as in "not my process; not my data."

CAPTURE 〉 DIGITIZE 〉 MANAGE 〉 PROCESS 〉 SEARCH 〉 ARCHIVE

- No defined interfaces - Not integrated
- Processes cannot be automated
- Data is stranded, unleveraged, at rest
- Wasted license and ps dollars
- Promotes tunnel vision

Capture to archive: an information flow

The best architectures integrate unstructured information into EIM data models to streamline processes across many disciplines. This represents the automation of 90 percent of an organization's information, which unleashes the power and value of unstructured data. To accomplish this, the 90 percent of unstructured information we have discussed must be understood through the five practices by which it can be managed: ECM, BPM, CEM, Information Exchange, and Discovery.

To better illustrate an information flow, consider Capture to Archive, a basic flow articulated graphically above. CIOs can either automate this entire information flow using software made to work together or by stitching together a dozen or so third-party providers. In an integrated EIM system, this information flow in the context of a vendor invoice exception resolution might look something like this:

1. Capture an invoice from a vendor.

   a. Business Process Management

   b. Enterprise Content Management

2. Execute an Accounts Payable (AP) process on this invoice.

   a. Business Process Management

3. Resolve a dispute on the invoice socially with the vendor. In this case, the AP clerk believes it to be a duplicate invoice with a new invoice number.

   a. Customer Experience Management

4. Fax the invoice with the issue back to a member of the vendor's accounts receivable team and keep a record of the "exception handling" communication.

   a. Information Exchange

5. Receive confirmation by email from the vendor that the invoice is correct and store the email message along with the exception-handling step in the BPM system.

   a. Business Process Management

   b. Enterprise Content Management

6. Perform a discovery on similar invoices to ensure this one is not a duplicate.

   a. Discovery

7. Close the process and archive the email to the EIM system, linked to the ERP transaction for future reference.

   a. Enterprise Content Management

   b. Business Process Management

If the systems required to handle this exception are integrated and structured to make the information flow as efficiently as possible for the employee, handling the exception is simple. If multiple records exist and there is no capacity to find similar unstructured artifacts easily, this duplicate resolution process can become very costly and inefficient for the organization.

2. Volume, variety, and velocity

The challenges of data fragmentation are further augmented by the nature of unstructured information, which can be described using three "Vs": volume, variety, and velocity. Enterprises need to pick information architectures to avoid the digital landfill of these three Vs. Information architectures help to manage the integration of data flows, the maintenance of an organization's data taxonomy, and how systems interact with each other.

VOLUME   VARIETY   VELOCITY

- Avoid the digital landfill
- Pick an information architecture
- Focus on what advances your business

The three "Vs" of unstructured information

Volume

The volume of unstructured information is extremely large. Some call it big data. The law of large numbers suggests that you need to pick a strategy on how to manage the volume. Do you try to manage it all? Do you try to manage it all for some period of time? Do you manage a subset of systems or data types? Do you set priorities and go after this a slice at a time?

EIM helps organizations to manage the swell of information in front of them. Through mechanisms like auto classification of content, semantic analysis, semantic navigation, search, and records management, an enterprise can stay afloat of the ever-flowing river of data their business needs to survive.

Variety

Structured information has its own language. One can speak this language to access the information and ask it questions or gain a response. That language is the Structured Query Language (SQL).

Unstructured information comes in many formats: doc, pdf, xls, tiff, wav, ppt, html, email, SharePoint® files, faxes, business processes; it has no single *lingua franca*. It is critical that EIM solutions be able to understand all of these different formats to "crack the code" and to connect to the information to gain insight, extract metadata, and to organize the information.

EIM creates a unified language by which one can speak to unstructured information.

Velocity

The volume of unstructured information is estimated by some to double every 90 days. In fact, there are automated programs now creating content! Based on sheer velocity, it's critical that organizations create priorities based on what data is important and what data is not, and that they control the pace of unstructured information retention and creation.

3. Security

Security is essential for unstructured information. This is reinforced by the public trials and tribulations of businesses where bad actors, inside or outside the company, have stolen or leaked critical information. This challenge is here to stay and will remain persistent.

The security threat exists at many layers: employees, projects, competitiveness, national security, reputation, brand, and in some cases, to the business itself. Consider some of the most recent publicized cases:

- HBGary Hacked
    - http://arstechnica.com/tech-policy/2012/03/the-hbgary-saga-nears-its-end/
- Nato Hacked
    - http://rt.com/usa/news/nato-anonymous-today-hackers/
- RSA Keys Breached
    - http://www.theregister.co.uk/2011/03/18/rsa_breach_leaks_securid_data/

Nortel had trade information leaked and went out of business as a result. WikiLeaks leaked classified information that intersected with National Security. BAE had Joint Strike Fighter designs stolen. MegaUpload went out of business. The examples are many and what these organizations had in common was the lack of a sound Enterprise Information Management strategy.

These security issues are not insoluble. They can be addressed by managing your information with EIM software. Properly deployed EIM solutions protect your data in the repository, at rest, over the air, and over the wire, and on the client through encryption, permission and access control, audit facilities, and numerous other stringent security capabilities all designed to deal with the complexities and risk associated with managing unstructured enterprise information.

4. Governance, compliance, and risk management

The requirements for governance and compliance will only increase, as governments create more and more laws and legislation. Creating a solid information architecture with EIM ensures security, governance, compliance, and risk management. By automating processes and integrating information around governance and compliance, organizations can transform risk into opportunity by being able to react to changes in regulations more quickly than their competitors.

Often, the ECM practice of EIM is implemented to help organizations adhere to regulatory requirements and mitigate the risk associated with the long-term management of documents, contracts, cases, and the other assets generated through their normal operations. This practice may be implemented voluntarily to leverage the intellectual property of the organization and mitigate risk or by regulatory requirement such as:

• **Rules 17a-3 and 17a-4 of the Securities Exchange Act of 1934** - "All records required to be kept by the Act and by Commission regulations shall be kept for a period of five years from the date the record was made..."

• **ISO 30300:2011** - "Managing records using an MSS supports cost-effective operational processes, such as ... information retrieval, information re-use, litigation and due diligence."

• **FDA Title 21 CFR Part 11** - "Persons who use closed systems to create, modify, maintain, or transmit electronic records shall employ procedures and controls designed to ensure the authenticity, integrity, and, when appropriate, the confidentiality of electronic records..."

"'Vampire data': Don't get bitten by data you didn't know you had."[11]

Each corporate information asset represents both risk and value to today's organization. Every email is a potential smoking gun and every contract the potential solution to a costly litigation. At the same time, unstructured information is today's oil and being able to capture, preserve, manage, and capitalize on it is the next frontier of competitive business. EIM acts as a force multiplier in helping organizations unlock the untapped value of unstructured information, while complying with regulatory requirements and ensuring that corporate data is safe.

Information is power

This is where it all gets very interesting. We've come from the discovery, capture, and digitization of information and moved through controlling it, extracting value, and providing insight, to building applications on top of it all. With the foundations of EIM well laid out, and with unstructured enterprise information well managed, a company's information becomes powerful through the use of a new category of enterprise software: information-oriented applications.

---

[11]Mike Miliard, *"Vampire data and 3 other cyber security threats for 2013"*, (31 Dec. 2012), Government Health IT, *http://www.govhealthit.com/news/vampire-data-and-3-other-cyber-security-threats-2013* (accessed 12 Oct. 2012).

UNSTRUCTURED ENTERPRISE INFORMATION

.pdf .ppt .doc .xls | fax | JULY 31

DISCOVER. CONNECT. CAPTURE. DIGITIZE.

CONTROL CONTENT	EXTRACT VALUE	PROVIDE INSIGHT	BUILD APPS
Records Management	ERP, CRM	Share	Cases
Classification	SCM, PLM	Social	Contracts
Metadata	Email	Search	Customers
Security	Other Repositories	Intelligence	Invoicing
			Approvals

PROCESS & DATA ORCHESTRATION

INFORMATION ARCHITECTURE

It's all about applications

Based on the challenges of unstructured information, when we consider the variety (as one of the three "Vs"), the ability to discover, connect to, capture, and digitize unstructured information within an Enterprise Information Architecture is vital. An enterprise with sound control over the variety of data within their walls and a robust Enterprise Information Architecture can start to deploy or build applications, which are purposefully designed to solve the problems of its workforce. The more effectively we can collect, find, and process information in the context of an application for our end users, the more effective we make the organization itself.

Follow the information

With an Information Architecture in place, unlocking the value of your major data objects through information-based, smart applications is the next step. We see a variety of major categories for unstructured data models: Suppliers, Employees, Customers, Assets, Financial, Cases, Projects, and Contracts—all worth building applications on top of.

SUPPLIERS	EMPLOYEES	CUSTOMERS	ASSETS
Orders	Recruiting	Correspondence	Physical or Digital
Invoices	Retention/Advancement	History/Transactions	Acquisitions to Disposition
Materials & Returns	Retirement	Install Base/Revenue	Management to Revenue

FINANCIAL	CASES/PROJECTS	CONTRACTS	...AND MORE
Audit, Compliance	Approvals	Legal & Templates	eMail & ERP
Regulatory, Fraud	Claims, Loans	Terms and Entitlement	CAD
Collections, CAPEX	Quality, Projects	Renewals and Revenue	Correspondence

Information-based applications

The list of potential information-based applications is inexhaustible; the only limit is the capacity to gather and manage unstructured information and the requirements of the business.

Linking EIM to business value

The "big picture" is all about linking enterprise information to business value. If you can't link enterprise information to business value, it's not worth automating processes. Whereas ERP and other structured data-source platforms have been optimized over the past 30 years, EIM is new and rich with business opportunity.

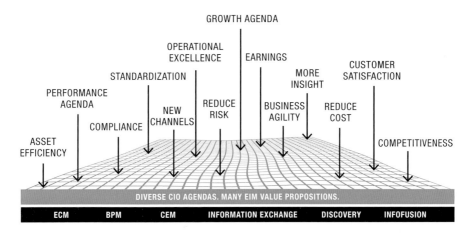

Creating business value with EIM

Over the last 20 years, OpenText has been helping tens of thousands of businesses unlock the value of their information. With two decades of experience and proven results, what we have learned is that corporate agendas vary greatly based on situational analysis and that CIO agendas can be diverse. With that said we have categorized a variety of value propositions through our two decades of customer successes.

Business Impacts				
ECM	**BPM**	**CEM**	**INFORMATION EXCHANGE**	**DISCOVERY**
Drive Information Reuse	Improve Process Efficiency	Ensure Brand Consistency	Discover Unexpected Information	Ensure Litigation Readiness
Locate Subject Matter Experts	Reduce Time to Market	Improve Message Effectiveness	Discover Unexpected Relationships	Actionable Information
Ensure Content Authenticity	Increase Customer Retention	Reach Audience Cost-Effectively	Foster Information Sharing	Speed Up Decisions
Ensure Content Security	Adapt to Business Changes	Grow Customer Acquisition	Reduce Digital Storage Costs	Information Action
Preserve Knowledge	Handle Organizational Changes	Improve Customer Service	Mobile File Access	Automate Knowledge Capture
Protect Intellectual Property	Reduce Transaction Cost	Web Management	File Share	Crisis Management

ERP Integration	Dynamic Case Management	Mobile Tools	Secure Share	Search
Improve Quality	High Volume Imaging	Mobile Knowledge	Forms Management	eDiscovery
Enable Compliance	Business Planning and Modeling	Web Content Management	Smart Billing	Content Analytics
Ensure Compliance	Process-Centric Applications	Media Management	Fax and Document Distribution	Semantic Navigation
Content Management		Social Communities	Cloud-Based File Sharing	Auto-Classification
Record Management		Customer Communications	Capture and Recognition	
Email Management		Portals	Managed File Transfer	
Learning Management		Mobile Web	Data Integration	

Unleashing the power of information

We've outlined the principles of the deep web, how enterprise information—both structured and unstructured—is all connected, the challenges of unstructured information, and the major opportunities to extract the most value from your enterprise information—after all, EIM is ultimately about unleashing the power of your information. So where do we go from here? What are the major steps in your EIM journey?

The EIM journey starts at capture and digitization and then progresses to building smart information-based applications. EIM is comprised of technologies for

1. **Enterprise Content Management (ECM)** solutions manage information throughout its lifecycle and improve business productivity, all while mitigating the compliance and legal risk and controlling the costs of growing volumes of content.

2. **Business Process Management (BPM)** solutions empower employees, customers, and partners with the processes and information they need to produce signature experiences and significant business results.

3. **Customer Experience Management (CEM)** solutions help organizations exceed customer expectations, reach new markets, and provide superior experiences across all digital touch-points.

4. **Information Exchange** solutions facilitate efficient, secure, and compliant data exchange inside and outside the enterprise.

5. **Discovery** solutions organize and visualize all relevant enterprise information to make it possible for business users to quickly find answers to questions and optimize the business impact of their decisions.

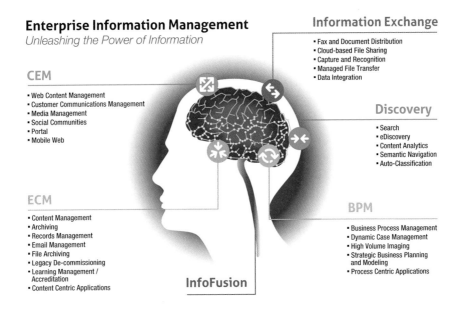

Enterprise Information Management
Unleashing the Power of Information

Information Exchange
- Fax and Document Distribution
- Cloud-based File Sharing
- Capture and Recognition
- Managed File Transfer
- Data Integration

CEM
- Web Content Management
- Customer Communications Management
- Media Management
- Social Communities
- Portal
- Mobile Web

Discovery
- Search
- eDiscovery
- Content Analytics
- Semantic Navigation
- Auto-Classification

ECM
- Content Management
- Archiving
- Records Management
- Email Management
- File Archiving
- Legacy De-commissioning
- Learning Management / Accreditation
- Content Centric Applications

BPM
- Business Process Management
- Dynamic Case Management
- High Volume Imaging
- Strategic Business Planning and Modeling
- Process Centric Applications

InfoFusion

EIM powered by five major categories; OpenText InfoFusion helps pull it all together

1. Enterprise Content Management (ECM)

ECM plays a key role in helping us manage this explosive growth of information across the enterprise and minimize the costs and risks related to unmanaged content. Basically, it manages any content object within an enterprise—electrical, digital, even physical content, …anything that can have a barcode attached to it. ECM solutions are a set of interrelated and integrated software products that manage the entire lifecycle of information—from creation and management to storage, distribution, archiving, and disposition—across the whole organization. And they do so while ensuring security policies and regulatory compliance mandates are followed.

There are several major reasons for an organization to look to ECM. One is to meet compliance rules. There are more than 100,000 compliance regulations across the globe just for content, and with so many different types of data today, it is no longer acceptable to count only some of your content. Another reason is to prepare for litigation and/or auditing. ECM enables an organization to find the right data and assemble it for a court of law or to quickly create a true chain of custody for a piece of information. And yet another top driver is to create a single source of the truth rather than deal with several versions of a document in several different locations.

The different types of assets ECM manages include office and PDF documents, CAD diagrams and models, contracts, case records, templates, faxes, blogs, and the entire stretch of unstructured data types that users create every day for everything from team meeting presentations to the almost 170 million emails that are sent every minute.[12]

ECM uses document and records management, email management, content archiving, search, contracts management, and other information governance capabilities to manage all of this information and produce significant and tangible results.

For example, one of the world's largest integrated energy companies was spending a great deal of time and money managing critical content throughout its lifecycle and was incurring tremendous costs related to outsourcing legal discovery. After employing an ECM strategy to govern content from creation to disposition, along with an early case assessment tool for the legal department, the company saved both time and money, improved efficiency, and strengthened their compliance program. Reliance on third-party legal teams during discovery has almost been completely eliminated; users spend less time applying retention policies and other information management tasks, which allows them to work on actual projects, and the overall storage and management costs around business content have been dramatically reduced.

ECM helps organizations take advantage of their data and use it to compete in the market, instead of allowing it to remain idle, at risk, and expensive to maintain.

Building on top of ECM as part of an EIM strategy ensures all content is managed safely and securely and helps unlock the untapped value of your organization's unstructured enterprise information.

2. Business Process Management (BPM)

The level of operational effectiveness and efficiency on which an organization runs can be determined through business processes. ERP systems are often at the core of transactional processes within most organizations—from financials and human resources to supply chain, customer relationship management, invoicing, accounts payable, and other critical aspects—and they do an excellent job of executing process and serving as the "system of record," but with the pace of business, the growing need to harness agility and adaptability to spur innovation, and pressure to continuously improve business processes to gain and

[12] The Marketing Bit, "Online for One Minute", TheMarketingBit.com, http://www.themarketingbit.com/infographics/online-for-one-minute/ (accessed 13 Oct. 2012).

maintain competitive advantage, organizations need more.

Gartner defines BPM as "a management discipline that treats business processes as assets that directly contribute to enterprise performance by driving operational excellence and business agility."[13] It's clear that this tool is about more than going through the motions of a process: it's about noticing where the bottlenecks are, if there's a black hole your resources are disappearing into, and how often performance meets organizational goals. BPM also ensures repeatable, structured customer service or case management, which are absolutely crucial to establishing a positive, memorable customer experience while maintaining compliance.

Like all assets, these processes need to be tracked in order to find the right balance of resource investment, effective performance monitoring, sound maintenance, and life cycle management that can drive operational excellence. The most critical areas that determine BPM success, however, are actually nontechnical issues, such as changing people's attitudes and assumptions based on building a new frame of reference or perspective for measuring business performance. These essential factors are as follows:

- Understanding the processes using business process modeling
- Using appropriate process metrics to measure process performance
- Analyzing processes to create options for performance improvements
- Convincing the stakeholders that the processes might need to be changed

Implementing sound BPM practices enable you to understand, monitor, and account for how your business is conducted. Whether managing millions of high-volume processes per day in cases like claims management or regulatory compliance or running a lower volume of extremely high-value procedures such as commercial lending approval or contract management, BPM allows companies to understand their operations, track the information that flows through those operations, recover costs, and optimize efficiencies.

The core transactional capabilities of BPM execute processes, and the next-generation tools it provides continuously improve them. The results of successfully extending BPM across the enterprise to allow for agile process improvement and strategic business modeling can be startling.

For example, the financial services arm of a leading car manufacturer receives more than 50,000 time-sensitive auto financing contract packages every month. Traditional transactional systems and ERP were unable to manage the workload and, more importantly, didn't meet customer service standards and compliance mandates. With dynamic case management and an advanced process management framework to complement core transaction systems, the organization has been able to process about 30 percent more

---

[13] Gartner Inc., *"Business Process Management"*, IT Glossary, Gartner.com, *http://www.gartner.com/it-glossary/business-process-management-bpm/* (accessed 2 Oct. 2012).

contract packages per month with increased accuracy. What's more is that they are doing it with 26 percent fewer staff. Another key benefit, according to the organization's head of contract processing, has been a significant improvement in customer satisfaction with the organization's lending and financing experience. This has improved both top- and bottom-line performance for the business by way of cost reduction, increased sell-through opportunities, and efficiencies.

BPM enables organizations to capture the output of processes like sold product, a resolved insurance claim, or a new drug taken to market, and it also provides a mechanism through which to assemble the context of the decisions and outputs of those processes.

Integrating BPM with the other EIM core technologies delivers significant business value from the vast amounts of unstructured information generated daily by organizations the world over.

3. Customer Experience Management (CEM)

An organization needs to have a customer presence to conduct business, and the better the customer experience, the stronger the business. CEM is a set of technologies that helps your organization offer the customer more than expected, reach new markets, and provide outstanding experiences across all digital touch-points. It includes the presentation, assembly, and interaction of your organization's information with your customer. CEM generates return from a corporate identity by helping to project a strong brand, conduct electronic commerce, and manage media assets. In fact, a company's survival depends on the proper management of the customer's full experience—from visiting the website and mobile app to consuming media or conducting a transaction and consuming brand material. So whether it's presenting a portal view of the systems within an organization to simplify and multiply their use throughout the employee base or managing your web and media assets, CEM creates and manages your organization's "presence" inside your enterprise and outside in the market.

Gartner defines CEM as "the practice of designing and reacting to customer interactions to meet or exceed customer expectations and, thus, increase customer satisfaction, loyalty, and advocacy."[14] Although some experts believe that the correlation between customer experience and loyalty are "likely overinflated,"[15] a relationship certainly does exist and they do depend on each other.

Business itself is built on relationships. To succeed, organizations must successfully reach out to new markets while fostering positive relationships with their customers, partners, and employees. This requires communicating consistent corporate positioning and messaging internally and externally online, in print, or via multimedia. CEM helps to create a richer, more interactive online experience across many channels, including websites,

---

[14] TGartner Inc., *"Customer Experience Management"*, IT Glossary, *http://www.gartner.com/it-glossary/customer-experience-management-cem/* (accessed 2 Oct. 2012).
[15] Bob Hayes, *"Is the Importance of Customer Experience Overinflated?"*, CustomerThink.com, *http://www.customerthink.com/blog/is_the_importance_of_ customer_experience_overinflated* (accessed 30 Sep. 2012).

mobile devices, and social networks without sacrificing the organization's requirements for sound and defensible information governance. CEM ensures the consistency of brand communication and messaging by effectively managing all brand assets throughout their entire lifecycle, automatically and on a self-service basis to improve efficiency and reduce errors in brand communication. Protecting intellectual property is another key element of brand management, and CEM technology, with digital rights management and other security features, ensures consistent and easy use of assets across digital channels while preventing unauthorized access and distribution. Broadly speaking, it gives the enterprise control.

For example, one of the world's best-known video game producers needed to control its brand globally, make assets easy to find and distribute, and create a consistent look, feel, and voice for all communications, campaigns, and programs around the world. Before deploying CEM, the company struggled with off-brand communications reaching consumers, issues with localization, and major brand-standard infractions. Now, with a central repository for all digital content, the organization can ensure the secure access and distribution of materials and quickly and easily roll out new campaigns.

The Social Enterprise is a vital part of CEM. With so many consumer social networks available, such as Facebook and LinkedIn®, employees are demanding access to the digital conversations that consumer social sites provide them. The challenge is that these social interactions can represent both value and risk to every organization. While they present new opportunities for engagement and productivity, much of the content generated is not moderated or managed by IT and falls outside of governance policies.

The loss of intellectual property or leaked information is also a huge risk for today's Social Enterprise. CEM provides a safe social harbor for organizations, which enables employees, customers, partners, and the public to interact socially in a forum that can be archived, moderated, managed, and explored for both value and risk. Social Enterprise capabilities also deliver a medium through which the organization can customize their social experience to suit their objectives and integrate with today's colloquial consumer platforms. Spanning this bridge in a way that is both compelling for end users and safe for the organization is critical in a world where the search volume on social networks has surpassed those on pure-play public search engines.

Your social organization, how it is portrayed, the management of the assets that portray it, the customer's digital experience, and the handling of their commerce—all of this is based on unstructured information and all of it is incredibly valuable. When customers engage directly with the company brand, conversion rates and customer loyalty soar. CEM allows marketing departments to transform the smallest exchange into a source of productivity, innovation, and revenue. It makes it possible to continually measure and refine programs using web and social analysis, sentiment analysis, and customer analytics to discover new opportunities and create relationships through self-service solutions, targeted customer correspondence, and communities.

CEM requires a combination of software technologies designed to make the most of your online marketing strategy and campaigns, manage your global brand, optimize social media, and produce effective customer communications.

4. Information Exchange

Information Exchange is a set of solutions that allows people inside and outside an organization to efficiently and securely exchange conversational data while the actual organization maintains compliancy, which means chat all you like—your bases are covered. You're safe. This data includes anything from electronic faxes and cloud services to Electronic Data Interchange (EDI) and large managed-file transfers. But Information Exchange isn't about managing the actual content objects (the document or email files): it's about managing the living and breathing conversations and communications that happen every day around an enterprise in various electronic formats.

A great deal of organizational data is exchanged during internal conversations between employees and external conversations among employees, customers, and partners. In fact, an information exchange can be described as a payload of data, moved between one or more parties for the purposes of communication, sharing, and/or transacting business. These services are the lifeblood of an organization's communications and generate truly massive amounts of data each day. This creates a very particular challenge: it's not practical to harvest, capture, and store every exchange an organization conducts, and it's not possible to manually sort through which data is worth storing and which data should be tossed. Often these exchanges sit and wait until their information payloads can be sorted through, but that's risky—important information could be missed because it's sitting in this virtual waiting room, by the time the information is sorted it could be out of date, or the "waiting room" could be compromised.

Usually, Information Exchange is tied to other practices such as ECM with very specific collection parameters that automate, archive, and monitor the exchanges. This way, the enterprise can maximize on its information without the impossible overhead of manually sorting or the dangers of leaving the data unattended or lost to a transient state. It allows information to flow at the speed of business and safely moves the data from where it is to where it needs to be—regardless of where it lives or what devices it is on—from anywhere at anytime and from user to user, company to customer, agency to constituent.

For example, one of the largest neuroscience research facilities in North America needed to overcome the barriers of location, department, and scientific discipline to provide the infrastructure necessary for communication and collaboration between researchers. It created a highly intuitive and secure web environment that allows for easy sharing of information and online collaboration, and this has accelerated time-to-market for new methods and pushed research projects to completion much faster than was possible even a few years ago. With the institute's new online collaborative workspaces, researchers are able to focus less on managing information and protecting its distribution for collaborative purposes and almost exclusively on discovering, developing, and delivering new treatments for brain disorders.

Information Exchange also helps protect against internal information leaks and cyber-attack. It helps find the gems in all the conversation that happens within and around the enterprise, and it protects what it finds.

5. Discovery

There are three ways to make decisions: (1) guess from somewhere in the dark, (2) hope for the best with half of the information, or (3) understand all of the information and what it means when it's together. To make inspired business decisions, we need to know all the facts. All too often, important decisions are made, and then, too late, more information turns up from a far-off silo that would have had a significant impact on the decision. Discovery is a set of solutions that links structured and unstructured information across multiple formats and sources, such as ERP systems, document management repositories, business applications, websites, and more, across the enterprise and delivers it in a tidy package. Organizing, combining, comparing, and visualizing information in new ways offers fresh insight to everyday business, which leads to new ways of thinking, and this provides organizations with a leg-up on the competition. It helps identify current and possible relationships, lurking risks, and new opportunities for growth.

Discovery analyzes large volumes of information in real-time with incredible accuracy. Not only does it capture, combine, and convert data across silos and formats, it automatically puts information into context and groups it for users, making query and analysis work much more efficient. It provides progressive search, semantic analytics and navigation, and categorization, all designed to mine, extract, and present the true value of enterprise information for decision making and analysis.

An example of this can be found at one of Canada's leading newspapers that leverages discovery solutions to deliver exceptional information search and exploration experiences on its website. In the past, readers complained about poor search and retrieval of information, a "clumsy" experience, and an overall inability to find what it was they were after in a timely manner. This had negative implications for the business, namely that visitors (potential subscribers) would move on to another source where they could get the news they were after, and this led to a loss of ad revenue as the visit times shortened and advertisers felt that readers needed a better experience or they were less likely to visit their site or act on their promotional offers.

The organization overhauled their website with a discovery solution to provide the semantic search and navigation capabilities needed to keep visitors on the site longer and provide a rich, meaningful search experience. Readers now report being able to find what they are looking for much faster and seem to like the "suggestive search" capabilities on the site that provide context and "further reading" on a predictive, proactive basis. Overall satisfaction and click-through rates for advertising have increased substantially and readership and "time-on-website-per-visit" rates are increasing steadily.

This non-intrusive solution eliminates the need for business users to sort and classify growing amounts of content or even, in some cases, know what they are searching for—the solution puts things in context and makes connections that might not have occurred to users. Managers and employees rely on information to do their jobs, and having these resources indexed and accessible significantly improves efficiency and employee satisfaction.

In addition, the expense and time that goes into traditional legal or other information discovery is very high. Having a set of tools available to filter through and make accurate the data sets retrieved in a discovery represents immediate savings for an organization. And with the incredible amount of data arriving and being created at organizations today, full text search simply can no longer sift through the mountains of information quickly or accurately enough.

Volumes of uncategorized content can be automatically analyzed to help highlight relevant topics, summaries, sentiments, and relationships to deliver more enriched information. Content analytics allows the enterprise to organize and interpret data streams in new and repeatable ways. And along with metadata, Discovery solutions like semantic analysis allow for the integration of data for a variety of reporting and analytic uses that provide insights for more effective business management. This set of technologies organizes and presents information from the enterprise to help users find answers to their questions, make better decisions, excite creativity, and make inspired business decisions to create competitive business advantage.

Twitter: @ankuronEIM

Ankur Laroia, VP of Global Premier Accounts, OpenText

…On antifragile organizations and the basics of EIM

I think we can all agree that volatility is the new normal. Organizations that don't react quickly to change are the most vulnerable to stressful and evolving market conditions. These same organizations usually have trouble accessing their information in a timely manner—or at all. Antifragile organizations are those that leverage information to manage—and even profit from—the disruptive forces in their ecosystems. The doctrine of EIM, effectively employed by a strategic CIO, can rapidly put an organization on the road to achieving antifragile characteristics. EIM and the strategic CIO are key catalysts in the new economy where business is becoming social, ideas and information are free flowing, and the lines between work, home, and play are constantly overlapping.

Enterprise Information Management (EIM) is a computing doctrine that supports a transformative leap in the way that enterprises organize, integrate, share, and describe one of their most important assets: intellectual capital, also known as information. Information, one can argue, is the second most important asset that corporations possess, right behind the people that create the information: the knowledge workers. The tenets of the EIM doctrine are not revolutionary—they are the result of an evolving, volatile market where new threats and business models appear and quickly harvest market share from traditional players that are slow to react and adapt. Fundamentally, EIM modalities strive to improve business performance and agility by increasing business insight, catalyzing operational efficiency, increasing transparency between organizational silos, departments, and divisions, and most importantly, being information centric, i.e., putting information to work by making it accessible and operational.

EIM focuses on a layered model. It begins with both the Business Analyst and the Developer. Coupled to both these roles is a set of robust development tools and extensible information-driven architecture. This is the foundation of EIM. On top of this core layer, rest five other pillars that make up the EIM model: Business Process Management (BPM), Enterprise Content Management (ECM), Customer Experience Management (CEM), Information Exchange, and Discovery.

EIM technologies have the potential to foster efficient business operations, reduce risk, and lower costs for regulatory compliance. The platform is inclusive of the entire ecosystem and value chain. It provides for intimate engagement with customers, suppliers, employees, and partners along with connectivity to the social enterprise. Unstructured data makes up 80 percent of corporate storage. By using the EIM framework to capture, manage, store, and operationalize unstructured data and turn it into actionable information, businesses can transform their information into strategic assets. Organizations that have the ability to leverage this insightful information in meaningful ways to exploit the business environment around them will become nimble and strong and outperform their competitors.

The evolution of Information Management

In many ways the future has arrived, and the five building blocks of EIM can help us meet it standing up. Information is different in almost every way in today's world, and if we don't rethink our data management strategy soon, we might end up taking a fall. EIM helps us prepare for and equip ourselves with new techniques to capture, store, access, analyze, and apply information in and around the enterprise to make better informed decisions, more efficient exchanges, improved productivity, and exceptional customer experiences. The right information still gets to the right people at the right time, but now it gets there faster and more accurately despite today's added challenges of mobility, the Cloud, increased regulations, IT consumerization, frequent security breaches, and an onslaught of structured and unstructured information coming at us every day.

Experts estimate that 80-90 percent of our enterprise information is unstructured[16], and a shocking 90 percent of that is unmanaged.[17] So…exactly which information are we managing? The same stuff we've been managing for years and years. It's true: we're doing all right with that, but for how long? (It's starting to fall apart already with the amount and variety of data coming at us every day.) And imagine what we could do if we had all of our information at our fingertips…everything laid out, organized, up to date, and in context.

EIM is the onramp to drive value

Investment in traditional structured systems like Enterprise Resource Planning Financials, Human Capital Management, Order Management, Supply Chain Management, Customer Relationship Management, and others is now meeting diminishing returns because it has been optimized. We've gotten almost all the value we can out of them. The discipline of EIM is our onramp to driving value from the untapped 90 percent of unstructured information in the enterprise.

In a recent survey, it was found that 95 percent of organizations agree "strong information management is critical for business success."[18] And with the amount of information that will have to be managed expected to climb by 50 percent over the next 10 years, the top concern of CIOs is information growth and making sense of it all once they have it.[19]

There is no avoiding this new generation of information. And every enterprise that is interested in survival needs a strategy that includes business value drivers, industry best practices, and an EIM plan that includes

1. ECM to manage your enterprise information throughout its lifecycle,

2. BPM to empower users with the right information at the right time,

---

[16] Mike Lynch, *"Data Wars: Unlocking the Information Goldmine"*, Business, BBC News, *http://www.bbc.co.uk/news/business-17682304* (accessed 4 Oct. 2012).

[17] Doculabs, *"Quantifying Return on Investment for ECM: A Methodology"*, Doculabs.com (2009), *http://www.doculabs.com/wp-content/uploads/downloads/2011/12/A-Doculabs-White-Paper-Quantifying-ROI-for-ECM1.pdf* (accessed 10 Oct. 2012).

[18] Forbes Insights, *"Managing Information in the Enterprise: Perspectives for Business Leaders"*, Forbes Insight (2009), *http://fm.sap.com/data/UPLOAD/files/Managing%20Information%20in%20the%20Enterprise%20Perspectives%20for%20Business%20Leaders.pdf* (accessed 24 Oct. 2012).

[19] Mark McDonald, *"2012 CIO Agenda"*, Gartner Inc., *http://www.gartner.com/technology/cio/cioagenda.jsp* (accessed 8 Oct. 2012).

3. CEM to help organizations exceed customer experiences and expectations,

4. Information Exchange to facilitate safe and secure data exchange inside and outside the organization, and

5. Discovery to organize and contextualize enterprise information and bring it to life.

With these sets of technologies, your organization can run the way it needs to run. There is no other enterprise like your enterprise. That's why you're still in business. And that's why you need maximum flexibility to carry out your unique strategy, to change your direction if you need to, and to react to the world around you. This is what you need in your toolbox to not only work in this new generation of information with all its volume and speed and surprises but to turn it into a world-class opportunity from which you never look back.

CHAPTER 2

ENTERPRISE CONTENT MANAGEMENT

CHAPTER 2

Enterprise Content Management: Governing the Power of Information

"Information workers, who comprise about 63 percent of the US workforce, are each bombarded with 1.6 gigabytes of information on average every day through emails, reports, blogs, text messages, calls, and more..." [20]

Unstructured information is at the core of any enterprise. And as we're learning, it's also one of the most valuable yet difficult assets to manage. Unstructured information represents 90 percent or more of an organization's data, and over the last decade, worldwide information has grown exponentially. The five exabytes of information that existed globally in 2003 now represents the amount of content we create every two days.[21] It truly is an explosion of information, and the effective management of it has become a key differentiator in today's competitive economy. While the growth of unstructured information provides an opportunity to set us apart from the competition, it also represents significant risk and cost for every business. Organizations need to address the explosion of data as a key competitive challenge as they face a digital realm that is growing in size, complexity, and value.

Information governance in the context of an ECM solution helps address the growth of information in all formats. The need to develop information governance policies that encompass the entire organization is extremely important and, in fact, a requirement for the effective creation, management, storage, classification, retention, and disposal of unstructured assets. Bringing the right information together within business processes and systems is critical in creating an efficient enterprise. Organizations need to transform how groups and business units work together. The way employees and these units interact is fundamentally changing and will continue to change, and we need solutions that are adaptable. Whether they provide new solutions for capturing, managing, searching, or analyzing information, ECM technologies must be easy to use, scalable, and adaptable to constantly changing business needs.

ECM is the fundamental practice of managing and extracting value from unstructured enterprise information.

---

[20] Andrea Coombes, *"Don't You Dare Email this Story"*, MarketWatch, The Wall Street Journal (17 May 2009), *http://online.wsj.com/article/SB124252211780027326.html* (accessed 3 Dec. 2012).

[21] M.G. Siegler, "Eric Schmidt: Every 2 Days We Create as Much Information as We Did up to 2003", Tech Crunch, 4 Aug. 2010, http://techcrunch.com/2010/08/04/schmidt-data/ (accessed 10 Sep. 2013).

The ECM and EIM paradigm

What is the practice of ECM, and how does it fit within the broader discipline of EIM?

ECM is the technology used for managing information throughout its lifecycle to improve business productivity, while mitigating the risk and controlling the costs of growing volumes of content within the enterprise. ECM manages information assets, such as Microsoft® Office® and pdf documents, email, CAD diagrams, contracts, case records, social and web content, and even paper documents—from the time this information is captured or digitized to when it's used in active collaboration, archived for long-term corporate memory or defensibly deleted. ECM ensures that information is current, protected, and governed within corporate and industry regulations.

EIM is made up of five principal practices: Enterprise Content Management (ECM), Business Process Management (BPM), Customer Experience Management (CEM), Information Exchange, and Discovery. Whereas ECM manages the unstructured content of an organization, EIM is the overarching discipline that brings unstructured content together to drive more value from content. In other words, EIM is concerned with creating efficient messages, identifying the receivers of this information, and understanding their information needs so that the receiver of information can take the appropriate action (or inaction) in a timely manner. ECM focuses on the capture and management of content, regardless of how it's used within the enterprise—ECM provides the foundational core for governing enterprise information.

The content lifecycle

Information is a critical enterprise asset, and it must be governed and appropriately described in all stages of its lifecycles. Simply managing content as it's generated and ingested into your organization's business processes is not enough. The ability to access this information is paramount and goes beyond simply viewing the correct version of a document. At a business level, the content should be managed in line with business objectives, and achieving this dynamic is where the tools and technologies of ECM come into play.

Content must also be managed within regulations that require the protection and preservation of content. As the number and complexity of regulations grow, content needs to be effectively managed by an ECM system, rather than placing the burden of these regulations on employees.

ECM facilitates and manages the complete lifecycle of content—in structured and unstructured format and in all locations that this information exists—from creation to expiry in the context of organizational processes. A holistic view of ECM in the context of EIM is the evaluation of the strategies, methods, and tools used in the preservation and management of content.

Twitter: @l_elwood

Lynn Elwood, VP of ECM Product Marketing, OpenText

...On arriving at the single source of the truth in 45 days

Organizations looking to put in place an Enterprise Information Management strategy should start with the foundation of ECM: managing content. ECM covers a broad spectrum of solutions and provides information governance for all types of content. ECM includes document content, like email, presentations, and faxes. It manages physical content, such as paper documents, boxes of files, and physical assets. It manages content in processes, such as contracts and invoices, and content on the web, such as sites, social, and blogs. (Anytime an executive is saying something on a website or in a blog, it's a record that's in the public domain, and it's something that needs to be kept.) ECM is really any kind of information. And with so much information, organizations need to have a single source of truth. They need to understand the information they have, use the high-value content in business context, and defensibly delete low-value, transient content.

All types of organizations need ECM to manage their information. In one example, a large public sector organization had a significant problem managing their growing content and quickly finding information to support litigation requests. They needed to manage their email—to find and keep the critical mail and to delete low-value mail to keep the volume down. Within 45 days from purchase, they had our ECM system running in the cloud, bringing in their email, classifying it with records management, and building in deletion of transient mail. They use our Auto-Classification to understand and classify content and our eDiscovery software to search. They can now find everything they need in litigation investigations. It really can be that simple!

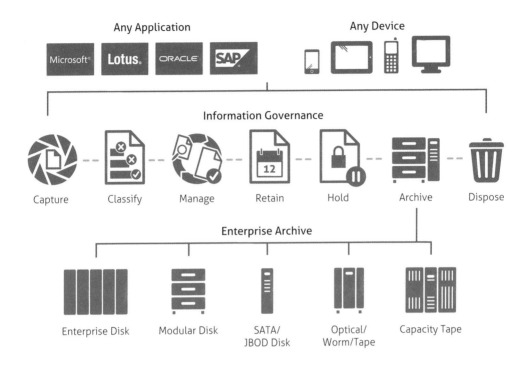

Complete Content Lifecycle Management from creation to expiry

Collaboration

Collaboration is more than a powerful way of solving problems: when practiced effectively, it's an essential success factor for any business. Time and time again, it has been demonstrated that groups accomplish more than individuals through the use of specific expertise and complementary skills. Collaboration generates a better result in a shorter amount of time than similar work completed by an individual. Many hands make light work. It sounds simple, but effective collaboration isn't easily achieved. Different geographical locations, inaccessible project information, serialized tools, and language barriers all have the potential to reduce or even eliminate the benefits of collaboration. ECM plays a critical role in meeting operational objectives by providing the tools necessary to collaborate in disparate environments. ECM streamlines processes to save time, cut costs, and organize the efforts of collaborators as a whole. This translates into benefits like the development of better products and services, decreased time to market, reduced discovery costs, lowered price points, reduced risk, effective governance, and so on.

"Information workers, who comprise about 63% of the U.S. workforce, are each bombarded with 1.6 gigabytes of information on average every day through emails, reports, blogs, text messages, calls and more..."[22]

Compliance

Corporations operate in an increasingly contentious landscape and under a growing number of government rules and regulations. The Sarbanes-Oxley Act, HIPAA, FRCP, and SEC/FSA regulations, to name a few, are drastically changing the corporate landscape. Regulations can be prevalent to an industry, but a number of countries and jurisdictions now have legislation that covers data privacy and data sovereignty, rules that strictly enforce who can access information and when it can be stored and accessed.

More than 100,000 rules and regulations wordwide and growing

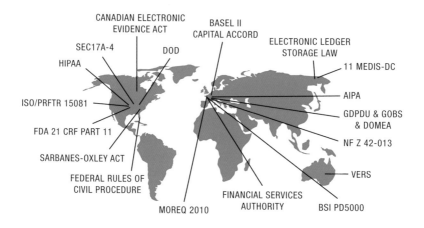

Global regulatory pressures

[22]Andrea Coombes, *"Don't You Dare Email this Story"*, MarketWatch, The Wall Street Journal (17 May 2009), *http://online.wsj.com/article/SB124252211780027326.html* (accessed 3 Dec. 2012).

Failure to meet these obligations exposes an organization to possible financial penalty, loss of reputation, and legal liability. Complying with these regulations can be painful and expensive, but the cost of neglecting these obligations far outweighs the cost of developing a successful compliance strategy. Taking a narrow view when creating a compliance system—one that focuses on one or two regulations against a subset of corporate information—can result in greater expense in the long run as new regulations take shape. It's vital to implement information governance as a major driver of success in your business, ensuring your compliance program is robust and adaptable so it can continue to grow with the delivery of each new regulation.

Protection from risk and risk mitigation is fundamental to every business, and this is where ECM becomes a key component of your overall compliance strategy. While compliance is not always a technology problem, information technology and the massive growth of unstructured content contribute to the risk of corporate exposure. ECM can help reduce the overall cost of compliance to the business through the following central tools:

Document Management – unites documents and business processes to ensure content authenticity, relevancy, and security with minimum time spent by end users.

Records Management – manages legal and financial risk by maintaining and disposing of content according to internally and externally defined policies.

Rights Management – protects sensitive and valuable content, preventing intellectual property theft via inappropriate use and unauthorized access.

An effective ECM strategy ensures that employees follow the proper business practices and that all content is suitably captured, stored, managed, and disposed of at the appropriate and legal juncture in its lifecycle. Compliance should not be viewed solely as a business expense—it should be viewed as an opportunity to review processes and make changes that benefit the entire company from both a cost and an efficiency perspective.

Cost savings

Growing volumes of information put increased pressure onto IT infrastructure. While IT budgets are flat or declining, experts estimate there is a 30-40 percent annual increase in IT costs due to the proliferation of information. As the acquisition cost of storage trends downward, operating costs are not following suit. Cloud offerings appear to provide infinite storage capacity at a manageable level of cost. However, as the volume of information grows, challenges are emerging to indicate storing content is only part of the problem.

Searches and queries take longer, confidential data can become accessible to unauthorized staff, and considerable effort is required to respond to eDiscovery requests or regulatory challenges.

Using an ECM Archiving solution, long-term storage costs are reduced by up to 40 percent through rationalization of storage infrastructure, smarter storage decisions, and decommissioning legacy systems. Some of the key archive features that drive costs savings are tiered storage, single-instance archiving (SIA), and compression.

Archiving provides an enterprise-wide repository for long-term retention across multiple storage devices. This means that the cost-appropriate storage device, depending on the level of access required, can be chosen at a software configuration level. A tiered approach to storing archived content supports a multitude of storage mechanisms, including optical media, hard disk, tape, and the Cloud. Content can be moved from online to near line or offline storage through a series of rules, enabling IT costs savings without impacting the applications using the archive.

Identical documents are at risk of being stored several times, especially in highly collaborative work environments. Within the context of an ECM solution, single-instance archiving ensures that organizations maintain identical documents in one instance. This can reduce storage space significantly, especially when managing email content with redundant attachments.

Finally, in order to save storage space, content can be compressed before being written to a storage system. Compression can be activated for each individual archive or content type. Important formats, including email and office formats, are compressed by default. Further savings can be realized through using ECM to consolidate content and decommission legacy systems, resulting in a potential 75-95 percent IT cost reduction. Other benefits include increased productivity of knowledge workers by ensuring rapid and ready access to information assets. As well, business disruption costs are reduced by up to 40 percent through improved compliance capabilities, processes, and enforcement monitoring.

ECM, when combined with Discovery offerings, creates a significant impact on organizational savings in all of the areas related to legal processing. Costs of collection, analysis, and review of electronically stored information during litigation can be dramatically reduced, in addition to the legal costs associated with culling, de-duplication, and external forensic discovery. Legal fines, sanctions, and penalties related to discovery violations can be reduced up to 45 percent.

While every organization faces different challenges and costs, savings can be realized in each through the deployment of ECM technologies.

Business continuity

The lifeblood of your organization is rooted in your intellectual capital, which is most often stored in the form of digital, unstructured data. Since access to this content is critical to daily operations, ECM plays a central role in ensuring business continuity. A strong business-continuity plan will result in the creation of centralized repositories where all critical corporate information can be consolidated and accessed.

The intellectual property of any organization needs to be kept as corporate memory, easily accessible when needed in business processes, search, and discovery. In some industries, critical business content needs to be kept for a significant amount of time, even as long as 100 years or more. Over time, document formats change, making the ability to transfer content into long-term data formats critical. Effective ECM has proven regulation compliant capabilities in maintaining critical business information for the very long term.

Records Management technology is used to classify content that should be maintained for the long term. It ensures that content is protected and stored on appropriate media so it's available and accessible by current and future systems. ECM abstracts the storage tier, enabling content migration across changing hardware technologies to be both manageable and cost effective.

An increasing number of organizations are looking to ensure that their corporate knowledge assets are maintained for the long term as part of their business continuity planning, and ECM technology plays a major role in helping the enterprise achieve these goals.

Capture of critical enterprise information

Ensuring that information is available for collaboration and compliant with internal and external policies helps to maintain business continuity, while at the same time keeping costs in check. These are urgent mandates for organizations today. To meet these mandates, all types of content within the organization must be brought into a centralized management scheme. It's not enough to simply manage email content alone or just email content and office documents without also managing all other information sources in your organization.

Courts of law have declared that all electronic information is subject to litigation review and discovery, regardless of whether the organization has it under formal management or not. When a lawsuit is filed, the state of the corporate website can become a discoverable information source—as can any social networking comments made by executives, corporate documents, email, file system content, or any other source of structured or unstructured information—all of these can be requested during a litigation review. As a result, electronic information is now being treated in the same manner that paper information has been traditionally dealt with. This drives a corporate imperative to be able to produce all information for review. It also dramatically increases the cost and risk of not managing this information effectively or keeping it unnecessarily and not deleting content when it's legally permissible.

Organizations that move beyond managing isolated types of content to managing all sources of corporate information are better positioned to manage their corporate risks and costs. They're able to drive process efficiency by bringing content together in a consistent way to serve business applications and processes. They are better equipped to apply consistent policy to content, driving defensible deletion when its active collaboration phase has been completed and regulation permits it to be removed from corporate memory. These capabilities and content management paradigms dramatically reduce the cost of storage and potential discovery processing.

ECM helps organizations manage all types of enterprise information, from the vast array of unstructured content types to structured data to paper content. Complementary Discovery technology allows organizations to access and manage other sources of data, such as those found in legacy systems, and bring all the critical enterprise information together for use within applications and business processes under a common information governance policy. Together these technologies reduce information overload by ensuring that only the most relevant content is captured, kept for the required length of time, and then deleted in compliance with regulations.

ECM and email

For a business, email serves many different purposes. It's a collaborative tool, a way of transferring and sharing information, and for many information workers, email is a method of storing information. Without a doubt, the vast majority of business information exchanged today happens over email. Email messages typically contain business critical information, some of it highly confidential in nature. A lost email message or the inability to find critical correspondence can severely damage the ability of a business to meet operational objectives. The loss of an information audit trail can hamper defense in the case of litigation and put the business in a state of non-compliance.

Estimates made in 2012 put the number of email accounts worldwide at over 3.3 billion, and these are expected to have a 6 percent annual growth rate to over 4.3 billion accounts by the end of 2016.[23] And this phenomenon is not isolated to particular portions of the world,

---

[23] Sara Radicati and Quoc Hoang, *"Email Statistics Report, 2012-2016"*, The Radicati Group, Inc., *http://www.radicati.com/wp/wp-content/uploads/2012/04/Email-Statistics-Report-2012-2016-Executive-Summary.pdf* (accessed 10 Dec. 2012).

although Asia Pacific is expected to see the most robust growth. In terms of segmentation, corporate accounts represent 25 percent of worldwide email accounts and are expected to grow at a faster pace than consumer accounts. This is driven largely by corporate initiatives to make email universally available in the Cloud and through mobile devices. In 2012 alone, estimates show over 89 billion business emails were transferred per day through corporate accounts.

The growth in email content is resulting in significant costs to the enterprise. Email-based information is stored multiple times, significantly increasing the volume of information found in email stores. Let's use an email with an attachment sent to 10 people as an example. Not only is the mail stored 10 times, but its attachment is as well. When we consider how much corporate memory and critical information is buried in email, it's easy to see why this is one of the first sources of content under review in both audit and litigation situations.

> *"Having all email in one location, being able to search in one place and put a legal hold in one location instead of potentially seven or eight, is huge for us on the legal end."*
>
> - Clint Wentworth, Records and information Manager, Nustar Energy

Some organizations have taken the approach of simply storing all email and using search to wade through it during litigation or audit review. This approach is extremely expensive and time consuming, and it greatly reduces the ability to respond quickly and cost effectively to official inquiries and litigation reviews.

Increasingly, organizations look to ECM technologies to help them more effectively manage email content as unstructured enterprise content. This is because ECM helps organizations store and manage email in accordance with compliance regulations, preserve provable chain of custody, and defensibly delete email to minimize archived volumes. Cost savings are realized through the de-duplication and compression of email in an archive, as well as in defensibly deleting email when it has reached the timelines and conditions spelled out by industry, country, and company regulations. Whether we manage our email within our own infrastructure or in the Cloud with an online mail offering such as Microsoft Exchange® Online or Google Mail, Email Management, Records Management, and Archive technologies can cost-effectively manage email content throughout its lifecycle. When the time comes to review and preserve large volumes of email, often for the purpose of audit or litigation, Discovery technologies such as Search, Auto-Classification, and eDiscovery can be used to find, evaluate, and preserve the content.

ECM and social media

ECM, when combined with social networking, has the potential to transform the way people work in your organization. Social media is the prevailing form of collaboration outside of the workplace, with sites such as Facebook, YouTube®, and Twitter® dominating the online social scene.

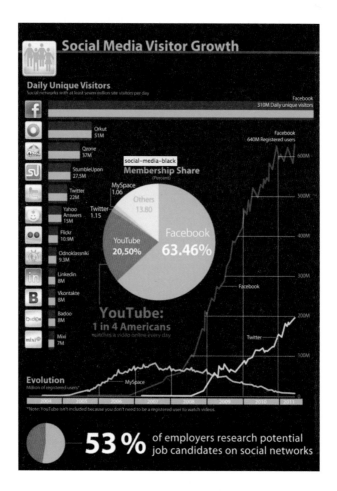

The growth of social media[24]

---

[24] SEJ, *"The Growth of Social Media: An Infographic"*, Search Engine Journal, Infographic Series, Social Media, Infographics, Spotlight (30 Aug. 2011), *http://www.searchenginejournal.com/the-growth-of-social-media-an-infographic/32788/* (accessed 10 Dec. 2012).

To adequately understand how prevalent social media is, consider the following statistics:
- One in every nine people on Earth is a Facebook member.
- 700 billion minutes per month are spent on Facebook.
- YouTube has over 490 million unique users a month.
- Over 30 billion objects are shared on Facebook every month.
- Over 400 million new Twitter accounts are created per day.
- In 2012, Facebook stated that it had an average of 526 million daily active users, an increase of 41 percent from the year before.

As most employees are consumers, many are very familiar with social networks. Many businesses today are using social network strategies as part of their overall marketing mix.

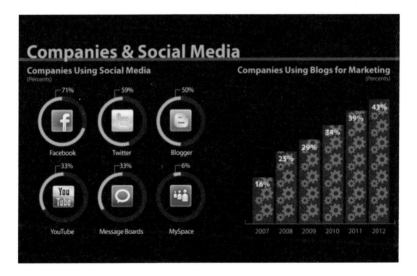

Companies and social media[25]

But what if the power of the social network, something that your employees are already familiar with, could be employed internally to foster content sharing and use of intellectual property?

---

[25] SEJ, *"The Growth of Social Media: An Infographic"*, Search Engine Journal, Infographic Series, Social Media, Infographics, Spotlight (30 Aug. 2011), *http://www.searchenginejournal.com/the-growth-of-social-media-an-infographic/32788/* (accessed 10 Dec. 2012).

With the introduction of Enterprise Social Networking (or the "Social Enterprise"), we're starting to see a dramatic shift in the fundamentals of corporate information flow. Email continues to be the central communication tool for most organizations and was once viewed as the enabler of employee productivity. However, with the rise of many-to-many communication that is inherent in social applications, it's become clear that email can inhibit effective collaboration due to its point-to-point and asynchronous nature. Without an internal social network, employees gravitate to external sources to collaborate on corporate work, something that poses its own set of challenges, as external social applications don't manage content in line with corporate policies. Whether it's the public nature of the information, the lack of a controlled repository in which to store the content, or the ability to preserve or search on this content, an ECM strategy is an integral component for effectively managing this data input channel.

Once deployed, social networking software is adopted more than 70 percent of the time. By integrating social networking software with an ECM deployment, *ad hoc* collaboration is embraced and user adoption is enhanced through the use of familiar tools. Social applications in the context of ECM can be used to follow people and capture and share user-generated content. Productivity within projects or case environments improves, while a "single version of the truth" is maintained for information workers and the organization as a whole.

ECM and file system content

In most organizations, a very large percentage of their unstructured data is stored on network and personal drives: "62 percent of organizations permit their users to store content—primarily files—locally, such as on the hard drive of a desktop or laptop computer. However, only 33 percent of these local content sources are backed up to a central location where they are accessible to the entire organization."[26] This information is, in essence, unmanaged, as content is duplicated and it's not clear where the most recent versions reside or how content can be consistently classified.

In an Osterman Research survey of small, mid-sized, and large organizations conducted during October and November 2012, nearly half of the typical organization's electronic content is stored on file servers (used to store electronic files, such as documents, videos, images, databases, etc.), while another 35 percent of content is stored in email systems, as shown in the following figure.

---

[26] Osterman Research, *"File Archiving: The Next Big Thing or Just Big?"*, An Osterman Research White Paper (Dec. 2012), SlideShare.com, http://*www.slideshare.net/emcacademics/analyst-report-osterman-research-file-archiving-the-next-big-thing-or-just-big* (accessed 6 Jan. 2013).

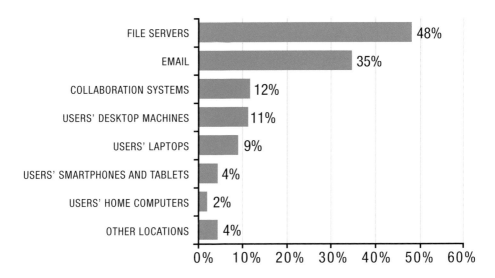

Distribution of electronic content in the typical organization[27]

Content on file systems can represent some of the most costly content within your organization as the work of finding, collecting, and preserving it for review is difficult, labor-intensive, and extremely time-consuming. The risk of missing some data stored on a particular hard drive is very high, and the impact of missing that data during a legal review can be devastating. As a result, many organizations are either using ECM to manage their file system content or are migrating this content into an ECM system, decommissioning the file system sources, and managing all unstructured information within their ECM infrastructure. File System Archiving as a solution is commonly used by organizations that wish to give their users ongoing access to a file system but want to manage content with the broader capabilities of ECM. In other situations, Information Exchange and Discovery technologies are used to analyze and migrate content into the ECM system and collect file system data for use in audit or litigation review.

ECM and legacy systems

Organizations typically have several systems managing their unstructured data. These information sources often become silos with information locked inside and only used within the confines of each system. These legacy systems can be costly and may present IT challenges as their technologies become older, obsolete, and more expensive to operate. Support costs inevitably escalate due to the technology, support, and training required to run these systems.

---

[27] Osterman Research, *"File Archiving: The Next Big Thing or Just Big?"*, An Osterman Research White Paper (Dec. 2012), SlideShare.com, http://www.slideshare.net/emcacademics/analyst-report-osterman-research-file-archiving-the-next-big-thing-or-just-big (accessed 6 Jan. 2013).

With flat or decreasing IT budgets, most organizations have projects underway to review their legacy systems and consolidate wherever possible to reduce costs and improve operational efficiency. An important consideration to take into account when reviewing these systems is whether their processes can be replaced and what to do with the information assets locked inside these systems. Information Exchange and Discovery technologies can reach into legacy systems, examine the content within them for corporate value, and migrate the data into an ECM system for ongoing management. Information Exchange technologies, such as Extract, Transform, Load (ETL) tools, allow for the ongoing operation of the legacy systems for the short or long term by bringing these systems together in a common interface. This enables users to do their work without regard for the system that is managing a given business process.

ECM and managing paper

Despite all the growth of automation and digital content, paper and physical content is still a reality in the majority of organizations. It used to be common practice to store boxes of paper with labels, ship them offsite, and manage the physical information about these assets in a disparate, often outsourced system with its own rules related to security, access, and the destruction of paper. Advanced ECM strategies suggest physical paper be managed in the same way that electronic content is managed: according to a common information governance policy.

Some paper-based content needs to be left in its physical form. This is common in professional services and legal industries. In such cases, paper is managed through mechanisms like a barcode attached to a box containing paper documents which "tells" the system what is stored in the box and where it's located. Using this method, content can be managed as a physical record within an ECM system, allowing it to be searched on and incorporated into business operations. Importantly, it can also be classified and managed throughout its lifecycle, which includes flagging it for physical deletion. This process for managing physical paper can be applied to any physical asset and organizations use it to manage assets of all types, such as artifacts of historic value and even microfiche.

Paper content that's digitized can be used most effectively within an organization's business processes. Scan, capture, and Optical Character Recognition (OCR) technologies help bring content into an ECM system where it is integrated with business processes. A common example of this is invoice processing, which involves scanning physical invoices, running them through business processes using OCR to translate content into digital format, processing payment of the invoice, archiving the paper and electronic invoices, and ultimately, the destruction of both. This is a common scenario that organizations address with ECM in a number of ways, often in connection with their ERP system.

ECM and ERP data

For many organizations, ERP systems are the most mature and established information technology discipline, driving the critical data operations of the business. ERP systems manage well-defined processes that revolve around structured information, organized according to well-understood business models and process paths. These processes, however, often need to reference and bring unstructured information into the context of relevant business processes. Consider a system for human capital management, for example. While much of the employee information is highly structured (such as payroll data), there is also the need to include unstructured content like resumes and letters with the employee file, a capability that can best be met with a combination of ERP and ECM.

Both unstructured and structured data within processes are well managed with an ECM system, which has industry-leading capabilities to combine structured ERP content, like data from SAP® or Oracle®, with relevant unstructured information. In the example above, the unstructured content associated with an employee file can be stored within an ECM system and searched on and included in a human capital management system. All of the employee information, structured and unstructured, can be managed within the constraints of corporate compliance through an ECM system, which holds replicated ERP data alongside other information contained in the ECM system.

ECM allows casual users to access information in familiar environments rather than having to learn to use new ERP interfaces for occasional access. One of the differentiating factors in organizations combining ERP with ECM is that users likely aren't aware of the underlying ECM system as they work with an ERP-based front end, processes, and systems. Critically, all of the value and cost reduction associated with ECM is provided in these use cases without impacting end-user experience in a negative way.

Understanding and classifying information

With the significant variety in types of information, organizations are challenged to understand and classify their content, driving its compliance rules and archival or deletion timeline. As part of a larger ECM system, Records Management can be used to track the classification of content and manage that content throughout its lifecycle. Records management classification is applied to content in a variety of ways, which are often used in combination to achieve full compliance. Content is assigned multiple classifications, and the ECM system ensures that this content is kept until the longest compliance deadline has been reached as per the definition of a classifications retention period.

A typical method for classifying content is asking end users to actively determine the classification. In the past, this was accomplished in a central group by one or more records managers who would review and determine how to best classify content. While this method provided highly accurate results, it hasn't been effective because records managers simply aren't able keep pace with today's growing volumes of content.

As information growth has made central records management groups ineffective at handling critical content, end users have been asked to participate in the classification of content. In some cases, this involves a user who understands content and applies a classification to it. While this method is effective for larger sets of content, it has challenges in terms of accuracy. While the average user may understand their email or document content, they are less likely to understand the records classification categories and requirements. They're also much less motivated to spend time classifying content as they focus on completing daily tasks. Most organizations find that this method is effective in classifying certain types of content through a set of knowledgeable workers and the records manager performing periodic audits, promoting compliance, and responding to questions from users.

> *"Now that we have a tool for managing electronic records, users don't have to worry about declaring a record and sending physical files to us. Records management is done behind the scenes, and it's done efficiently. It's a win-win situation for the records department and for users."*
>
> - Michelle Vanallen, Supervisor of Records Mnangement at Santee Cooper

Classification can be built into business process and applications. As the system models an automated process, it provides a link to the appropriate classification for content within the process. All content that participates in the process is then automatically assigned a given classification and managed consistently as a set of information. This is a powerful and accurate method of classifying content, reducing time invested by records managers and removing the need for end users to understand and apply classifications.

Increasing volumes of information are driving the need for the automation of classification. As large volumes of content are brought into an ECM system, there is a need to classify the content outside of business processes. The volume for email, for example, is far too high, and it's not practical to ask end users to review and classify this data. Automatic classification provides significant benefits in this situation. An Auto-Classification solution can be used to review high-volume content, gain an understanding of the information, and automatically apply a records classification to it within the ECM system. With the accuracy level and auditability provided through this Discovery technology, large volumes of content can be brought into the ECM system, classified, and then managed through its lifecycle, delivering savings and risk reduction for the enterprise.

Retention and deletion of content

With growing volumes of information and storage requirements, keeping everything is not a viable or affordable option for the enterprise. How, then, do organizations decide what to keep and what to delete?

The same logic used to classify content can be used to drive the retention schedule for content. Organizations need to ask the pertinent question: "Is this content something that needs to be kept for the long term or is it transient content that can be deleted from the system when the active collaboration phase has completed?" Corporate policy and regulatory and industry requirements may dictate how long certain types of content need to be kept, and these can be described in the classification applied to the content.

Content classification not only triggers how long content is kept, it also indicates why that content has a given lifecycle. This can be linked to the process that is followed for the review and deletion of content. It's not enough to simply apply a retention timeline to content: retention needs to be associated to classifications. Consider the example where Human Resources (HR) and invoice data must both be kept for seven years in a given industry. If a simple retention schedule without reason is applied to that content, when the HR legislation changes to indicate records need to be kept for ten years, it won't be possible to change the retention period for only that subset of content. Comprehensive retention and classification ensures that the retention period for content can be easily updated when policy or legislation changes and indicate what legislation drove the change.

Some corporate information assets need to be kept for the very long term, remaining in corporate memory for a hundred years or more, as mentioned earlier. This is an area where ECM and Archive excel, keeping content secure over the long term, allowing it to be moved to cost-effective or permanent storage, changing permissions as appropriate, and handling renditions so the content continues to be readable.

Deleting content is something organizations need to do carefully and within policy. With ECM, deletion can be carried out based on the retention assigned to content by its classification. Since there can be multiple classifications applied to content, all retention periods must be reached before the content is deleted from the system.

In addition, when a delete request occurs, the system first checks if the content has been placed "on hold" due to audit or litigation review. If the content is on hold, it will be deleted from the end user view but retained in the system until the hold has been removed so that it continues to be available to auditors and legal reviewers. The combination of classifications, retention schedules, organizational process for review and deletion, and respect of litigation hold provides organizations with the ability to delete content knowing that their actions are defensible in a court of law.

Information security

While productivity and efficiency demand that people share and collaborate with business information, organizations must ensure that critical information is protected from threats both inside and outside the firewall. Information availability, confidentiality, and integrity must be ensured in such a way that productivity is not negatively impacted.

A comprehensive ECM solution is designed for high-security environments, with the flexibility that allows organizations to configure security according to the level they require for each information asset. Content is protected when it's at rest inside the organization through encryption and authentication at the repository level, ensuring only authorized systems and users are able to gain access. Permission control ensures that users see only what they have permissions to see. Even in search results' titles and associated abstracts, content isn't visible to unauthorized end users. Access rights can be applied at the group or individual level to specific types of content and to different stages in the lifecycle of content.

Extended information security can be applied and enforced through an ECM system. With security clearance capabilities, content is designated as secured above and beyond standard permissions to a set of clearance requirements. When individuals request access to information protected with additional security, Directory Services authenticates the individual, checking for additional security-specific identifiers that can include elements such as nationality, security clearance, and business role.

Data sovereignty and privacy legislation in many countries and jurisdictions requires that content must be stored and accessed only in data storage systems located in those countries. When content is marked with security clearance restricted to a given geography, the ECM system will ensure that it's stored in that geography and those users are able to access it only when they are physically in that country.

Throughout its lifecycle, all content in an ECM system is tracked and all actions audited and logged. Chain of custody is preserved and with the archive server, additional security features, such as timestamps and integrated logging, provide more granular security and audit capabilities. Tracking and monitoring ensure administrators are aware and notified of any access concerns, and the administrator can extend the events that are monitored.

Content in business context

Organizations look to their information systems to solve their business challenges, manage their business processes in the most efficient way possible, and ensure competitive advantage through operational excellence and innovation. Virtually all business functions have content associated with them. If the systems put in place make it easy to find the right information in the context of a business process, productivity of knowledge workers can be increased by up to six percent.

"One of the first questions they ask you in a deposition is, 'Do you ever deviate from policy?'… If you say yes you have another three hours on the stand. The minute you deviate from policy you open the door to massive damages."[28]

Systems implemented to solve critical business problems can range from simple workflows to highly complex and long-running processes and complete business applications. These systems require knowledge worker collaboration and decision making as well as automation wherever possible to ease the burden on workers and ensure consistency. Within business processes and applications, ECM plays an important role in ensuring correct information is made available, actions on content are tracked and audited, and security is maintained. Business Process Management (BPM) combined with ECM drives timely decision-making and enforces compliance with corporate policy. As all organizations face increasing levels of litigation, pressure to prove consistent compliance to policy is increasing. This must be accomplished while maintaining efficiency and ease of use for end users.

The ability to create and work with business processes is built into ECM. Organizations use processes to review and approve document sets, create and manage procedures, manage projects and cases, and more. Virtually every organization uses ECM workflows to automate business processes. Some organizations have the need for a high volume of processes or cases, interconnectivity with other systems, and *ad hoc* and very complex processes. These organizations look to BPM offerings together with ECM to meet their process needs.

[28] Andrew Conry Murray, *"Ease the Pain of E-Discovery"*, Global CIO, Information Week (30 May 2009), *http://www.informationweek.com/global-cio/legal/ease-the-pain-of-e-discovery/217700666* (accessed 30 Jan. 2013)

Beyond process management, there are dedicated business applications built to solve specific sets of business problems. These systems provide a rich environment, which drives all aspects of the business case inclusive of the content, processes, user environment, and the documentation—often in context of an industry. Examples of these applications include Contracts Management, Regulated Documents, Vendor Invoice Management, Engineering Document Management, Employee File Management, and Learning Management. These applications extend the core ECM environment to help organizations more effectively meet their specific business needs.

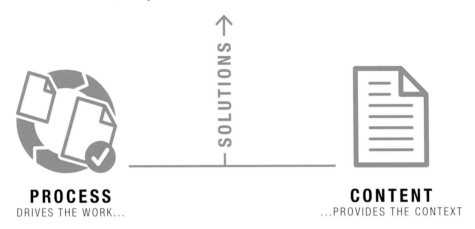

UNIQUE BUSINESS VALUE

PROCESS
DRIVES THE WORK...

CONTENT
...PROVIDES THE CONTEXT

ECM + BPM delivers business value

User acceptance of and ease of use with an ECM system are paramount in driving productivity gains. People need to be able to do their work and access content in every environment they work in. One of the guiding principles in effective ECM is to foster user adoption through seamless integration into user environments. This entails letting people work in their environment of choice, while content management is driven by business actions. When the user is working within an ERP system, for example, content from ECM is brought into that interface to work according to their ERP system; when they are in Microsoft Office®, the system mimics the desktop application; when they are on their mobile device, it works according to the user experience defined by the device. When they are working in a business application, then, they are focused on the business, and content is invisibly managed within that environment. In some cases, users aren't even aware they are using an ECM system because the capability is provided as a native extension of the user interface.

Governing the power of information

Experts estimate that over 80 percent of data in organizations is unstructured and is growing at a rate of over 36 percent year over year.[29] Furthermore, estimates put the amount of unstructured data in an organization that is unmanaged at 90 percent.[30] While an ECM initiative can be seen as costly based on incremental investment considerations, what is the potential impact of not managing over 90 percent of the data in your organization? Lack of management can manifest itself in the inability to assess critical business data, which results in customer service delays or significant compliance-related threats—bringing your business to a halt. In general, the value in ECM can be segmented into the following five major buckets:

1. **Increased revenue** through improved competitive analysis and insight and decreased product release cycles that result in competitive advantage
2. **Mitigated risk** through compliance and efficient legal defense/proceedings, reducing the cost of discovery and increasing accuracy in findings
3. **Reduced expenses** by effective collaboration and information sharing, resulting in better use of employee time and improved productivity
4. **Business continuity** through uptime of key business processes and ensuring quick disaster recovery when necessary
5. **Business transformation** by providing better service to your customers based on timely access to critical information; supporting business process re-engineering by making content available in context of the relevant business process

As the amount of unstructured information grows exponentially and in corporate importance, the need to have an effective ECM strategy in place to optimize the value of content and reduce risk is becoming more critical. Access to increasing amounts of information will require a comprehensive and proven ECM solution that can address the increasing demands for backups and auditing, tighter security, compliance, data classification (metadata), protection from threats of litigation, effective risk mitigation, and discovery technologies. OpenText ECM brings content to the fingertips of information workers, integrates critical content with business processes, and ensures compliance with external regulations and internal policies—delivering a seamless experience across multiple environments to manage content and unleash the power of information across your organization.

[29] Ray Paquet, *"Technology Trends You Can't Afford to Ignore"*, Gartner Inc., *http://www.gartner.com/it/content/1503500/1503515/january_19_ tech_trends_you_cant_afford_to_ignore_rpaquet.pdf* (accessed 10 Nov. 2012).
[30] Doculabs, *"Quantifying Return on Investment for ECM: A Methodology"*, Doculabs (2009), *http://www.doculabs.com/wp-content/uploads/ downloads/2011/12/A-Doculabs-White-Paper-Quantifying-ROI-for-ECM1.pdf* (accessed 10 Dec. 2012).

CHAPTER **3**

BUSINESS PROCESS MANAGEMENT

CHAPTER 3

Business Process Management: Accelerating the Power of Information

"We create 2.5 quintillion [10¹⁸] bytes of data every day, with 90 percent of the data in the world created in the last two years alone." [31]

Imagine a world in which business processes were integrated with multiple enterprise systems, from capture solutions to correspondence management, and they incorporated data from systems of record, provided mobile user experiences, and enabled customer self-service within the context of the Business Process Management (BPM) solution. Information would flow smoothly throughout the organization, it would be where it is supposed to be, and decisions could be made with all the necessary information. That world is not far: EIM delivers the unique opportunity to incorporate business processes and case management applications into a larger, more comprehensive context to empower employees, customers, and partners with the processes and information they need to exploit opportunity and produce significant business results.

Key drivers for BPM

The way that organizations manage business processes determines operational effectiveness, efficiency, and ultimately, success. EIM enables organizations to bring together previously distinct solutions for content management, process definition and execution, discovery, and information exchange and capitalize on it. EIM changes the way that organizations think about business process and the role that people and information play in transforming the business.

ERP systems are often at the core of transactional processes within most organizations— from financials and human resources to supply chain, customer relationship management, invoicing, accounts payable, and other critical operations. ERP systems do an admirable job of executing process and serving as the "financial system of record," but with today's pace of business and the growing need to harness agility and spur innovation while continuously improving business processes (or risk losing the competitive advantage), organizations need more.

---

[31] Larry A. Bettino, *"Transforming Big Data Challenges Into Opportunities"*, Information Management, April 18, 2012, *http://www.information-management.com/newsletters/big-data-ROI-IBM-Walmart-USPS-10022342-1.html* (accessed 22 Apr. 2013)

Enterprises that look for opportunity in information—the ones that take full advantage of information assets to empower people, fuel processes, and drive results—have embraced advanced BPM and Case Management capabilities to enhance operations. On top of the core transactional capabilities that BPM provides, organizations have next-generation capabilities to not only execute processes but to continuously improve them.

The results of successfully extending BPM beyond its traditional role across the enterprise to allow for agile process improvement and strategic business modeling can be substantial:

• **QSuper**, one of the largest providers of retirement investment products in Australia, replaced a legacy workflow system with OpenText Case Management to support all of their business processes. Powerful analytics track day-to-day performance of staff and high-level information management. QSuper's solution enhances their basic administration system by linking member information with work that is both in progress and completed, and in doing so provides a 360-degree view of their customers. Having this single-member view significantly improves the level of staff knowledge about members and their interactions with QSuper, which has led to a 38 percent reduction in effort required to manage cases across business units.

• **Nationwide Building Society** is one of the largest financial services institutions in the UK and the largest building society in the world. OpenText process and case management solutions have enabled Nationwide to re-enter the market to sell ISAs, a type of tax-efficient savings account, after having to withdraw entirely due to process issues that had created massive recurring costs and that became too burdensome to maintain when coupled with mandatory government regulations. After implementing OpenText process and case management, Nationwide re-entered the market just two years after withdrawing entirely, and they have secured a 25 percent share of the market, while simultaneously eliminating 8 million pieces of paper, saving 200 temporary jobs, and lowering associated IT and infrastructure costs.

Process and case management solutions can be used to replace manual, paper-intensive processes and breathe new life into rigid line-of-business systems, to provide visibility and manageability into mission critical processes, to improve customer service and reduce operating costs through self-service applications, and to link core data, documents, and processes.

BPM as a top CIO priority

Delivering business solutions was the number one IT strategy in the 2012 Gartner CIO Agenda Report.[32] The team from Gartner® Inc. asked CIOs to identify not just their IT priorities but also their technology and business priorities for the upcoming year. Topping

---

[32] Mark P. McDonald and Dave Aron, *"Amplifying the Enterprise: The 2012 CIO Agenda"*, Gartner Inc., *http://www.gartner.com/id=1901814* (accessed 5 Apr. 2013).

the list for the second year running are priorities like increasing enterprise growth, attracting and retaining new customers, reducing enterprise costs, and creating new products or services—all of which can be addressed with process and case management solutions.

CIO TECHNOLOGY PRIORITIES FOCUS ON THE CUSTOMER EXPERIENCE					
CIO TECHNOLOGIES	RANKING OF TECHNOLOGIES CIOs SELECTED AS ONE OF THEIR TOP 3 PRIORITIES IN 2012				
Analytics and business intelligence		5	5		
Mobile technologies			6	12	12
Cloud computing (SaaS, IaaS, PaaS)				16	*
Collaboration technologies (workflow)	4	8	11	5	8
Virtualization	5				
Legacy modernization	6	7	15	4	4
IT management	7	4	10	*	*
Customer relationship management	8	18	*	*	*
ERP applications	9	13	14		
Security	10	12	9	8	5
Social media/Web 2.0	11	10		15	15

2012 Gartner CIO Agenda Report: #1 delivering business solutions
(not ranked)*

The Gartner survey demonstrates that CIOs' top technology priorities, as outlined in the graph above, match very closely to an EIM strategy in general, as well as with the capabilities of OpenText process and case management, specifically.

Analytics is a core capability of effective process and case management solutions, through the capture of key process metrics and the presentation of that information in the form of reports and dashboards. Prior to implementing BPM, many organizations struggle with the creation of reports because it's a manual and time-consuming exercise for IT departments. With real-time analytics built into a BPM platform, reports can be both created and modified by those who need the information. According to the Director of Data Center Operations at a leading Irish pension and insurance provider: "We can now immediately see which teams are under pressure and which have excess capacity and can re-distribute the work accordingly. This has enabled us to handle 60 percent more queries this year, with fewer people, in comparison to last year."

BPM and workflows are not the same

Many organizations often characterize BPM and workflows as one in the same. There are many similarities between the two, especially related to information, work, and content being set in motion, but workflows are a subset of BPM. While both are effective at improving efficiencies, it's important to understand when and where to deploy a workflow and where full BPM delivers a more effective solution.

Workflow: travel approval request

To illustrate the differences, let's consider a travel approval request, which can be supported by a straightforward workflow. Typically this sort of request is initiated manually by the person who wants to travel and is done so by capturing some basic information: where they need to travel to, when the travel is likely to occur, what the approximate cost is going to be, etc. The request is forwarded to a manager, who reviews the details and carries out some manual tasks, such as checking with the employee to determine if the meeting can be held virtually via conference call or web meeting.

Depending on the cost involved, the manager may be able to approve directly or it may require a higher-level approval, from a business unit leader for example. The end result is simple: either the request is approved or it isn't, and that disposition is the end of the workflow. If the outcome isn't to the employee's liking, their recourse is simply to start a new request with a stronger justification.

TRAVEL REQUEST CREATED   MANAGER REVIEWS REQUEST   BU LEADER REVIEWS REQUEST

APPROVED?   12   BOOK TRAVEL

REJECTED?

MANUAL TASKS:
Check with employee to see if meeting can be held via conference call or web meeting etc.

NOTIFY EMPLOYEE

Travel request is a good fit for workflow

BPM: loan processing application

Now let's consider a loan processing application, a process that is effectively managed using a BPM system. At face value this process is similar to submitting a travel request: an application for a loan is received by a bank, a processor reviews that application and checks the details provided, passes the information on to a loan underwriter, and the request is approved. The funds are issued to the customer or the application is rejected and the customer notified.

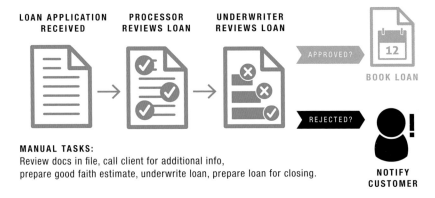

LOAN APPLICATION RECEIVED   PROCESSOR REVIEWS LOAN   UNDERWRITER REVIEWS LOAN   APPROVED?   12   BOOK LOAN   REJECTED?   NOTIFY CUSTOMER

MANUAL TASKS:
Review docs in file, call client for additional info,
prepare good faith estimate, underwrite loan, prepare loan for closing.

A simplified loan application

Is a loan processing application a good fit for a workflow solution? Let's think about it. Firstly, how did the application arrive at the bank? Most likely the applicant filled out an application form, possibly a paper-based or online one, or perhaps it was mailed or scanned and sent as an attachment to an email. Possibly there was a third-party involved, such as a local agent, who faxed the application form to the bank. These multi-channel inputs all trigger the same process but do so using different technologies, and the incoming content must be stored somewhere and treated as a case by the financial institution—perhaps tied to other processes initiated by the same customer.

This is just the beginning of a complex business process. In a real-world process, work rarely moves seamlessly from start to finish. What if the applicant has failed to complete the form correctly? Does the bank simply reject the form? Probably not: this is a potential new customer who they want to treat with respect. They would most likely contact the applicant and ask for the form to be re-submitted. And if the applicant has forgotten to provide supporting documents, the bank asks for that additional information to be sent. This outbound communication and the need to match the updated incoming information with the original application requires additional technology.

The loan processor doesn't make an arbitrary decision at this point. They rely on information from other systems (maybe the applicant is already a bank customer, so their history will be available), and they need to receive, send, and integrate information from line-of-business systems into the process. Additionally, the loan processor may have guardrails set around their decision paths that are in line with corporate governance policies or industry regulations.

We also need to consider that the loan processor will be part of a team, one that is managed to ensure that internal Service Level Agreements (SLAs) are being met and that applicants don't take their business elsewhere if processes are too slow. Inefficient processes result in revenue leakage, which calls out the importance of visibility into the flow of work: where the bottlenecks in the process are, for example, along with key areas for improvement.

The level of visibility

This level of visibility isn't just important for loan application processing. It relates to other processes in other departments such as future product launches. Let's say that Marketing is planning to launch a new loan product with a goal of increasing the number of customers by 20 percent. What will the impact of 20 percent more applications have on the processing team? Will new resources be needed to process the work? Will SLAs, or worse still, regulatory requirements be breached because of the inability of the loan underwriters to review loan applications on time? Business process and case management solutions are able to track performance metrics related to each operation spanning across multiple departments for improved visibility into the business. The metrics can also be used by the BPM solution to simulate potential outcomes of various "what-if" scenarios, allowing for better planning of future activities.

There is tremendous value to be gained from being able to deliver customer centricity through presenting a single view of the customer, including all past transactions and all documents sent to and received by them, and to potentially streamline some of these processes and communications using a self-service portal, a mobile app, etc.

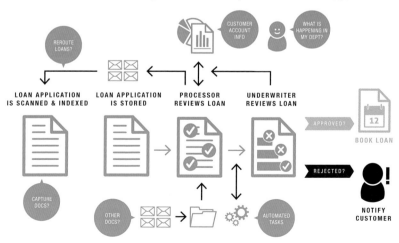

Complex processes are best addressed with process and case management

Processes like the loan application example above can be delivered by a workflow, but a BPM suite that supports Dynamic Case Management (DCM) handles complex processes much more efficiently. This efficiency can be amplified into cost savings in the context of an EIM suite (with all of the process elements integrated from a single vendor) to dramatically reduce total cost of ownership and administrative and integration requirements. The breadth of process complexity implies that the nature of the business problem needs to be carefully considered before attempting to simply apply a technological solution.

BPM case management: structured and unstructured processes

Another key principle that underlies complex business processes is that there is another spectrum of structure. On one hand, there are the processes that are highly predictable and repeatable and that lend themselves to supporting straight-through processing. These are structured processes. The abovementioned loan example could fall into this category because many of its functions can be automated—and it's possible to assess an application and grant a loan without any user interaction at all.

On the other hand, there are unstructured processes, such as those driven by users who are knowledge workers, and are by their nature collaborative and content-driven. Consider medical diagnosis cases, for example. Each one will consist of a different patient with different symptoms and potentially fundamentally different treatments involving a simple diagnosis on the spot through to tests, referrals, examinations, medical imaging, and more. The use of the word "case" above is deliberate; this is where case management fits in to the BPM landscape.

It's important to note is that the majority of processes fall somewhere between being structured and unstructured. Few are entirely unstructured, and few are completely structured. Just because a process is considered highly structured doesn't mean it can't be content-rich or benefit from a case-based approach.

It could be argued that this spectrum also represents a change in thinking over time and that future emphasis will be on the value of process and case management suites rather than traditional process management approaches. When workflows and process management first came to the fore in the early 1990s, the typical approach was to model every aspect of every process and then to execute that process. The thinking was that it would be possible to incorporate all of the knowledge of everyone involved in the process. To make this approach work, every possible exception path had to be mapped out, which often led to a circuit-board style process or, in the worst case, one that resembled a tangled mess.

The result of this process "over-engineering" was difficult to maintain and almost impossible to modify when business conditions changed and forced users to follow a pre-defined course, even when certain steps were not required or when an inevitable, unexpected exception occurred.

The result of previous approaches to mapping processes was that the solution failed to meet the needs of both the users and the organization. Fortunately, focus has shifted to the end user and both technologies and methodology have followed suit. In many process cases, the individuals involved are knowledge workers, and their knowledge adds value to the processing of work items. This change in focus has meant that it's often more effective to provide a basic process framework and allow the users to apply their knowledge to determine whether steps, activities, or tasks are required. The delivery mechanism used to solve this kind of process is a BPM suite with support for DCM. A multinational organization has deployed process and case management solutions to manage retail claims from over 11,000 retail outlets. Because each claim or dispute was unique there was no predictable path for managing the claim.

BPM and DCM

DCM is vitally important because it has opened up the possibility to automate and manage processes that have up to now been seen as impractical or impossible to achieve with traditional BPM approaches.

Instead of being forced to model every exception path, we can use DCM to automate those processes where the exception is the rule. It isn't that we don't want to have the same visibility and repeatability on processes that fall below the waterline; it's just that the nature of the work is different and more dependent on the knowledge of the people involved because it's highly variable.

BPM and DCM: life insurance policy
Using a DCM approach means being able to quickly automate and manage work by providing a compliance and governance framework to process and measure work, and at the same time allowing the knowledge of the users to be harnessed. Take, for example, the process of selling a new life insurance policy. The applicant has provided the usual information: name, age, gender, lifestyle information, financial details, etc. This information is used to perform a risk assessment. Each applicant will of course be different, and it's these differences that the knowledge worker will take into account, even though the process at a simplistic level is the same.

A DCM approach models a higher-level version of the process and provides the knowledge worker with the tools needed to ensure that all types of processes can be effectively managed and resolved. Good examples of these are *ad hoc* tasks. In the example of applying for life insurance, it may in some circumstances be necessary to request that a medical assessment is carried out. This is something that the insurance representative will not personally attend to. Instead, the system allows the representative to trigger a medical assessment task, which is then assigned to the correct resource or team with an associated deadline. At the same time, the system may be configured to automatically launch a new structured process associated with this task. For example, it might be a process to contain the activities needed to schedule the medical check, organize for a doctor or nurse to make a visit, review the results, etc.

What does this actually mean? Instead of taking many months to model and analyze every process in the organization and then many more months to implement those processes, users can dramatically reduce the time required to complete a process for greater time-to-value. Once implemented, the information generated in a process can be used to refine and optimize processes and to gauge where improvements are needed for greater visibility into operations.

One large life insurer has implemented DCM to gain heightened visibility into their operations by addressing all areas of operational processes, including new business, underwriting and claims, and policy and customer management for both their retail business and their group businesses. This exercise took just over six months from start to finish. Prior implementations of a workflow/BPM solution typically took 18 months and failed to support complexity or flexibility by automating only one group of processes involved in group claims, for example, or retail underwriting.

Customer-centricity with DCM

While DCM evolved out of existing BPM suites, a fundamental shift has placed the case at the center of the process, rather than focusing on the process itself. A case may be contained within a process or in many processes, either sequentially or simultaneously. A case may initiate a process or may not even have a thing to do with any process at all.

BUSINESS PROCESS MANAGEMENT	DYNAMIC CASE MANAGEMENT
THE PROCESS IS PRIMARY	THE DATA OR CASE IS PRIMARY
Normally the process is pre-determined and static.	Case object is core to storing data.
Data flows through the process.	Data tends to remain persistent for a long time, possibly forever.
Data ia an asset of the process.	Processes are an asset of a case.
	Sub-cases are an asset of a case.
	Sub-cases are not always predefined and can be defined on the fly.
	Tasks may replace processes.

BPM and DCM: not two sides of the same coin

All of this has particular relevance when you introduce the concept of customer-centricity. More and more organizations are embracing the mandate to be more customer-centric in order to better understand their customers and provide better customer service, ultimately deriving greater value from their customers.

DCM can assist organizations that are becoming more customer-centric by offering a case view of their customers and related entities. We call this a single view of the customer. What this entails is that a persistent case folder is created for each customer. This case folder describes the customer using personal information like name, address, phone, email, customer number, etc., and it acts as a master container for links to documents sent and received, cases either completed or in progress, and process work currently underway.

Each folder provides links to related people or objects that are relevant to the organization. These will vary based on the industry or usage, but using insurance as an example, they will include links to a folder for each policy the customer has, the broker or adviser that the customer used, any family members who also have policies with the company, etc. In a healthcare organization, this might be a link to a folder for a healthcare worker, a general practitioner, a hospital, etc. For LA County's DNA Tracking solution, the DNA of offenders is tracked and coordinated across 40 law enforcement agencies.

These links are bidirectional, so for example they could start with one person, link to their doctor, and then expand to include any other patients served by that doctor. These interdependencies or relationships are of great value to the enterprise. For many organizations, the data that describes individuals is locked away in legacy systems that don't provide the capacity to build links. With mergers and acquisitions commonplace, many organizations will have multiple line-of-business systems. A life insurance policy, a motor insurance policy, and home insurance in a customer's wife's name might be buried or hidden. The customer service opportunities presented by a customer-centric approach are many.

BPM and people

The critical links in the effectiveness of a process are represented by the activities, wants, and needs of all the people involved in the process. From conception to operation and then on to adaption, process success is determined by the ability of people to interact with processes in a simple, personal, and meaningful way. While many of these needs remain largely unmet, someone is still required to

1. identify which process will be improved and determine the KPIs that accurately reflect the desired outcome of the process.

2. design the process model by figuring out what tasks must be performed, which dependencies exist, and how work will "flow" through the process.

3. build an executable process model, automating tasks and even activities where possible, integrating with other systems and embedding active documents where needed.

4. perform the tasks and activities of the process, deal with daily nuances that occur, and adapt to *ad hoc* requirements that often involve other people and resources to "get the job done".

5. oversee process operations, making strategic decisions to adjust resources to work demand, staff availability, and priority assignments.

6. review process performance, develop line-of-sight into trends and patterns, predict emerging challenges, and identify new opportunities for improvement.

7. provide strategic oversight, make strategic decisions, and "piece together" the big picture to ensure the organization remains on track to achieve goals and shareholder value.

All of these provide critical links for process success. If any are missed, the entire process is subject to a high degree of risk and uncertainty. Each person involved in providing these links has individual preferences, behaviors, organizational styles, and approaches to work performance. Personalization is a natural part of all things that people do, and this critical observation is what brings the insight needed to take control of process results and realize the full potential of BPM.

By supporting varying roles and activities and including the ability for people in the process to personalize their experience, process success can be achieved on a predictable and consistent basis. This is called persona-based BPM.

Persona-based BPM

BPM user types

People in a process can be classified into common user types. The three user types of builders, participants, and managers categorize people into groups that exhibit similar characteristics and have common purposes.

Builders

Builders are involved in determining what will be done and how, when, and why it will be done. They set the stage for process operation, as well as shape the process to achieve desired outcomes. The builder view is a construction view. Builders often belong to the IT organization or, when the tools or solutions permit, are senior users with the ability to build by configuring the solution to meet their needs.

Participants

Participants do the real work required by the process, handling the day-to-day tasks and activities that are part of each process. Participants have by far the most "face time" with the process, as they are the ones who are living in the process every day. It's suffice to say that a poorly constructed process—from the perspective of its participants—will result in ongoing frustration, anxiety, and wasted resources as the people in the process struggle to find ways to work around inefficient or inappropriate process design. The participant view is a perspective of work performed on an ongoing, daily basis.

Managers

Managers provide oversight, guidance, leadership, and direction in a process. Managers must view each process as an aggregate of work for a given range or domain of the organization. It's the managers' responsibility to make critical observations that result in the directing of participant focus and work prioritization to ensure overall outcomes are met in a desired manner. The management view is a "big picture" perspective of the relationship between demand, resources, outcomes, and context that support the decisions made.

Builders, participants, and managers have defined roles within the overall perspective of process and are dependent on each other to achieve process success. Only when the interrelationships are molded into a composite view of process can the value of process be consistently realized.

BPM implementation

Another key capability for a successful BPM implementation is fast and easy deployment, along with the flexibility to adapt to constantly changing business conditions. Early workflow and BPM implementations were long to deploy and rigid to adapt when conditions changed.

Rapid deployment doesn't entail the ability to technically create an application as quickly as possible using a given toolset. It should take other elements into account, including understanding process flows or determining the optimum user experience to meet specific needs. The point is that business changes every day, and systems and applications need to be able to support these changes.

Effective process and case management solutions are designed to support both rapid deployment and changes when business demands it. State-of-the-art dynamic process applications deliver a set of pre-built processes and request types and empower users to build new processes, add and configure work types, change SLAs, and add new tasks themselves without any IT intervention. This flexible approach lays a foundation for the future of BPM.

More than process execution

A lot of emphasis is placed on the execution of a process. This makes sense because it's the tangible culmination of effort. But it's also important to consider where the process fits into the larger context of the organization's strategic goals and objectives. In the BPM landscape, there are three key areas of focus: strategy, analysis, and execution—and these should be addressed in combination.

STRATEGY & ENTERPRISE ARCHITECTURE	PROCESS ANALYSIS & OPTIMIZATION	PROCESS EXECUTION & MANAGEMENT
Goals and objectives	Modeling	Design
Enterprise models	Simulation	Integration
Relationships & future state	Optimization (Six Sigma, SCOR, ITIL…)	Automation
		Metrics and monitoring

Build a unified BPM platform

Strategy

Strategy includes defining the mission of the organization, setting key objectives, taking an inventory of critical assets (systems, people, data, products, customers, suppliers, services, etc.) and outlining plans for growth or consolidation across these assets. To address an enterprise strategy, organizations need to be able to build strong, cohesive strategic modeling function (an enterprise architecture) to enable the creation of the big picture. It gives visibility into the interrelationships and dependencies of critical business assets and allows organizations to use this enterprise model to identify the key processes that impact objectives.

Analysis

Gaining this understanding is critical and can't be done without analysis and optimization. Analysis and optimization enable organizations to analyze and propose improvements to processes through initiatives such as Six Sigma, Lean, ISO9000, etc.

Organizations need to be able to model all of the sub-processes, people, systems, data, services, resources, and interdependencies associated with a single process. Users need to work on, share, and manage process models in a collaborative environment, while having access to a rich set of built-in optimization capabilities to ensure everyone is working toward the optimum process outcome. A leading pharmaceutical company uses BPM to help define business processes and unify its information systems to break down barriers between organizational and geographic divisions and improve collaboration and innovation.

Execution

Once the right processes have been identified and optimized, they can be executed. Process analysis capabilities allow interchange directly with process and case execution engines and critically complete the loop by delivering key metrics and visibility into process performance to feed back into business strategy.

Social and mobile BPM

Two related areas that are growing in importance today are mobile access to BPM and apps to effectively support consumer applications like the social networks of Facebook or LinkedIn.

Today, it is essential for knowledge workers to be able to initiate a process using a mobile device. Field workers (such as healthcare workers, claims adjustors, etc.) must be able to interact directly with processes while they are out of the office using mobile phones and tablets. They can check the status of their claims, applications, complaints, and queries through the devices that are always available from any place at any time.

Social capabilities promise to revolutionize BPM. Instead of the traditional lists of work, to-do lists, watch lists, my work, team work, and more, each user now has the ability to personalize their "feeds" to provide links to what they feel is important. From the work that is assigned to them to system events such as approaching deadlines and tasks that need to be completed, users can instantly access the related case or work to complete these tasks.

BPM in an EIM context

Enterprise BPM is never implemented in isolation. While a workflow system can legitimately reside without connection to any other capabilities (consider the travel request example mentioned earlier), this simply isn't possible once a system is managing a critical business process. Documents will be received, correspondence will be sent, sometimes on paper, sometimes via a myriad of electronic formats—and all of these documents will need to be stored and managed. Data will be imported and exported from any number of line-of-business systems and supporting information will be searched for and indexed. Process metrics will be presented not just to users of the BPM system but to managers and executives. And external customers will want to initiate, participate, and check the status of their requests from convenient applications or devices of choice.

EIM presents the opportunity to meet these objectives through a single vendor solution, with process and case management capabilities connecting all the critical elements required.

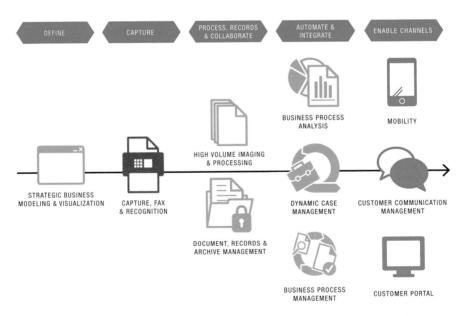

Integrated process, content, information, discovery, and customer experience

Twitter: @brianwick

Brian Wick, Director BPM Product Marketing, OpenText

...On how knowledge workers engage with information

The way people engage with processes is changing. People are shifting toward increased usage of social media techniques and rich media to make business decisions, and this is evident in numerous service delivery workflows that span both inside and outside an organization. This can add efficiency and productivity to getting work done. But there is a downside. When workers collaborate across multiple communication mediums, making decisions and working through issues, the organization often doesn't have a record of this information, which is inefficient and makes it extremely hard to ensure it's meeting regulatory requirements and internal information governance mandates.

Organizations are working hard to set up environments where the process workarounds (untamed spreadsheets and Access® databases) are reduced and communication mechanisms are provided within a controlled environment. The new process automation and case management solutions provide these capabilities by offering integration with information sources, virtual workspaces, and collaboration and communication tools to give knowledge workers what they need to do their jobs. They also capture instant messaging, email, and content sharing within the context of a process or case and manage that information so it can be retained and retrieved in accordance with the organization's retention policies.

In addition to this, there is now a variety of new devices being used to access information in a way that was not possible before. The current generation of knowledge workers is likely to be very connected and wants to engage with their work across PCs, laptops, tablets, and mobile devices—whenever they want. So organizations are working hard to create multi-channel on- and off-ramps to capture and present information in the way users want to see it.

Finally, today's knowledge workers are far more self-sufficient in accessing information over the web than previous workers, and they gravitate to self-help as they can often find a resolution how they want, when they want, and on the device they want. So in many workflows, especially those engaging customers or other third parties, organizations are providing more knowledge-base, FAQ, and self-help capabilities to make it easier for users to search and find information on their own. Now organizations must expand how they engage with users, inside and outside the firewall with multi-channel and multi-device solutions, and capture and retain information across all channels. The new generation of BPM solution vendors is responding with new solutions to make this far less complicated 71 and far more cost effective than before.

Enterprise Content Management (ECM)

Almost every business process will contain some form of content. From an insurance claim form on paper to an application form for a job, these documents must be managed and stored, treated as records, and ultimately archived or deleted. A world-class ECM solution should have all of these capabilities, within an information governance framework, integrated with process and case management solutions.

Customer Experience Management (CEM)

CEM incorporates a wide range of capabilities including customer portals, mobile interaction environments, and Customer Communications Management. A key facet of any customer-facing business process is the ability to communicate back with those customers. Frequently there will be the requirement to request more information (e.g., if the loan applicant has failed to provide a credit history or has incorrectly completed the application form). There are also regulatory requirements to keep customers up to date with the most current information, such as providing them with the status of a life insurance claim every 20 working days. Proper CEM solutions can be used to enable creation of regular documents, such as updates, statements, utility bills, and so on, as well as to support the *ad hoc* correspondence requirements common to many business processes.

Information Exchange

Information Exchange products are used primarily to bring documents and associated data into the BPM and DCM systems for use in processes and cases. Some products can be used as both the entry point to a process and as an output channel, while others provide class-leading Optical and Intelligent Character (a.k.a. hand-writing) Recognition (OCR and ICR), which can be used to automate the capture of information required to drive the business process to support straight-through processing.

Discovery

Business processes and the users who do the work being managed by a process are reliant on the information they have available to them. It's impossible to process an insurance claim without understanding exactly who you are dealing with, the nature of the claim, whether they have a valid policy, and the terms and conditions of that policy. A strong discovery solution provides robust search capabilities across the various case, process, document, and content management systems that are connected to support the work that is being processed. Further capabilities are provided using content analytics that not only search information contained in unstructured content but glean meaning and context from it.

Putting it all together

To put all of the above into context, imagine a claim being made on an insurance policy following a vehicle accident. The claimant uses a mobile phone to record images of the damaged vehicle, including the exact location of the incident, and immediately initiates their claim. They send repair estimates by mail, as faxes or as attachments to emails that can be recognized, indexed, and matched to the claim case folder. The claims processor can request additional information and send status updates via email, fax, letter, or even via text messaging and publishes the information to the company's customer self-service portal.

Meanwhile, the progress of the claim with respect to company KPIs and regulatory requirements can be both reported on and used to ensure that those KPIs are not missed by automatically adjusting the priority of work as deadlines approach. And as the business changes, the process can be further optimized and validated against strategic objectives using process analysis and enterprise architecture capabilities. This entire experience is best delivered from an integrated EIM suite, with dynamic process applications available on-premise or in the cloud.

> *"Smart process applications have the power to improve a firm's cost structure, revenues, profits and return on assets if implemented correctly."*[33]

Smart process applications

OpenText EIM represents a coming together of core capabilities in the five key technology areas. And OpenText is not alone in recognizing the need for the next generation of enterprise software: Forrester® Research, Inc., has recently published a report introducing the concept of smart process applications that "make collaborative processes the next frontier for software."[34] Forrester identifies five key components of a smart process app— specifically that they contain imported or embedded data and content relevant to the business activity; they are able to capture incoming documents, forms, and faxes related to the business activity, while supporting multi-channel output of information; they have embedded analytical tools to support the business activity; they offer a collaboration platform so that the people involved in the business activity can get their jobs done; and that all of this is underpinned by a core platform of process and case management.

---

[33] Andrew Bartels and Connie Moore, *"The next frontier for software: Smart process applications fill a big gap"*, KMWorld, 30 Oct. 2012, *http://www.kmworld.com/Articles/Editorial/Features/The-next-frontier-for-software-Smart-process-applications-fill-a-big-gap-85806.aspx* (accessed 15 Mar. 2013).
[34] Andrew Bartels and Connie Moore, et al., *"Smart Process Applications Fill A Big Business Gap"*, Forrester Research, *http://www.forrester.com/Smart+Process+Applications+Fill+A+Big+Business+Gap/fulltext/-/E-RES77442* (accessed 2 Apr. 2013)

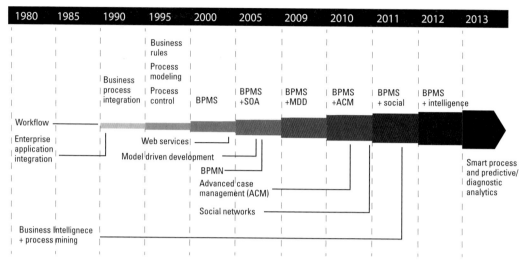

Source: Forrester Research, Inc. Smart Process Applications Fill a Big Business Gap, August 2012

Workflow evolves into smart process applications

Accelerating the power of information

Forrester has been mapping the evolution of BPM from the early days of workflow in the 1980s as additional capabilities have been incorporated to include model-driven development, web services, case management, and ultimately smart process applications. A smart process application is an application for the EIM portfolio with key BPM capabilities extended to include content management, collaboration, analytics, customer communications, capture, etc.

As we move from traditional enterprise suites and packaged applications to the world of smart or dynamic process applications, it's important to recognize that none of this would be possible without BPM at the core but that the genuine leap forward are the opportunities offered by EIM—the bringing together of business processes, enterprise content, customer experience, discovery, and information exchange.

CHAPTER 4

CUSTOMER EXPERIENCE MANAGEMENT

CHAPTER 4

Customer Experience Management: Experiencing the Power of Information

"When dealing with people, remember you are not dealing with creatures of logic, but creatures of emotion." [35]

At a commencement speech in 1995, Steve Jobs attributes the beautiful design of multiple typefaces and proportionally spaced fonts of the Mac, and likely the personal computer as well, to a calligraphy class he happened to attend in college. We have since witnessed Jobs moving from Apple® to NeXT and Pixar to Apple again with a common theme: designing an exceptional user experience.

Steve Jobs did not predict the future: he invented it.[36] The advancements in technology in the last 20 years have revolutionized our lives in small but powerful ways. We have seen the evolution of the telephone connect people miles apart and the personal computer change the way we store and process information. With the connected dots of the Internet, we're now able to share those data stores, bring transparency to processes, and connect strangers with similar interests in global communities.

In this interconnected world, terabytes of data are generated by document and photo sharing, comments and reviews, and across mobile devices and business applications. The latest definition of big data barely touches on the oceans of intricate details, like aspect ratios, login preferences, or social graphs that get captured in the digital footprints left behind as people engage with business and each other. Creativity has become a necessity and a social norm; Pinterest (a virtual pin board) is making the Amateur Gourmet famous and television commercials have mere seconds to catch the viewer's interest with the 30-second skip button.

Customer Experience Management (CEM) is designed to thrive within this ocean of data, offering organizations a new way to listen, learn, and proactively respond to the audience's needs. CEM helps you reach out to your markets and customers instead of forcing them to come to you. It helps to create a rich and consistent digital presence across the many channels required to remain relevant, engaged, and helpful to partners, customers, constituents, and employees. Most importantly, it allows organizations to extract value from

---

[35] Dale Carnegie, *"Dale Carnegie Quotes"*, Thinkexist.com, *http://thinkexist.com/quotation/when_dealing_with_people-remember_you_are_not/171139.html* (accessed 30 Apr. 2013).

[36] Debra Lavoy, *"Steve Jobs Did NOT Predict the Future. He Invented It"*, CMSWire, *http://www.cmswire.com/cms/social-business/steve-jobs-did-not-predict-the-future-he-invented-it-018192.php* (accessed 5 Apr. 2013).

managed content and bridge the chaotic world of social interactions with the secure data repositories behind the firewall.

There are many facets to explore when adopting CEM practices, including how the method of audience interaction has shifted, how business priorities have changed, and how social, mobile, web, and context-rich communications have a positive impact on end users and businesses alike. There are also many challenges and rewards to consider, mostly attributed to capturing, managing, and distributing information to multiple touch points in a variety of formats.

Customer Experience Management

Although the "consumerization of IT" hit the newsstands back in 2004, we are only now seeing it come to fruition. Today, context-enriched experiences are simply expected by consumers and employees alike. A relevant and timely experience will lead to a convenient affinity to buy. A restaurant will place a vivid picture of its hot holiday coffee to drive sales in the winter and swap it with a frozen beverage in the summer. Information about successful sales is shared with other stores to obtain similar results.

While there are multiple definitions by industry analysts for CEM, they all converge on a similar idea: exceeding customer expectations to improve business results. The CMO pursues a great customer experience to influence customer satisfaction, brand value, and revenue opportunities. The CIO may be looking to reduce the operational cost of creating, managing, and securing the latest app or supporting multiple mobile devices across the organization. This struggle between the line-of-business and IT is exacerbated by consumer influence. CEM maintains a focus on revenue achieved by obtaining a 360-degree view of the customer while presenting a single face to many audiences across many different channels.

When tied in with the ability of EIM to manage, process, exchange, and discover information, CEM solutions can immediately expose, personalize, and socialize information that is relevant to suit audience needs. Security, governance, and process transparency are an integral part of a comprehensive CEM solution. CEM empowers people inside your company to efficiently create relevant experiences both inside and outside the firewall and across each stage of the customer interaction.

CEM creates relevance across the customer lifecycle

Building the information experience

Imagine sitting in the movie theater at the first matinee of *The Wizard of Oz* in 1939 watching in awe as Dorothy steps out of a black and white scene and into full Technicolor. The addition of color to augment fantasy is a brilliant device in the movie that enriches the storytelling aspect. Today, rich media and personal messages bring life to otherwise non-descript structured data. We are bringing our users from the black-and-white, one-size-fits-all, text-based world into the Technicolor of a personal, dynamic experience.

These experiences give users the right information—product, company, account, and thought leadership content—for their needs. Experiences enable them to ask questions or interact in other ways that make sense, whether it's visualizing a paint color, browsing how-to videos, getting a problem resolved, or adding services to their account. Each of these activities is an information experience that connects people inside your organization to someone you care about—be it customer, partner, investor, or just a passerby.

Each piece of media becomes more valuable as details get attached to it—people share it, rate it, download it, etc. A great information exchange lets you tell your story to the audience (in full color) and encourages your customers to tell theirs. It brings you together to form a conversation. Take, for example, a prospect who watches a video posted to YouTube and follows it to a website for more information, purchases a product featured there, receives a personalized thank-you receipt, and goes on to connect via their customized customer self-service portal for help or maintenance information. Each of these experiences was orchestrated to maximize engagement, capture their preferences, and facilitate a seamless buying experience. The value of this information experience can then be optimized across three areas:

1. **Empowerment:** Employee productivity is enhanced using personalized collaborative experiences.

2. **Reach:** Reach more people and grow business through transmedia channels.

3. **Insight:** Collect and present analytics to optimize each experience, while ensuring governance and brand consistency.

Understand expectations

A successful information experience will inform, engage, persuade, and preserve an audience's attention. But creating a successful experience means getting to know customers better than ever and pivoting from a "they come to us" mindset to a "we go to them" mindset. It's about anticipating their needs, concerns, and desires and designing to serve them. Organizations are adapting, changing their approach and perspective, and evolving how they communicate both internally and externally. They are becoming more proactive than reactive to changing audience needs, meeting the consumer on their preferred device, and communicating with them via their preferred medium, from email or print to social media, websites, etc.

Your audience wants to feel known to you regardless of how they enter into the conversation with you (phone call, walk-in, website visit, partner referral). They have an attitude of "if the news is important, it will find me", and this requires organizations to shift their thinking about the communication channel they employ to connect: mobile apps aid knowledge sharing, YouTube replaces TV ads, Twitter is a PR and customer support lifeline. With statistics like those below, organizations that don't make this paradigm shift will likely lose market share over time:

- 64 percent of people are more likely to buy from organizations that help them via social media channels.[37]

- 27 percent of companies active in social media report increased profits.[38]

- Sites that contain social media enjoy a 55 percent increase in web traffic.[39]

Attract and maintain interest

Attracting customers to interact online is only the first step of the information experience relationship. Your organization has to then invite them back for a deeper conversation, set up for their next visit, and the next visit, and so on. Designing a high-touch, universal experience that is consistent and relevant to an individual at the moment they want to engage, at their location, and on their terms can seem daunting, but CEM enables

---

[37] invodo, *"ComScore"*, invodo.com, *http://www.invodo.com/resources/statistics/* (accessed 21 Mar. 2013).
[38] Ben Hicks, *"Increase sales by integrating social media and email marketing"*, Signal, *http://blog.signalhq.com/2013/07/08/increase-sales-by-integrating-social-media-and-email-marketing/* (accessed 10 Jul. 2013).
[39] Rick Burnes, *"Study Shows Business Blogging Leads to 55% More Website Visitors"*, Hubspot, *http://blog.hubspot.com/blog/tabid/6307/bid/5014/Study-Shows-Business-Blogging-Leads-to-55-More-Website-Visitors.aspx* (accessed 15 Apr. 2013).

Twitter: @mmaddox2Tx

Marci Maddox, Senior Director of CEM, OpenText

...On successful customer experiences that create a utopia of end-users

When the internet first came online, organizations were quick to test the waters and put their message out into the market. They used the same old "one to many" communication style they'd been using for a century and were pleased to see it worked. For a while.

The big shift now happening in marketing communications is to send out a message at a one-to-one level. It's the end user who now has the power to demand their preferences— when they receive the information, which style they prefer it in, and how they get it. The organization's ability to respond quickly to those requests determines whether or not they earn the right to continue that relationship with the consumer.

From a marketing perspective, organizations are looking at ways to elevate their brand and increase the loyalty and advocacy they have with their customers. The end goal is to get to a utopia of end-users recommending the brand on their own simply because they had such a fabulous experience. This means less effort for a marketing team to promote their brand and more consumer loyalty and advocacy.

Additionally, customers are demanding better self-service. A lot of consumers have angst about this. They really do want to be loyal, but what if they have a problem or an issue? They don't want to feel abandoned by the organization they trusted with their business. Good customer support does not just stop after a customer is gained. The relationship should continue with ongoing support and evolve into even more loyalty.

The digital channel has made great strides in one-to-one communication. We would like to see it evolve into mindful, contextual, and dynamic personalized communication. This is the kind of communication consumers want from organizations. And at the heart of building these one-to-one relationships is information. If you're going to grow intelligently, you need to look at the information available to you. Making sure you understand where that information is, how it is being used, and where it has already been sent is key to creating a successful and pleasant customer experience.

because they deem it easier for the department to manage their own communication silo rather than trying to coordinate cross-functionally. This communication approach misses the opportunity to connect different points of view of the same customer together for a complete 360-degree picture. It also introduces cultural and integration challenges to the IT group, ill fated to support the whole system. With the right customer communication solution in place, each team is able to reach their target audience cost effectively, without losing the impact or delight of a personalized invoice or strategically placed promotion in a search result list.

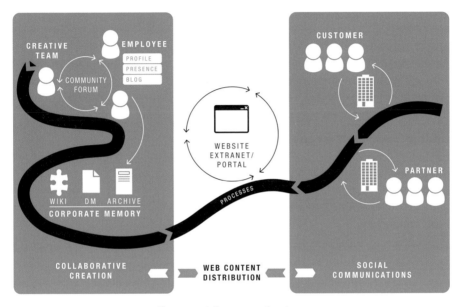

Context-rich communications

New challenges

With each of these new opportunities created by CEM technologies comes a challenge to balance structure in the context of a line-of-business need. Today's CIO must mitigate the risks associated with opening new lines of communication, meet the demands to produce mobile apps quickly, and control the security and permissions of burgeoning data stores.

Complexity in engaging audiences

EIM helps CIOs with the alignment of information domains through management, process, and discovery. CEM reflects a similar complexity in that it facilitates the internal collaboration use case as well as the external social community interaction. The web meets behind the firewall. Teams inside the firewall must touch teams outside the firewall, and a CEM solution should connect these activities back to the business.

Visionary organizations that embrace this connection resemble a learning entity; they watch how their customers and markets engage with them, which areas have the greatest revenue or customer satisfaction impact, and then enable that information to be used more pervasively and effectively. One utility company adopted this methodology and offered its customers relevant marketing programs based on their water, gas, or electricity usage. If a customer were experiencing higher than normal heating consumption, the system would automatically insert an energy audit offer in their next billing cycle. This fee-based service would identify and fix leaking windows and door seals that allowed the heat to escape or cold air in. The ROI was reduced heating bills in the coming months—a win-win situation.

Citizens have unique needs as well. One local municipality analyzed website navigation patterns to discover visitors abandoning the site after failing to find common answers and forms online. The city organized the website according to their internal department structure, rather than by the external citizen perspective. After redesigning the website to place a menu of frequently requested items at the top of the page, the city received fewer calls and more customer compliments about the online services.

Exceeding customer expectations

Most companies establish benchmarks for customer satisfaction, always striving to improve or maintain leadership recognition. Why? Because study after study shows that happy customers buy more and tell their friends to buy more as well. It's all too easy to like a business, tell others where you are shopping via check-ins, or search for recommendations from your community.

In the spirit of Jim Collins' book, *Good to Great*, good companies accept that there is a proportional mix of happy, satisfied, and unsatisfied customers using their products or services. But great companies set a higher bar. They understand that moving from meeting customer needs to exceeding their expectations will likely result in a purchase and create a repeat customer who will share their great experience with their friends.

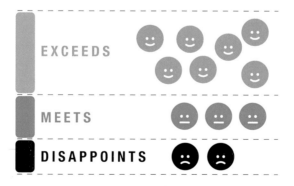

Exceeding expectations improves customer retention

Thus the network effect is put into motion. Similar to the telephone, the value of online social networks is multiplied as more people adopt it.[41] Opportunities to create an extraordinary experience can be easily identified if you know what to look for. Every interaction between customers, partners, and employees shapes their experience. With the social network effect in place, imagine the impact hundreds of positive recommendations can have on your brand identity. Likewise, the toll just one negative review can take.

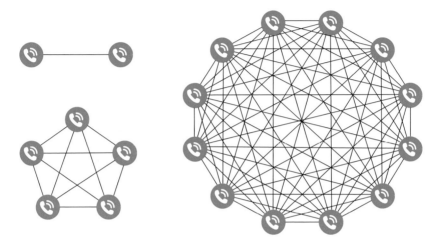

The network effect

With the barrage of stimuli competing for their attention, how do you make every experience positive, rich, personalized, and available to your constituents across any channel? To move from meeting expectations to exceeding expectations, organizations need insight about their customers.

- How do they interact with the company?

- Why do they buy a product or service?

- What do they think of the brand?

Being consistent in the actions that differentiate, such as offering no-questions-asked returns like Zappos® does, will be recognized.

Finally, you don't need to ask for permission to exceed customer expectations. Instead, you should be proactive. There are many ways to surprise and delight a customer simply by watching and listening to their actions.

---

[41] Definition and image courtesy of Wikipedia.

New priorities

Once we accept that the consumer is entreating a personal relationship no matter the device or application they're using, marketing can define, refine, and continuously improve touch-points with a concerted laser-like focus. A new set of priorities is in order to choreograph and orchestrate the content, processes, and technology required for more effective customer experience management.

The changing nature of the workforce

To maximize the impact a CEM strategy can have on the business, a recent study by Aberdeen Group, Inc. found that every employee in the organization must understand the influence they have on the customer lifecycle. Organizations that tie CEM initiatives to employee objectives have seen up to a 10 percent increase in customer satisfaction and customer revenue.[42] One auto company in the US stated: "One of the building blocks of our CEM activities involves creating engaged employees to improve our customer interaction results and even support new product development efforts."

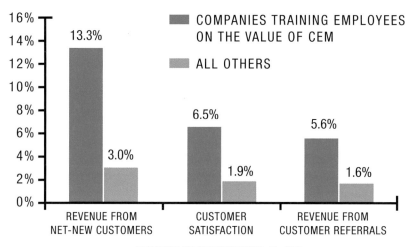

Linking CEM to employee objectives

To achieve such results, an organization must be open to change, such as offering team access to new tools and supporting a "bring your own device" (BYOD) policy. Every process must evolve to leverage the omni-channel and tap into the collective knowledge inside the organization to deliver the best customer experience possible.

[42] Aberdeen Group, *"Customer Experience Management: Using the Power of Analytics to Optimize Customer Delight"*, Research Preview, Aberdeen Group, *http://www.brandchannel.com/images/papers/531_aberdeen_group_wp_customer_experience_management_0911.pdf* (accessed 15 Feb. 2013).

Online marketing automation

Content Marketing—such as website copy, messages delivered via Twitter, or personalized promotions on invoices—has grown to become a vital component of an interactive marketer's strategy. In the online world where endless engaging content is just one click away, effectively delivering high-quality and relevant experiences are necessary for gaining and maintaining people's attention. Yet marketers must beware of burning out their relationships with their community with an irrelevant barrage of information. Savvy interactive marketers are using online marketing automation to help them reign in the chaos of information overload and turn out more effective campaigns. CEM can help form a better relationship with customers by orchestrating personalized and multichannel communications through automated processes.

Connected conversations

Non-profit, government, and commercial organizations alike are transforming traditional methods of self-service and commerce to bridge the needs of the organization with the demands of the consumer. One example of this is the OpenText Cloud-based online collaboration system used for the 2010 G-20 Summit held in Canada. Promoting an open and constructive online dialogue before, during, and after the annual meeting, the two social networking sites, one internal and delegate-driven and the other a public accredited press site, had to be secure, mobile, always on, and globally accessible. The self-governing community facilitated multilingual senior-level collaboration, requiring very little training for the busy delegates.

From a commercial perspective, the sales funnel of the 1990s has an opportunity to transform from a model that loses track of 90 percent of interested prospects through a series of qualify-out steps to an orbital model that promotes close active relationships and looser connections to the broader interested-but-not-yet-committed crowd. The less interested parties may someday become customers or influencers or give insight into key markets, but in the meantime, organizations can continue rich narratives or an exchange of ideas through social links. In the end, each connection (or friendship) with each member of the community helps build brand equity and expand a circle of influence.

Forget the Funnel!

ACQUAINTANCES: BE MEANINGFUL

COMMUNITY: BE VALUABLE

EVALUATORS: BUILD CONFIDENCE

EMPLOYEES: BE EXCELLENT

CUSTOMERS: BE HELPFUL

THE MARKET: BE OF INTEREST

Sales funnel is replaced by an orbital model

Changing the nature of information revenue flows

Today, content is much more fluid, flowing dynamically throughout an organization. The content streams are interconnected, interrelated, and interdependent. Yet production environments remain fairly linear. If a video or image is created, it moves through a process to get to an end-point and is published for consumption. People, processes, and technology support these specialized production and publishing environments with linear workflows and direct output to dedicated channels. Information flows, or structured content processes, incorporate CEM and unstructured information to address revenue opportunities differently.

> *"Being able to surface relevant content is critical to help our audience understand the news that affects them on a daily basis. From a business perspective, it helps further that engagement where you've got users consuming more pages that are more relevant to them on a more regular basis. So the faster we can surface that information to them via search or automatic triggers through Semantic Navigation, the better it is for us as a business."*
>
> - Craig Saila, Director, Digital Products, *The Globe and Mail*

Marketing activities

To deliver a new project, product, or service to market, there are usually multiple cross-functional steps that push information, rights to usage, marketing, and communications out to different audiences. A social community site helps organizations stay abreast of market shifts. Videos help generate interest and create awareness for new product releases. One home improvement store, mired in old marketing techniques, generates its Sunday circulars 18 weeks ahead of time to promote inventory. This information process proves useless in a national disaster like a hurricane, where stores in that region need to quickly advertise generators or storm shutters rather than the holiday lights planned weeks ago. Having instant visibility to the right inventory in the region and quickly publishing it to print, web, or social channels could make a difference in helping victims in a timely manner.

The social enterprise

The organization has evolved beyond its four walls to act like an organism, able to take ideas from the social realm and apply them to corporate culture. A social enterprise can engage its employees, customers, partners, and broader networks on a variety of topics, achieve hard cost savings, and help mitigate risk in social media participation. Take the popular social site Facebook, which offers a profile of interests, updates on activities, connections to friends, and endorsements of liked content. Now apply these principles to a corporate project. Imagine if you had access to a pool of talent, with examples of other projects they worked on, recommendations from people you have worked with and trust, and visibility into their skills and availability. Staffing that project for success could be a lot easier using a social-based process.

Semantic discovery

Data that is resident but untapped can be analyzed for trends: news feeds, social feeds, web properties, or content sources can be monitored to generate alerts based on a pattern, event, or trend. If an objective is to attract the largest possible audience to a website and keep them there for as long as possible, online marketing activities can be enhanced with intelligent content discovery. Semantic navigation exposes meaningful key terms to guide Search Engine Optimization (SEO) practices and display ads based on their inherent meaning. This relational content connects audiences directly to their interests, resulting in stickiness and increased customer loyalty.

Sales readiness

The final information process to get a boost is the sales portal. At each prospecting stage, different information is needed to promote the sale toward closure. The traditional shared file folder has evolved to embrace social and mobile capabilities. At OpenText, our sales team has mobile access to a single sales resource page with consistent branding, recent discussions, and links into Salesforce® automation tools all at their fingertips. Organizing a unified experience that helps sales people be more productive translates to success.

The OpenText sales portal

Experience-driven information strategy

CEM helps orchestrate different experiences that exceed customer expectations, reach new markets, and facilitate data access across many interaction touch-points.

From capture to archive

OpenText is the only organization to approach CEM by connecting systems of engagement with systems of record.[43] CEM is the bridge between the tip of the iceberg of external information and the plethora of data existing in the deep web. OpenText helps capture audience expectations, process requests, search for relevant content, and archive the web and social activities for analysis after the fact. OpenText rationalizes the digital chaos into a discovery and archive approach, synchronizing the movement of assets and correlating descriptive data, like time of day, visual preferences, or recommendations, through a single solution.

---

[43] Geoffrey Moore, *"Systems of Engagement and the Future of Enterprise IT: A Sea Change in Enterprise IT"*, AIIM, *http://www.aiim.org/futurehistory* (accessed 10 Jan. 2012).

Audience experience and governance

A comprehensive information strategy influenced by the audience experience can help CIOs and CMOs turn unstructured data sources into levers of competitive advantage and profitability. Imagine CEM contemplating big data information through a prism. Depending on the angle (the audience type) or intensity of light (level of interaction on the asset), the picture will be different. Add in permissions and connections to other data, and you have a complex world evolving. To help manage the explosive growth of information and the related costs and risks associated with unmanaged content in social media or on mobile devices, a CEM information security solution is in order.

A second consideration for an information strategy is governance of social media. The risks associated with enterprise and government participation in the consumer world of social media are on the rise. On one hand, this communication medium can reach the widest berth of interested parties. On the other hand, comments made by an external (or even internal) individual on a social media page that violate governance policies may go unnoticed until it's too late. One financial institution had a user comment get flagged by a federal security agency, which prompted a subpoena of all posts ever made by that individual on the corporate website. Had this organization archived their social content, the discovery process would have been straightforward. A CEM solution helps organizations to create a richer, more interactive online experience, crossing the boundaries between websites, mobile devices, social networks, internet channels, etc., without sacrificing information governance requirements.

What can CEM Measure?

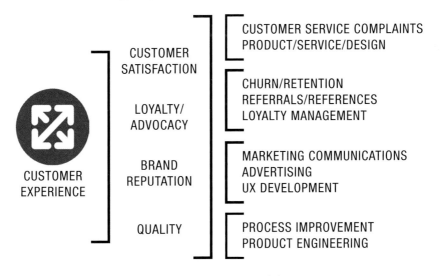

CEM offers an enriched view of the customer

CEM offers an enriched view of a customer or citizen only if a company has organized its collection of digital assets on multiple axes. Similar to a card catalogue in a library, automatically analyzing and indexing assets with linguistic markers can help speed up search results and reduce the cost of sharing and recommending similar materials the reader would appreciate.

Organizations can gain better business insight of an individual or market to improve responsiveness and effectiveness across department boundaries. With proper measurement and analysis, they can offer a better alternative before the visitor realizes they have encountered a problem or improve the experience on their next visit. For example, some may find submitting an auto insurance claim to be quite overwhelming and vague. The insurance company wants to make this process as fast and hassle free as possible—perhaps creating a mobile app that not only offers customers access to their policy information online but also supports the creation of an auto claim. Step by step, the driver is prompted to fill in details of the accident, upload pictures of the scene, find towing services within a five-mile geographical location, and receive a confirmation email that the claim is in process. Customer care is alerted to the new submitted claim, they initiate a courtesy follow-up call, and they remind the driver to view the claim status online— and share the mobile app and their experience with their social network. CEM crosses departmental boundaries to streamline the content experience.

Measuring value

Architecting an experience-driven information strategy should be coordinated with mandated business goals. According to a recent survey of marketing executives, the value of CEM centers on customer retention, customer satisfaction, customer response time, and the total customer lifetime value.

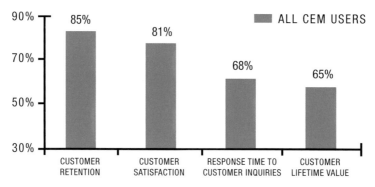

PERCENT OF RESPONDENTS INDICATING AS VALUABLE METRICS TO
MEASURE CEM PERFORMANCE, N=252

The value of CEM

Leaders want to quickly access and relate all elements of a customer interaction with all the internal knowledge their employees have about not only the customer but also the processes used to interact with a customer. Key measurements include the following:

1. Improving Revenue Opportunities

• Increasing conversion rates

• Increasing customer profits

• Connecting to new customers

• Estimated 20-30 percent reduction in cost per lead

2. Increasing Customer Satisfaction and Retention

• Increasing self-service

• Reducing cost to reach customers or communicate effectively

• Building customer loyalty

• Estimated 15-25 percent increase in revenue per visitor

3. Growing Brand Value

• Increasing awareness

• Increasing sentiment

• Estimated 20 percent reduction in time to market for updated messaging

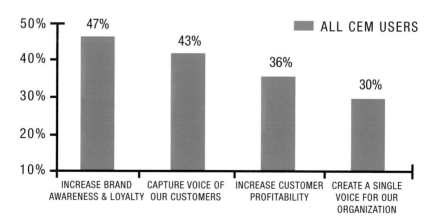

Key measurements of value

A springboard to new ideas

Every business or government need is different, but one theme rings true: turning information from managed content into business opportunity is paramount. It is possible to accomplish more with your brand, to manage digital assets for syndication and align public and private controls of information through a single EIM approach.

Online marketing: improve the web experience to grow revenue

A compelling online experience gives visitors dynamic, personalized, relevant, and engaging digital information—delivered on whichever device they prefer. This is achieved by adding rich media, social interaction, mobility, and Web 2.0 functionality to an online presence. Enabling visitors to interact through blogs, user comments, chat, and rich media such as video and slide presentations—on a laptop, kiosk, or smartphone—will help keep them engaged for longer periods of time and increase the likelihood that they'll make a purchase or call the sales team.

Global brand management: control brand and expand reach

By delivering the tools needed to better manage communication and brand perceptions in a Web 2.0 world, CEM helps the enterprise to become more transparent about their business. Greater transparency leads to a perception of authenticity within a target audience, which strengthens brand. To do this successfully, a business must be able to publish rich media, deliver information to mobile devices, manage user-generated information, and incorporate information governance into the whole process.

Social business: create a culture of productivity, expertise, and innovation

Internally, CEM allows companies to create secure, community-based environments and use our social nature to foster innovation, boost productivity, and reduce the need to travel for meetings. It provides a new, more efficient model for collaboration, one that connects knowledge workers to the people and information important to them. It also enables businesses to listen to consumers, monitor conversations relevant to the business, and respond in more proactive ways.

Customer communications management: strengthen relationships and profitability

How a company communicates with its customers can make or break its relationships with them. It's important to take advantage of every interaction and opportunity to build trust and increase loyalty. Delivering personalized, relevant communications helps strengthen those relationships, leading to increased revenue and share of wallet. This includes selective inclusion of promotions in bills, personalized invoices, or targeted messages sent just at the right time.

Self-service portals: improve satisfaction and loyalty

The ability to find information fast is one reason customers become loyal to a favorite online business. With government agencies, constituents are seeking the same level of service that they experience with companies they buy from. Employees also now expect self-service in many aspects of their job. CEM allows you to create engaging apps that provide convenient access to information for customers, constituents, employees, or partners. And it can help reduce costs by establishing online self-service centers that enable people to complete transactions online instead of contacting a call center or standing in line.

Experiencing the power of information

CEM focuses on delivering business outcomes by delivering optimized, personalized, and contextual experiences to all stakeholders. Organizations can significantly improve their business impact by creating new markets and fostering vital relationships between customers, partners, and employees through business solutions for online marketing, social business, optimized customer communication management, and global brand management. Business insight is enhanced through the continuous measurement of web and social interactions, semantic connections, and customer or citizen activities.

Organizations are using CEM to create engaging communications through secure self-service solutions, targeted customer correspondence, and well-connected communities—and to streamline their processes with the more effective distribution of information using automated processes and self-service. Brand value is preserved with consistent digital rights usage and auditing across multiple channels. Finally, CEM helps to ensure information security and information governance by implementing solutions designed for compliance, archiving, and meeting privacy requirements.

From technology to processes, CEM helps organizations exceed audience expectations, extract value from managed content, and bridge the chaotic interactive online world with the secure data repositories behind the firewall. As the connections to data grow, so will the opportunities for extracting more value from it. In the context of EIM, Customer Experience Management, when integrated with Enterprise Content Management (ECM), Business Process Management (BPM), Information Exchange, and Discovery, helps organizations unleash the power of their information.

CHAPTER 5

INFORMATION EXCHANGE

CHAPTER 5

Information Exchange: Extending the Power of Information

"The latest batch of cyber attackers (is) delving deeper into the cyber warfare and cyber terrorism space. They have a rapidly evolving ideology and agenda—namely, they are coming to destroy the secure network, erase pertinent data, wreak havoc with physical equipment, and ultimately take your company down." [44]

As a practice of Enterprise Information Management (EIM), Information Exchange is a set of technologies that facilitates the efficient, secure, and compliant flow of information inside and outside the enterprise from any sender to any receiver in any format. Information Exchange encompasses the entire B2B value chain, facilitating an enormous (and ever-increasing) volume of transactional and conversational data through a host of mediums—from electronic faxes and Cloud services to file sharing, Electronic Data Interchange, and Managed File Transfer.

Information Exchange is different from Business Process Management (BPM) and Enterprise Content Management (ECM) in that it focuses on the secure capture, processing, distribution, and sharing of information between internal and external stakeholders as opposed to addressing business information and governance policies on a predominantly "inside the firewall" basis. This difference does not make organizational challenges less daunting, however, and the prospects for reducing cost and generating value and opportunity are just as strong.

In fact, significant business value can be realized with Information Exchange by implementing a comprehensive, global, and Cloud-based approach.

The new era of Information Exchange

Information Exchange doesn't manage data objects that behave as a document or an email would: it manages transient, communicative exchanges of information in different formats across processes and people, both inside and outside the firewall. This is the conversation of an organization—the language of an enterprise—internally among its employees and externally with its customers and partners (and all along the supply chain). An information exchange can be described as a payload of data, moved between one or more parties for

---

[44] Health Data Management Staff, *"The Four Horsemen of Cyber Security Threats in 2013"*, Information Management, *http://www.information-management.com/news/the-four-horsemen-of-cyber-security-threats-in-2013-10023736-1.html* (accessed 17 Jan, 2013).

the purpose of communication, sharing, or conducting business. These services generate truly massive amounts of information and often are tied into other practices such as ECM with very specific collection parameters.

Information Exchange is the lifeblood of a company's communications and represents a very steep challenge for overall EIM initiatives because of the sheer volume of data generated on a daily basis. It's not tenable to harvest, capture, and store every exchange an organization conducts. Some exchanges live in a transient state where their information "payloads" are disposed of on a post-transaction basis, even though auditing these transactions for compliance reasons is often required. This poses great risk (and processing burden) to organizations. In a sense, managing certain Information Exchange processes is like panning for gold, where the dirt must be separated from the ore—or the unessential from the essential.

But which exchanges are dirt and which ones are gold? Manually dealing with the disposition of information exchanges is simply not possible, and the effort and expense of the monitoring required to carry it out effectively is financially prohibitive. So combining Information Exchange services with ECM and Discovery practices allows for the automation, archiving, and monitoring capabilities to make the most of the information exchanges created by an enterprise, without the overhead of accommodating them manually or the risk of leaving the data unattended or lost to a transient state.

The challenges of effective Information Exchange include managing enormous and mounting volumes of data, controlling costs with diminishing budgets, ensuring compliance and security, and improving agility and responsiveness for the business. And while these are significant challenges, there are also opportunities for progressive organizations that embrace a comprehensive approach to Information Exchange. These opportunities include increased efficiency and decreased costs by outsourcing to Cloud services, automation to streamline information exchange processes, establishing an optimal B2B communication framework, and a keystone for executing a successful EIM strategy.

With this in mind, let's explore the various stakeholders across the enterprise—what they should consider focusing on and, more importantly, what's in it for them if they successfully deploy a sound Information Exchange strategy.

> Xavier Chaillot

Twitter: @xavierchaillot

Xavier Chaillot, VP Marketing for IX, OpenText

…On securing information in motion

Every organization needs to exchange information. Whether it is with their customers, suppliers, partners, or third-party vendors, information exchange is happening constantly. And information on the move is information at risk.

Because of this constant exchange of information, companies need to be sure they are in control of their data at all times. Imagine you want to share some type of business information with someone, for whatever reason. There are many ways you can do that today, but very few of these methods are secure, compliant, and enable you to share large amounts of information while retaining complete control. So what do you do? Imagine your organization wants to automate your electronic supply chain. You need to normalize your data to ensure you can communicate with another tier, even if you have no idea how that tier is set up or what type of system it uses. Again, what do you do? In both of these cases, an information exchange (IX) solution can help you achieve the security and control you want.

IX helps control information that is in motion. Information at rest is not the problem. As soon as information leaves a repository, what happens? What happened during the exchange? Who received the information? What did they do with it? All of these questions are concerns any CIO must address when thinking about their company's information. No EIM strategy is complete without IX. The exchange of information is the conversation that underlies all of your information activities. It doesn't matter what type of information you are working with: if you are working with it, it is alive and in motion, which means it needs to be controlled, managed, and secured.

Information Exchange stakeholders

As with other aspects of EIM, Information Exchange requires a host of players representing departments and roles that stretch across the enterprise and around the world. Unlike other categories that support EIM, though, there is an added layer of complexity for Information Exchange professionals: Information Exchange involves a large number of external parties or participants in business processes versus the largely internal stakeholders of other EIM disciplines such as ECM or Information Discovery.

So what should forward-thinking organizations that want to capitalize on the significant and tangible benefits of Information Exchange do? Who are the key stakeholders? What are their roles and challenges? What's in it for them?

Chief Information Officers

According to the results of a recent IDG Research survey[45] of large-organization CIOs and IT executives, the top two concerns and areas of budget spend for the business are (1) ensuring information security across both internal and external processes and participants and (2) making sure that the systems that capture, manage, and exchange business information are available at all times.

Identifying the core challenges is one thing, but executing on strategies that overcome them is proving to be a highly complex, frustrating, and daunting task for a variety of stakeholders.

Controlling the exponential growth of information is a well-known issue for CIOs, but in recent years that challenge has intensified. New ways of exchanging information and a host of new devices for creating and sharing information have led to increased security concerns; "rogue" information exchange between employees, partners, and customers; and the ever-present specter of regulatory compliance. In short, securing, controlling, and integrating all the systems that capture and manage information has become a colossal undertaking.

INCREASING BUSINESS PRODUCTIVITY	80%	26%	55%	12%	2%	5%
GROWING REVENUE	77%	43%	34%	15%	1%	7%
IMPROVING THE QUALITY OF INFORMATION	75%	24%	51%	18%	3%	4%
REDUCING COSTS/IMPROVING EFFICIENCY	74%	33%	41%	18%	4%	4%
IMPROVING CUSTOMER SATISFACTION	74%	30%	44%	20%	2%	4%
INCREASING BUSINESS AGILITY	66%	22%	44%	26%	4%	4%
IMPROVING EMPLOYEE ENGAGEMENT	64%	15%	50%	25%	7%	4%
CREATING COMPETITIVE ADVANTAGE	63%	26%	36%	22%	9%	7%

Improving the quality of information one of the top three business objectives for CIOs and IT executives[46]

[45] OpenText and IDG Research, *"Unleashing the Power of Information"*, IDG Research, *http://resources.idgenterprise.com/original/AST-0079214_OpenText_li_0115_FINAL.pdf* (accessed 1 Mar. 2013).
[46] *Ibid.*

"Do more with less budget and fewer resources" has long been the motto of IT departments, but the economic crisis, unprecedented competitive pressure, and other market factors have put an end to traditional "workarounds" and reassignment of people and money. This new reality is forcing CIOs to explore new horizons of cost efficiencies and elimination of stale, expensive approaches to information exchange in favor of a holistic approach. Progressive organizations are executing on strategies that treat all information exchange methods and systems under one umbrella as opposed to the point-by-point, application-specific mentality.

Are you getting the most of your business data?

CIOs should explore ways to exploit the value of enterprise information [47]

According to industry research, exploring and exploiting opportunities in the Cloud is on the agenda of more than half of today's CIOs. The cost-reduction benefits tied to IT administration and infrastructure management are a primary driver of the "move to the Cloud" model, but there are other areas of tangible return. Many point to an increased ability to focus on innovation rather than channeling time, resources, and money to less visible and valuable contributions to the business. Others indicate significant improvements in efficiency and effectiveness of IT resources, while increasing "responsiveness to the business" as significant drivers of a Cloud-based model. In short, as CIOs explore ways to demonstrate their IT department's ability to contribute to business transformation initiatives, many are finding that the Cloud holds a great deal of promise.

Chief Compliance Officers

For years, the focus of Chief Compliance Officers (CCOs) and security officers was to develop information governance strategies that shored up transactional data (inbound via fax, email, etc.), as well as what is known as "information at rest"—information that has been captured and requires policies applied for storage, retention, archiving, and ultimately,

---

[47] OpenText and IDG Research, *"Unleashing the Power of Information"*, IDG Research, *http://resources.idgenterprise.com/original/AST-0079214_OpenText_li_0115_FINAL.pdf* (accessed 1 Mar. 2013).

disposition. With more information to manage, along with more systems, devices, and information-driven processes, compliance and security officers are now faced with the high risk associated with "information in motion."

There is a higher risk in managing information that fuels processes, is shared between multiple parties, and moves across more systems and devices than before—making the traditional "capture and keep everything" mentality a standard of the past. Information in motion presents new challenges for compliance and security officers, particularly because some of the parties involved with information exchange processes are outside of the corporate perimeter, or firewall, and are not subject to the standard compliance mechanisms and tools that regulate internal users.

What if you could?

AN INTEGRATED EIM STRATEGY WILL DELIVER **BETTER** RESULTS, RELATIONSHIPS, AND IT INFRASTRUCTURE.

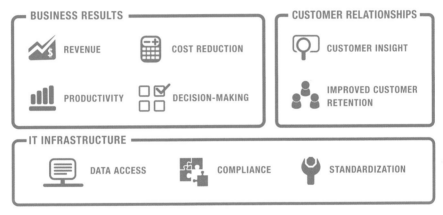

The business value of effective Information Exchange[48]

The evolution of Information Exchange adds an element of increased risk. Controlling information that is not centrally located exposes that information to potential leaks of regulated data or highly valuable intellectual property to malicious third parties. CCOs must control information across business systems like SAP, Oracle, and Microsoft. After all, everything is connected, and combined Information Exchange solutions, such as fax and document distribution, file sharing, and transactional content systems, present a holistic approach that is more effective than a separate solution.

---

[48] OpenText and IDG Research, *"Unleashing the Power of Information"*, IDG Research, *http://resources.idgenterprise.com/original/AST-0079214_ OpenText_li_0115_FINAL.pdf* (accessed 1 Mar. 2013).

> *"If you experience a data destruction attack, everyone will know once your systems are down. In other instances, the stakes will be too high; the threat will be insurmountable without help from security consultants and government entities. We've already seen an increase in the number of breaches where clients have been notified by a government entity or security firm that they've lost sensitive data; we expect to see that trend only accelerate in 2013."*[49]

Line-of-business managers

In the case of Line-of-Business (LOB) managers, "knowing what we know is no easy task" is a common refrain in the age of a highly-dynamic IT landscape, a landscape that includes a growing number of repositories, new ways of capturing and exchanging information, and the mass of content that spans all of them. What LOB management is really looking for is an easy, fast, and centralized way to seek out and share not only the information across the systems and stores they have direct influence over but all sources of information. The elusive "single version of the truth" and the ability to securely share that information in a way that lines up with governance policies and regulations (without unnecessary or cumbersome manual tasks) is the chief success factor for LOB management.

Improving productivity with fewer resources is the mandate for all directors and LOB managers. But as information keeps growing both in size and volume and security requirements increase, traditional information exchange mechanisms, such as email, fax, or file transfer, have shown their limits at the expense of the business itself. By looking to tools that will help them overcome those limits and adapt to the changes of a dynamic and global reality, LOB managers and directors can enable a truly safe, rich, and swift platform for information exchange.

Opportunity

As the secure and efficient exchange of information becomes an increasingly daunting task, what can organizations take away in terms of hope? Is there a silver lining to the gray clouds that shroud the efficient management of Information Exchange?

For organizations that take advantage of a central, comprehensive approach to Information Exchange, the answer is yes and the opportunities are significant and tangible.

EIM is an approach that allows content to flow at the speed of business in a governed, secure, and efficient way to give organizations competitive edge, spur innovation, and increase revenue-generating opportunities and cost efficiencies. As part of a holistic EIM strategy, Information Exchange offers a set of applications and capabilities to facilitate

---

[49] Information Management, *"The Four Horsemen of Cyber Security Threats in 2013"*, Forecast, Information Management.com, 27 Dec. 2012, *http://www. information-management.com/news/the-four-horsemen-of-cyber-security-threats-in-2013-10023736-1.html* (accessed 6 Jan. 2013).

efficient, secure, and compliant exchange of information, both inside and outside of the enterprise, regardless of format, in context of collaboration, and integrated with business processes.

Driving value across the enterprise

The following are key areas of business value that are impacted by a holistic approach to Information Exchange:

- **Optimizing the reliability, reach, and cost efficiency of the electronic B2B supply chain.** Advanced Electronic Data Interchange (EDI) capabilities can cross the communication gaps that hinder effective process execution.

- **Cutting the cost of B2B information exchange processes.** Automate workflows, speed communications, and facilitate compliance with security and records-keeping mandates, all while lowering costs of information exchange, such as fax-based processes, by up to 70 percent. Additionally, enterprises can significantly reduce the administrative burden of B2B information exchange by moving the management of systems (fax and document distribution, data integration, file sharing, etc.) to the Cloud.

- **Efficiently sharing and managing vital high-volume data exchanges.** Being able to safely and cost-efficiently manage the flow of large files through Managed File Transfer (MFT) is a source of enormous cost savings compared to traditional approaches like FTP.

- **Improving flexibility without sacrificing security.** The ability to reach customers, employees, and other stakeholders across the entire B2B value chain using a variety of mediums—including email, SMS, voice, and fax—without having to manage separate processes and systems for each, delivers substantial efficiencies and productivity improvements.

- **Safely and easily sharing files in the Cloud.** Today, there is easy access to many public file-sharing apps and tools. To ensure security and compliance, organizations need to implement tools and processes to share, synchronize, access, and manage information in the Cloud.

- **Increasing compliance and security of information.** Extending governance policies across all information channels to maintain a fully transparent audit trail and manage the flow of information in a defensible manner strengthens the ability of organizations to confidently address regulatory inquiries and litigation calls.

- **Accelerating business processes.** With a sound Information Exchange strategy, organizations remove geographic barriers to increase process velocity and accelerate the exchange of enterprise information with anyone, anywhere, on any device.

The building blocks of effective Information Exchange

A flexible approach that allows organizations to rapidly deploy Information Exchange is critical to driving overall EIM success. This includes B2B supply chain and business systems integration facilitated by EDI, the management of large files inside and outside the organization with airtight security and complete audit tracking supported by effective MFT, and the automation of business-critical fax and electronic document distribution to increase employee productivity and lower paper-based operational costs. On such a platform, information exchange between the enterprise and end users is integrated, collaborative, and secure.

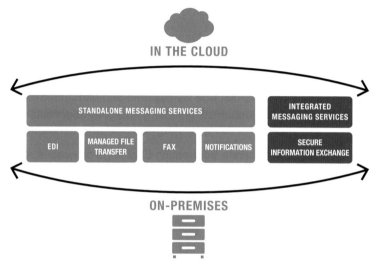

The building blocks of effective Information Exchange

Cloud-based file transfer and messaging

Today's high-risk environment demands an Information Exchange solution that protects valued content while enabling organizations to fully benefit from it. Inactive information is neither useful nor safe—the power of information comes from the ability to securely share it. For most organizations, the safe transmission of confidential and sensitive data is of the utmost importance, and as a result, the requirement for a secure information exchange continues to grow.

Cloud-based file transfer and messaging capabilities combine enterprise-level security with collaborative features and the flexibility of the Cloud. The result is a technology that helps organizations exchange information with customers, partners, and employees easily, securely, and collaboratively from any device and any location.

EMAIL IS UNSECURE AND LIMITED BY SIZE

**SECURE INFORMATION EXCHANGE WITH MESSAGES,
DOCUMENTS AND EXTREMELY LARGE FILES**

Secure Information Exchange with messages, documents, and large files

The secure exchange of messages, documents, and files results in a communications stream that is as easy to use as email, yet meets the security and audit trail requirements of today's enterprise for compliance and governance. Superior protection of sensitive data is ensured by encryption during file transfer. End users are empowered to collaborate effectively and transparently using threaded messages that include file uploads with multi-layered security.

Reliance on the limited ability of email is reduced, as is overall cost, by moving complex Information Exchange infrastructure off the premises. Information flow is unimpeded, improving efficiency and productivity as organizations exchange messages and information in a trusted, integrated, and collaborative Cloud environment.

Cloud-based file sharing
With Cloud-based file sharing, enterprises can share and synchronize files across the entire organization for access to accurate information without sacrificing the stringent demands for information governance and security.

Businesses can't let their users upload and store files in just any Cloud. The influx of free file-sharing apps has come with both the advantage of cost and the risk of security breaches, leaks, and exposure to improper handling of private or sensitive information. Cloud-based file-sharing systems give the enterprise a simple, fast, reliable, and highly secure way to share, access, and manage information in the Cloud, without sacrificing the simplicity and familiarity of public file-sharing apps.

Enterprise-class file-sharing solutions are flexible (both Cloud-based or on-premises) and offer secure file sharing to simplify the content management experience. Users can easily access, share, and store information across all the devices they use, without sacrificing the records management rigor and security demanded by an organization's internal policies and industry regulations.

A leading provider of diagnostics is using Cloud-based file sharing to improve their review process. They used to take 10 to 14 days on average to move documents through their review process. With the new system, their turnaround time has been reduced to half at five to seven days. This has also resulted in a much higher volume of documents being processed per year. The solution has enabled a more efficient and automated document review process. Administrative efforts have been significantly reduced and faster document turnaround times have resulted in increased production and efficiency.

Fax and document distribution solutions

Everything to do with capturing, controlling, and managing business processes related to facsimile-based information—core fax-driven processes to multi-function device management, email and desktop faxing, fax automation, and compliance and security measures for fax operations—is supported in an effective Information Exchange portfolio.

Organizations can capitalize on significant cost and efficiency gains by deploying fax and document distribution solutions as part of their broad Information Exchange and EIM strategies. Fax and document distribution solutions automate time-intensive, manual, paper-driven processes to reduce paper-based operational costs, increase employee productivity, and decrease the risks associated with unsecure communications. A complete portfolio of solutions includes secure document management, email and desktop faxing, automated faxing, and printer integration.

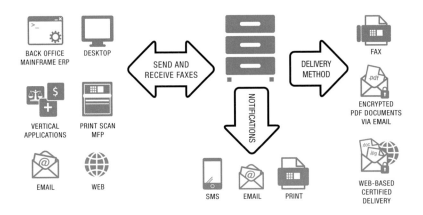

Comprehensive fax and document distribution

A complete portfolio of solutions will include

- **Document Management** to handle all of the inbound documents and data in an organization's electronic file cabinet that lets users securely file, archive, and find every document, no matter its original source.

- **Security and Compliance** to comply with internal and external regulations so a business can prove they are in compliance with the information security standards that govern their business.

- **Email and Desktop Faxing** to consolidate fax with email, documents, and desktop applications so employees can communicate more effectively by bringing technologies together in a centralized location.

- **Fax Automation** to streamline the exchange of information to improve security and reduce costs while optimizing overall fax-driven business processes.

- **Multi-Function Printer Integration** to save a significant amount of money and boost employee efficiency by integrating MFPs and MFDs through the industry.

In the healthcare industry, for example, switching from a manual-based solution to a fax and document distribution solution enables organizations to securely send, receive, and store confidential information about patients, providers, and insurers. Their secure information exchange includes admittance documents, physician orders, claims, payment and remittance advice, claim status, lab reports, prescriptions, and more. For many clinics and hospitals, Information Exchange technologies provide a vital bridge between paper and digital worlds. Secure fax and document distribution fully supports regulatory compliance and provides an easy, familiar path for digitizing paper health records so they can be incorporated into electronic health systems of record.

Capture and imaging solutions

This category of offerings provides organizations with the ability to capture paper documents and transform them into digital content for interpretation and processing. Capture and imaging solutions help organizations capture digital document images, email attachments, and faxes using sophisticated character recognition, document transformation, and data extraction software to reduce manual keying and automate paper handling for increased process velocity and improved information exchange.

Often, business documents are tied to document-centric processes like order management, accounts payable, and contract management. The speed, efficiency, and cost-effectiveness of these processes are driven by the integration of structured information (data from business or ERP applications) and unstructured information (such as emails, images, documents). Capture solutions bridge the gap between the structured and the unstructured world. By extracting business-relevant data from documents with technology based on optical character recognition (OCR), a collection of pixels is transformed into actionable information.

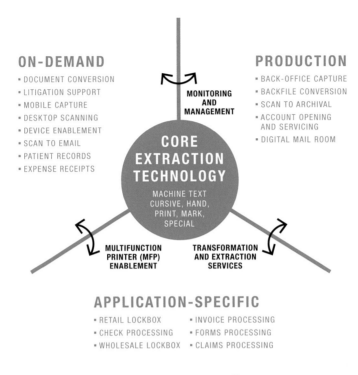

Capture solutions[50]

Capture and imaging solutions enable organizations to promote business efficiency, ensure wider accessibility, and support employee productivity. By eliminating the high cost of processing paper, organizations can realize a substantial, measurable ROI. The cost and time spent on storing and retrieving paper is reduced and productivity is improved. In addition, knowledge workers can now get to the information they need faster without needing to sift through volumes of paper documents.

A range of applications and solutions for capture and imaging supports broad Information Exchange and EIM strategies and is comprised of

- **Information Capture and Imaging Offerings**, which automatically capture and interpret paper documents, scanned images, email, and faxes using the most advanced document and character recognition capabilities available to turn documents into machine-readable information.

- **Imaging Tools and Solutions**, which provide a complete approach for capturing and viewing business documents from various sources, such as scanners, faxes, email,

---

[50] Alan Weintraub and Craig Le Clair et al., *"The Forrester Wave™: Multichannel Capture, Q3, 2012: Vendors Move Toward Mature Service Offerings"*, Forrester Research, *http://www.forrester.com/The+Forrester+Wave+Multichannel+Capture+Q3+2012/fulltext/-/E-RES78702* (accessed 14 Jan. 2013).

and other office applications, and linking them to all types of business objects within enterprise applications.

Once again, businesses can't let their users upload and store files in just any Cloud. The influx of free file-sharing apps has come with both the advantage of cost but also the risk of security breaches, leaks, and exposure to improper handling of private or sensitive information. Enterprises need a simple, fast, reliable, and highly secure way to share, sync, access, and manage their information.

Data and information integration

By enabling organizations to capture, transform, integrate, and migrate information across the enterprise, data and information integration solutions help consolidate and transform data and content throughout the entire information ecosystem. The ability to combine and contextualize information from any source (in a way that is seamless and transparent) has unequivocal business value. However, in today's global economy, an ever-expanding proliferation of data sources—structured, semi-structured, and unstructured (on top of the various formats and software applications they reside in)—has brought about a new mindset.

Companies can no longer simply analyze information with traditional views of data in structured databases or focus solely on content and its lifecycle. The emergence of 2.0 technologies, global competition, strict compliance policies, and the most intelligent consumer yet, has created a whole new world of information needs that requires analysis and context alongside traditional takes on corporate data. In order to compete, organizations must understand the full scope of enterprise information, breaking down silos and managing relevance during its lifecycle.

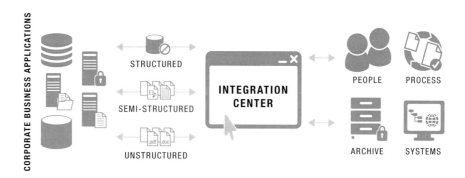

Integrate business systems to capture, transform, and deliver enterprise information

and accelerates file delivery, enabling global users to efficiently collaborate to improve productivity and agility and reduce risk.

Extending the power of information

From extending governance policies and best practices across channels to ensure compliance to removing barriers by accelerating information sharing through mobile devices, Information Exchange is redefining enterprise conversations. Within the next decade, we'll see a closer alignment of Information Exchange capabilities with ECM, Discovery and content analytics technologies, business process and case management applications, and mobile solutions.

With Information Exchange, the enterprise can safely share information across business systems and devices, from user to user, from anywhere at any time, without having to worry about data integrity or security—to get the right information to the right person quickly, unleashing the power of the information—whether on premises, across mobile devices, or in the Cloud.

CHAPTER 6

DISCOVERY

> Stephen Ludlow

Twitter: @ludlow_at_work

Stephen Ludlow, Director Program Management, OpenText

...On using search and content analytics to control electronic information

To me, EIM is the natural convergence of numerous facets of information management and technologies to solve problems that we haven't been able to solve in isolation. Almost every conversation I have with customers evolves into an EIM discussion. Organizations are trying to address the risks and costs associated with having unstructured information, but more than anything else, they are looking to improve user productivity and business processes that touch both top and bottom lines. The conversation often starts with tactics to address specific pain points, but as the audience broadens to include business stakeholders, legal, and IT—and the list of pain points grows—organizations begin to see the benefits of charting an EIM strategy to holistically address the source of many of their issues.

One of the big issues in information management right now is how to control electronic information. Electronic information is proliferating in volume, in the variety of sources it stems from, and in the different ways it is being consumed. Instead of becoming simpler to manage, it is becoming increasingly difficult to understand, control, and make available to the right people at the right time.

Search and content analytics are becoming critical in controlling information and determining what is valuable and what isn't. Search and content analytics are beginning to act as an early warning system for organizations to proactively address information risks. This is, in part, why companies should look into ways to better organize and control their information. OpenText has applications that use search and content analytics to unlock information from isolated silos and help to automate activities that users would find time consuming or impossible. These applications package search and content analytics with business logic to solve specific problems in EIM, such as classifying huge volumes of legacy and uncontrolled information, enriching metadata to improve website search, and collecting and culling Electronically Stored Information (ESI). This is one of the ways companies can mitigate the risks associated with managing large amounts of unstructured information.

Discovery aggregates and integrates content across an organization within a larger EIM context—providing access to content that is trapped in silos—and synchronizes this content to reduce the burden on end-users. Discovery technologies deliver non-intrusive solutions that eliminate the need for business users to sort and classify growing amounts of content or, even in some cases, recognize what they are searching for. Managers and employees rely on information to do their jobs and having content indexed and accessible significantly improves efficiency, productivity, and employee satisfaction.

Discovery technology is also the honey that makes your web properties sticky and enables users to find what they're looking for, helping to monetize content and generate revenue through longer visits and more completed transactions.

Organizations across the globe are unleashing the power of their information with Discovery solutions to improve decision-making and drive business outcomes to create competitive business advantage.

EIM needs Discovery

Within the context of an EIM solution, a centralized ECM repository plays a fundamental role in helping organizations realize the value of Discovery solutions. While Discovery technologies work to identify content that has value, an ECM system enables this content to be accessed, managed, and archived. Moving large quantities of unmanaged content into an ECM repository not only reduces storage costs, it enables content to be classified and retention policies applied, allowing for eventual disposition and further cost and risk reduction.

For Discovery applications, ECM with its associated Records Management (RM) capabilities provides a single source of the truth, which is critical when Discovery is used to provide insight and decision-making support. ECM with RM capabilities also delivers a single source of policy that Discovery applications can extend into the information silos found in most organizations.

If we consider the time, money, and effort invested in Customer Experience Management (CEM)—another category of EIM offerings—Discovery technologies can be used to effectively measure and apply analytics to understand the impact and return on investment in CEM technologies. CEM programs deliver volumes of information in many formats. Clickstreams, social media interaction, and eCommerce transactions are well complemented by Discovery applications to help organizations process, enrich, analyze, and help to visualize critical customer-based information. CEM activity and data is becoming both a showcase and proving ground for Discovery technologies.

Discovery stakeholders

Discovery technologies can be applied to problems that impact both the top and bottom lines in an enterprise. Embedded in the basic definition and use cases for Discovery are the concerns of the key stakeholders, including the Chief Legal Officer (CLO), Chief Compliance Officer (CCO), Chief Marketing Officer (CMO), and Chief Information Officer (CIO).

Chief Legal Officer and Chief Compliance Officer

Completing proactive and reactive audits is a requirement to fulfill the litigation and compliance obligations of the CLO and CCO. Organizations require the investigative capabilities of Discovery to search, analyze, and collect information for eDiscovery. Additionally, Discovery, with its ability to help users find and act upon content, helps to enforce information governance policies on large volumes of content.

Chief Marketing Officer

For the CMO, Discovery provides a deeper understanding of the customer, measures the effectiveness of marketing, and monitors the mobile, social, and web trends that impact their brands. Discovery can be used to explore variances and relationships between data, including third-party information. By analyzing this information, organizations can learn more about customers to understand their needs and deliver a more tailored, satisfying customer experience. Insight into customer needs, personas, and behavior gives organizations the ability to make faster, more accurate and cost-effective business decisions. Discovery helps CMOs monitor their campaigns and brands, profile their target markets, gather and analyze competitive intelligence, and launch more effective marketing programs to drive revenue and increase customer retention.

Chief Information Officer

The CIO is increasingly wearing many hats in the enterprise and has a lot at stake when it comes to exploiting the capabilities of Discovery technologies. Thanks to the combination of consumer technology and the "consumerization of IT", the CIO is significantly more concerned about user satisfaction and productivity and has become the voice of the end-user. Discovery improves operational effectiveness by automating and integrating processes and technologies. Reducing complexity and cost by rationalizing applications and decommissioning legacy applications is top of mind with many CIOs. To this end, many CIOs are using Discovery as a tool to identify and assist in the defensible deletion of content to control storage costs.

The CIO is also the owner and architect of the EIM vision within the organization. For this reason, it's the CIO specifically who focuses on Discovery as part of a larger vision to manage all of the information in the enterprise. Discovery capabilities are integrated and actionable, and to be effective, they should not be treated as an afterthought in a technology stack.

Discovery use cases

Discovery applications have been designed to solve defined business problems. The applications support myriad use cases and best practices to maximize business impact. The technologies typically fall into two camps: those that impact the bottom line by supporting good information governance practices and those that impact the top line by improving productivity, providing actionable insight, and monetizing content.

Discovery and good information governance practices

Many different stakeholders are often concerned about distinct aspects of information governance, which is why it's so hard to find common ground when it comes to the applications and policies that govern information. This is why projects become skewed to focus on one particular set of issues, especially when legal, IT, and records and information management departments have not been engaged. The following table illustrates key stakeholders and their differing information management concerns:

Stakeholders	Information Concerns
Legal	Risk
IT	Cost
Line of Business	Value and Productivity
Records Management	Risk and Value

Key stakeholders and their information management concerns

In order to achieve balance in your information governance programs, policies and systems should address the concerns of each stakeholder group listed above. This is especially true when we consider that the business can be looked at in two ways: (1) using content to make money and (2) the impact of policies and systems on end-user adoption and productivity.

Discovery can help organizations strike this balance in a series of applications that address the risk, cost, and value of information all while ensuring the end-user productivity is maintained or improved.

eDiscovery: litigation hold

The requirement to place litigations holds on content is based on the Legal Discovery obligation to suspend regular deletion policy on documents and materials that are related to the subject matter of anticipated litigation. This means that for content under Records Management control, where content is regularly deleted as per policy, it's necessary to be able to immediately suspend the disposal of this content.

Records managers and litigation support personnel must be able to quickly set rules around the information placed on hold. These rules can range from the vague to the very precise, the simple to the complex. The capacity to defensibly adjust the criteria of the hold as more information about the matter becomes apparent is also critical.

In the recent Apple Inc. vs. Samsung Electronics Co. Ltd. patent dispute, an inability to preserve email and other data almost resulted in the jury receiving adverse inference instructions against both parties. An adverse inference instruction means a judge will tell the jury to assume missing documents were favorable to the other side. In this dispute, the magistrate judge initially ordered an adverse inference instruction against Samsung for its failure to stop the automatic deletion of email. However, the judge later found Apple had also failed in its data preservation duties and ordered identical adverse inferences instructions against both parties.

eDiscovery: early case assessment, collection, and culling

Legal teams can utilize Discovery capabilities to connect to disparate data sources and quickly index content and metadata. A quick assessment can provide valuable information on the basic facts, key custodians, and the volume of content that will need to be collected, processed, and reviewed. This information can then be used to determine a strategy for the matter, as well as providing the preliminary cost and risk information that can shape the decision to settle or proceed with the matter.

After a case strategy has been determined, the same Discovery technologies can be used to perform the required actions upon the content under index. Based on search results, content can be collected from various data sources and preserved. These data sources include desktops, file servers, Microsoft SharePoint, live email servers, and more. This is a particularly critical step when working with unmanaged content where no in-place litigation hold is possible.

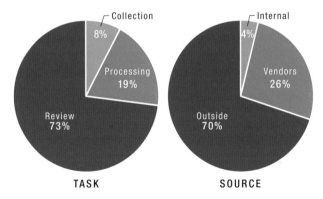

Where eDiscovery costs come from[54]

[54] Nicholas M. Pace and Laura Zakaras, *"Where the Money Goes: Understanding Litigant Expenditures for Producing Electronic Discovery"*, Rand Institute for Civil Justice, *http://www.rand.org/content/dam/rand/pubs/monographs/2012/RAND_MG1208.pdf* (accessed 26 Jan. 2013).

Discovery and "enterprise search"

Discovery and "enterprise search" are very different things. Enterprise search is a term that is used so often that it's difficult to pin down a clear definition. It's in this absence of a definition that enterprise search becomes all things to all people. Unfortunately, enterprise search has garnered a lot of hype, a lot of expectations, and an awful lot of disappointing or failed deployments. This can be explained in part by the "Google" phenomenon, where end-users express their search requirements as "we want something like Google."

> *"How can Amazon.com monitor my customer data so closely that it knows what book I want next, but after five years of daily use, my enterprise search engine doesn't get that I work in HR in the Chicago office?"*[55]

As Leslie Owens from Forrester Research so eloquently points out, simple, single-box search is not an effective way of getting information to users when they're searching for content within their organization. There is a reason why Amazon® knows what book we want before we do. They have used Discovery (and big data) technology to create an application that solves a specific business problem.

The idea that Discovery capabilities need to be tuned to solve specific business problems lies at the heart of a good EIM strategy. Rather than deploying generic search capabilities, organizations that deploy Discovery applications to solve targeted and specific problems will be more successful in their deployments and will be able to more easily correlate their return on investment.

Discovery technology

The platform

Discovery in EIM requires a platform to discover, analyze, and act on information sources throughout the organization. The platform provides a common set of features and functions that can be leveraged by multiple Discovery applications. A platform reduces the costs and complexity associated to having multiple indexes, multiple connectors, and separate hardware for the individual Discovery applications found in most organizations. A typical organization will have one or more indices for eDiscovery applications, one index for enterprise search, and multiple indices embedded in ECM applications.

---

[55] Leslie Owens, *"Semantic Technology in the Enterprise"*, Forrester Research, *http://blogs.forrester.com/leslie_owens/12-04-18-semantic_technology_in_the_enterprise* (April 2012).

The basic requirements for a platform include the following:

- **A unified index of enterprise information** to make it discoverable and to ensure analysis and decisions are based on precise and complete information.

- **Integration services** to provide authorized access to enterprise repositories and the capacity to index and act on that content.

- **Indexing and content enrichment** must support multiple use cases and support the requirements for speed, completeness, and analysis. Indexing can vary from light-weight passes to extract basic file metadata for a quick understanding of the composition of large volumes of information to deep indexing, during which content is enriched with semantic analysis to identify facts and relationships and detect sentiment, patterns, and trends.

- **Capabilities to facilitate the rapid development and deployment of applications and utilities** for EIM. Because many different enterprise information applications share common requirements, a rich set of APIs and a set of reusable widgets can be used to develop applications for specific use cases and user roles.

Discovery-based applications

The role of the Discovery-based application is to address specific business problems with the following technology:

- The right set of features and capabilities derived from search, connectors, integration, content analytics, and visualization.

- A User Interface (UI) that has been created specifically for the personas that will use the application.

- Embedded processes to address business problems.

- Appropriate permissions, security, and roles to support the different personas that interact with the business process.

Discovery-based applications are already replacing generic search capabilities in most organizations. eDiscovery and Knowledge Management applications are some of the first applications that have been adopted. Unfortunately, most of these are stand-alone and require their own infrastructure, index, and support. The true value of both Discovery-based applications and a Discovery platform lies in the ability to solve specific business problems on a common infrastructure to control costs and support requirements.

Where to start

This chapter has outlined a large variety of potential use cases for Discovery technologies. This could represent a challenge when it comes to determining where and how to start if there are multiple use cases that are attractive to the CLO, CMO, and CIO in your organization.

For most organizations, the decisions can be broken down into a few simple steps:

1. **Document and assess the opportunities.** What will have the greatest impact on the organization: a top-line or bottom-line focused project? Does your organization's litigation profile include a large number of high profile cases? Is your marketing organization having difficulty attracting and maintaining visitors? Are poor decisions being made due to an inability to locate and analyze information?

2. **Perform a risk assessment.** Where does the largest cost and risk exist? This is typically the starting point, especially for information governance initiatives. Where is the largest potential for lost opportunity? This is the usual starting point for top-line projects, where time-to-market can make the difference in giving you competitive advantage.

3. **Create a business case.** What will the pay-back period be for the project? In today's economic climate, projects don't move forward without a scrutinized business case. Create a business case based on cautious and optimistic impacts on the business.

4. **Engage with and gain the support of the right executive.** Work with them to validate the business case and risk assessment.

5. **Develop a roadmap.** The nature of Discovery applications prescribes overlapping functionality applied to different use cases. Developing a roadmap of supported use cases will serve to manage expectations and also clarify whether a best-of-breed or a platform strategy should be used. Consider the impact each will have on long-term maintenance, support, and infrastructure costs when developing the business case.

Discovering the power of information

For all the current use cases and existing technologies, Discovery as a category is truly in its nascent stage. It has only been in the past few years that we've seen the combination of search, content analytics, and two-way connectors that make Discovery possible. As a core set of capabilities that can be extended into applications to solve real-world problems, Discovery is an area that will see significant investment, adoption, and innovation.

EIM practices and technology will continue to grow in popularity and importance for the next decade as organizations look to reduce cost and risk and extract value from the untapped

90 percent of information that is unstructured inside organizations. Discovery technologies are a critical component EIM along with the combined ability to perform actions on massive amounts of enterprise information, aggregate and integrate information across enterprise technologies, and provide insight into volumes of content.

As EIM practices and technology mature, Discovery will continue to play a dual role. Common capabilities such as connectors, processing, indexing, content analytics, visualization, and the ability to act on content will be ubiquitously available for EIM technologies. At the same time, because of this ubiquitous availability, Discovery-based applications and features will be added to EIM suites of software to address specific use cases and challenges. These applications will continue to impact both the top and bottom lines.

Discovery in the Cloud
In the rush to save money by moving applications and content to the Cloud, organizations have forgotten the lessons of the past. In the same way organizations created archives with no thought to how content could be deleted or in the same way transactional imaging and BPM systems where developed with no thought to Records Management, organizations are doing it all over again in the Cloud. The first causalities are email and Microsoft Office documents that have been moved to the Cloud with no regard for retention, disposition, and eDiscovery. Other types of content will follow, including critical records like invoices and HR records. Discovery technology offers hope that technology might help save us, but the future will bring the ability to extend Discovery beyond the bounds of the firewall to discover, analyze, and act on content in Cloud applications, extending centralized policy, access, and eDiscovery to content sources stored in the Cloud.

Discovery technologies will continue to be a critical arrow in the quiver of EIM practitioners looking to unleash the power of information in order to protect their organization from risk and cost, make end-users more productive, and improve decision-making by unlocking the value found in enterprise information.

CHAPTER 7

INFORMATION GOVERNANCE

CHAPTER 7
Information Governance: Holistic Governance, Compliance, and Risk Management

"By 2016, 20 percent of CIOs in regulated industries will lose their jobs for failing to implement the discipline of Information Governance successfully." [56]

We know the volume of information is growing significantly, continuing on an exponential growth path. For the enterprise, there is obvious growth of content within the firewall in email, file systems, corporate systems of all types, and even on paper. At the same time, there is also an explosion of high-value content outside the firewall in wikis, blogs, social commentary, and customer interactions.

In some areas, issues of information access are impairing the business. Systems that rely on paper are a prime example and still exist in many organizations. When information is dispersed and copied across many environments, it becomes increasingly challenging to collaborate on this information, difficult to ensure access to the latest version of content, and impractical to automate processes.

There is value in understanding data and turning content into meaningful enterprise information that can be used to optimize the business. When information is brought together in standard processes, analyzed, categorized, and understood, that "new and revitalized" information can drive significant insight and competitive advantage.

Consider the case of an international firm bidding on a large capital project. There are two ways to create a response to the tender: start it from scratch or reuse one from previous projects. If information from similar projects is understood and can be easily reviewed and assembled, then the response to the tender demonstrates the experience held by the organization and offers a significantly higher chance of success.

As more is written about big data and the competitive advantage of understanding and utilizing enterprise information more effectively, corporate executives outside of IT are focusing on information and process. They are recognizing the value of corporate information both inside and outside the firewall. In forward-thinking organizations, critical

---

[56] Bill O'Kane and Andrew White, et al., *"Predicts 2012: Information Governance and MDM Programs Gain Traction"*, Gartner Inc., *http://www.gartner.com/id=1856616* (accessed 12 Jul. 2013).

business information is now recognized as a corporate asset that needs to be protected and cost-effectively managed and leveraged for maximum value to the organization.

Information Governance

There are many definitions of Information Governance, but at the heart it is about effectively using and managing an organization's information assets to derive maximum value, while minimizing information-related risks. It applies to all corporate information, regardless of form, function, or location. This includes structured and unstructured information and ranges from content on file systems and email to information within productivity and line-of-business systems on web, social, and mobile environments.

Information Governance is labeled in different ways. For example, it's sometimes referred to as GRC or Governance, Risk, and Compliance, and it's often discussed in conjunction with archiving, retention, preservation, and disposition of business information. While it does incorporate these elements (as well as aspects of Records Management), it goes well beyond them to encompass all policies and methods of managing information throughout its lifecycle from creation or capture and classification through management to long-term archival or deletion. It involves policy, process, and technology aspects of information stewardship.

Governance is about leveraging information to conduct business. As such, a critical part of Information Governance is ensuring that the right information is presented to the right people at the right time. It follows that governance starts with understanding the organization's information needs. Governance is based on answering the following questions:

• Why is the information needed?

• Who can (and should) use information?

• How can they use the information?

• When can they use the information?

• Where can they use the information?

• What can they do with the information?

Information Governance aims to balance value with the risks and costs associated with corporate information. Often driven by the legal or compliance executives in an organization, the aspects of legal risk, compliance to regulations, and electronic investigation are paramount. The Records Information Management (RIM) groups are normally key stakeholders in the governance process as they define and implement management of critical corporate records. Elements of security, efficiency, and cost are key factors for the technology groups. All of this must come together with key business objectives, such as increased competitiveness, agility, and profitability.

Information Governance Reference Model (IGRM)

Linking duty + value to information asset = efficient, effective management

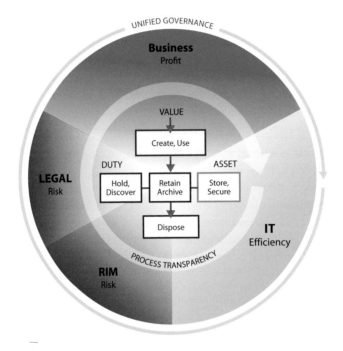

Duty: Legal Obligation for specific information

Value: Utility or business purpose of specific information

Asset: Specific container of information

Information Governance Reference Model (IGRM)

Corporate impetus

While there are several reasons for organizations to consider Information Governance, regulatory compliance is the most significant business driver:

"Regulatory compliance is the No. 1 driver for data management in the eyes of business leaders—70 percent of data management professionals in the Q1 2013 Data Governance Online Survey consider it a critical or high priority. However, data management organizations that keep pace with the business see another benefit to their actions: business innovation."[57]

---

[57] Michele Goetz and Henry Peyret, et al., *"Data Governance Equals Business Opportunity. No, Really"*, Forrester Research, *http://www.forrester. com/Data+Governance+Equals+Business+Opportunity+No+Really/fulltext/-/E-RES83342* (accessed 20 May 2013).

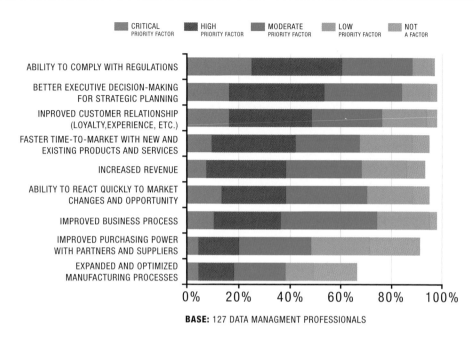

■ CRITICAL
PRIORITY FACTOR
■ HIGH
PRIORITY FACTOR
■ MODERATE
PRIORITY FACTOR
■ LOW
PRIORITY FACTOR
■ NOT
A FACTOR

ABILITY TO COMPLY WITH REGULATIONS

BETTER EXECUTIVE DECISION-MAKING
FOR STRATEGIC PLANNING

INPROVED CUSTOMER RELATIONSHIP
(LOYALTY,EXPERIENCE, ETC.)

FASTER TIME-TO-MARKET WITH NEW AND
EXISTING PRODUCTS AND SERVICES

INCREASED REVENUE

ABILITY TO REACT QUICKLY TO MARKET
CHANGES AND OPPORTUNITY

IMPROVED BUSINESS PROCESS

IMPROVED PURCHASING POWER
WITH PARTNERS AND SUPPLIERS

EXPANDED AND OPTIMIZED
MANUFACTURING PROCESSES

0%   20%   40%   60%   80%   100%

BASE: 127 DATA MANAGMENT PROFESSIONALS

Compliance is the key driver for Information Governance

Regulatory compliance

There is an increasing number of complex regulatory and legislative mandates driving the way organizations manage their business content. Examples of these include the following:

• **Protection and preservation of content** – In some industries, information must be kept (archived) for 50 or 100 years.

• **Defensible deletion of information** – Some content, such as personnel data, that is related to an incident can fall under defensible deletion within defined timelines.

• **Specific Records Management regulations** – Some regions have different regulations, often based on very lengthy and complex implementation and feature requirements specifications.

• **Privacy regulations** – These exist in most regions with increased oversight of types of information stored by organizations, what is shared, and where information is stored. The proliferation of Cloud implementations is causing scrutiny and extensions of this type of regulation inclusive of data sovereignty legislation that requires organizations to ensure information is kept within specific geographical regions.

Failure to meet these types of regulations can result in significant financial penalty, legal liability, and loss of reputation.

Security

Security is one of the top concerns for CIOs, and it drives action. Typically when we think of security, we think of external or internal threats, which involve explicit or inadvertent actions that compromise the integrity of an organization's information. In the context of information, we need to flip this perspective and consider the information itself to be the object that may catalyze a security event.

When information needs to be retained for litigation or compliance purposes, it's imperative to ensure that the information remains intact, pristine, and not only defensible but discoverable and unmodified. Information that is not in this condition with the requisite controls and discovery mechanisms becomes a threat to the organization. It could be the defense of a lawsuit or audit or the data required for submission to bring a new drug to market—in either case, losing or compromising the information represents a financial and/or competitive risk to the enterprise.

The value of information must also be considered in the context of security. Protection of corporate Intellectual Property (IP) is an increasing concern for IT organizations as confidential information, plans, and corporate competitive advantage is housed in electronic format. Threats from both inside and outside the company must be considered as information is protected throughout its lifecycle. No organization wants to find itself exposed through WikiLeaks or other breaches of security causing loss of IP.

Another security-related consideration is the need to ensure disaster recovery. While it is a regular function of IT organizations to consider backup and recovery in all situations, this type of project will also cause examination of the importance of key information and systems and the need to ensure that critical Information is protected from loss.

Organizational effectiveness

Increasingly strategic CIOs and business leaders look to Information Governance to drive improvements in many areas of organizational effectiveness. Consolidated, categorized, and analyzed information is used to drive a deeper understanding of success factors, business trends, and better strategic decision-making. Well-governed information, together with consistent processes, drives greater process velocity and allows organizations to bring products and services to market faster and more effectively than their competition. The more information is brought together for analysis and decision-making, the greater the opportunities for the organization to strategize and innovate.

Information Governance has become a top priority for line-of-business executives as they recognize the opportunities it provides for their business to excel. They join the ranks of their IT and compliance counterparts in recognizing the value of effectively managing their enterprise information.

Compelling events

While innovative CIOs and many other business leaders strive to achieve Information Governance under ideal circumstances, it's often a compelling event that impacts the business and drives these stakeholders to take action. For example, organizations that have faced a major lawsuit or experienced the eDiscovery process with disparate systems often struggle to identify critical information within their systems, uncovering masses of duplicate and sometimes irrelevant data. Sorting through enterprise information for relevant business records can lead to excessive spending on legal reviews, and in many cases, the organization will face fines related to their inability to defensibly show they have produced all information in a timely manner. The same can be true of an electronic investigation related to a regulatory audit. When an organization has faced one of these situations, the cost and business disruption factors are often the drivers on information governance initiatives.

Another example is when an organization within their industry or a related industry is subject to litigation, public scrutiny through audit, or a security breach. As they observe (and often benefit from) the cost to their competitors, organizations typically begin to evaluate the cost and risk factors and start to implement processes and systems for Information Governance.

Holistic is better than tactical

As illustrated in the figure below, the key goals of Information Governance programs within organizations include savings on storage and infrastructure, unimpeded knowledge sharing, and the ability to respond quickly to investigations of all types. Consider how hard it would be to realize these gains if the systems implemented for Information Governance spanned only one or a few departments and projects.

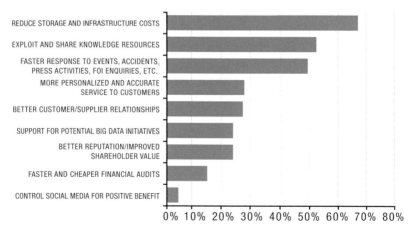

Benefits of good Information Governance

Once an Information Governance system is implemented, storage and infrastructure savings are perhaps the easiest benefits to realize—even if the system is in only one department. Of course, more significant savings can be realized when the system is broadly implemented. Let's consider how.

A large amount of content is duplicated across any given organization. A single document may be stored on the file system, sent to several people in emails, stored in a document management system, and published on the web. When an information governance system is implemented across the enterprise, the technology archives and manages content across all environments, maximizing the value that can be realized across enterprise systems. Archiving technology ensures that content is stored only once and more secure access provided to it from within systems and environments. The storage and infrastructure savings are multiplied with each content source that is brought under governance.

When corporate information sources are consolidated through central governance, there is a level of consistency that is not possible with disparate systems. Policy can be consistently set and enforced across all the content sources under governance. If information is managed across many systems, there are several approaches to how it is managed, searched, kept, or deleted. When an electronic investigation (audit or legal review) is initiated, many systems will have to be examined, information identified, and the policy dictated around that information well understood and documented. If policy is maintained centrally, then one central source of policy will need to be understood, documented, and defended. All information sources governed by that central policy can be searched once and information returned. This approach results in significantly less cost and time invested, in lieu of examining each and every different system of record for corporate information.

However, a central policy does not necessarily mean that all information needs to be physically stored in one system. With robust Information Governance technology, there is flexibility to maintain policy in one central location and manage the content either centrally or in the source system. Many organizations choose to put most of their managed content into an Enterprise Content Management (ECM) system, physically storing content to realize benefits such as infrastructure and user experience consolidation. However, some types of content may be left within their native system with policy managed centrally through ECM. Examples of this may include content within the file system, Microsoft SharePoint, or line-of-business systems in use within the organization.

Information Governance policy must be defensible in order to pass audit and legal review. This includes all parts of the policy from creation to management to disposition. When organizations have disparate systems and no overall governance, content deletion becomes very difficult and is seldom carried out effectively. Before content can be deleted it must be well understood and the corporate value of it assessed. A high percentage of organizations are not able to do this because they do not have complete governance in

> Liz Kofsky

Twitter: @lizkofsky

Liz Kofsky, Director, ECM Product Marketing, OpenText

...On adding value across the enterprise

Organizations have become extremely proficient at generating and collecting information. From emails to marketing collateral to financial statements and beyond, it's growing at staggering rates. But what are many organizations doing with it once it's served its purpose? In the absence of having a thorough information governance program, they've defaulted to dumping it en masse into an archive. Now they can compress, de-duplicate, and encrypt to their heart's content, but in very short order, they're going to want to cost-effectively access and retrieve pieces of that information in its original context—something that's next to impossible unless well-planned information governance policies were in place beforehand.

Chances are the optimal solution could already be roaming your hallways. By bringing your records manager and their knowledge base into the loop and having them collaborate with the IT, Legal, and Compliance teams on a comprehensive information governance program, your organization can extend pre-existing best practices to all its enterprise information and define capture, classification, retention, preservation, archiving, and disposition parameters in an easily accessible, defensible structure.

One of the areas where this cross-functional collaboration can be hugely beneficial to an organization is Enterprise Archiving. In the modern business environment, compliance and legal requirements obviously play a huge role, but effective information management also adds significant value to product development, process improvement, disaster recovery, and more. To achieve this, every email, every R&D report, every accounting ledger, every HR comment, every piece of content needs to be governed, and the best way to do that is to make it part of an existing process that is behind the scenes and reaches across the entire enterprise.

We all know the regulatory and legal climate of the business world has changed drastically: the systematic management of corporate records has become a core element of a compliant, defensible EIM strategy. Accordingly, the practice of records management has evolved from marginalized afterthought to essential survival tool. An organization's very existence can hinge on its ability to provide timely, accurate responses to compliance, regulatory, or discovery obligations.

place. They are faced with either keeping everything (the most common approach) or deleting content without being clear about the consequences.

Keeping everything means higher and higher storage and infrastructure costs. And there is no reason for that. According to research, the average organization needs to hold on to 1 percent of their information for legal holds, 5 percent to meet regulatory requirements, and 25 percent for business analysis and insights. By implication, 69 percent of all the information held by organizations can be thrown out, without suffering negative consequences.[58] One of the key benefits of implementing Information Governance is reduced storage and infrastructure costs. Moreover, hoarding everything significantly increases the cost of electronic investigation as content must be searched, examined, and reviewed from all of the sources where it is stored. With the dramatic growth in content volume, this approach becomes less and less tenable. The route to avoiding this is defensible deletion. This can be done when content is brought under governance, understood, classified, and then managed consistently.

Organizations that implement Information Governance across the full enterprise realize stronger gains. They bring projects together and plan holistically, even though implementation may occur in phases. Some progressive organizations work Information Governance into the requirements of each project, and this ensures business and IT alignment and Information Governance growth with each corporate initiative.

> *The goal of information governance is to strike a balance between the competing priorities in the creation, ongoing use, retention, and disposition of content.*

Challenges

While it's clear that there is good reason to focus on Information Governance, many organizations do not believe they have reached a significant level of data maturity to date. "In fact, only 15 percent rate the data governance maturity as high or very high—defined as incorporating both business and IT, with top-level support and spanning major parts of the organization."[59]

Why is that? Well, it's because Information Governance isn't easy. It takes time and broad consideration.

Organizations have information stored in silos—fragmented across the enterprise in disparate line-of-business systems, email systems, productivity tools, and Enterprise

[58] Lorrie Luellig, *"A Modern Governance Strategy for Data Disposal"*, CIO Insight, *http://www.cioinsight.com/it-management/inside-the-c-suite/a-modern-governance-strategy-for-data-disposal.html/* (accessed 12 Jul 2013).

[59] Michele Goetz and Henry Peyret, et al., *"Data Governance Equals Business Opportunity. No, Really"*, Forrester Research, *http://www.forrester.com/Data+Governance+Equals+Business+Opportunity+No+Really/fulltext/-/E-RES83342* (accessed 20 May 2013).

Resource Planning (ERP) systems, inside and outside the firewall. As companies acquire and merge, more systems and management methods are brought into the organization.

Interoperability of systems across many vendors is complex. Ask any IT group, and they'll tell you that APIs for connecting systems vary considerably, information and metadata are categorized differently across systems, and search and process automation are difficult across different systems. All of this makes Information Governance more challenging.

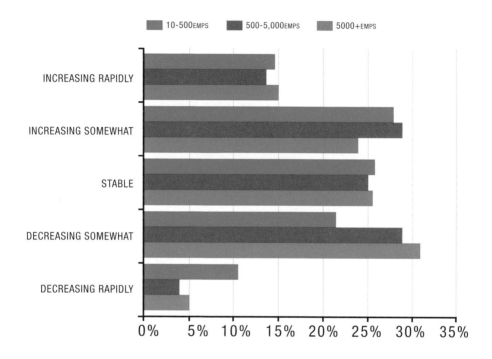

Volume of paper records in organizations surveyed

Progress toward the "paperless office" is slow. In a recent study, 42 percent of the organizations surveyed reported the volume of paper records is still increasing.[60] Paper continues to be a factor in most organizations. While paper is one of the most mature content types and many organizations do have retention and disposition policies around paper, they don't always have the same policies applied across paper and electronic content. Information on paper is largely isolated from efficient electronic processes, is poorly collaborated on, and causes bottlenecks when collaboration does occur.

---

[60] Doug Miles, *"Information Governance: records, risks, and retention in the litigation age"*, AIIM, *http://www.aiim.org/Research-and-Publications/Research/Industry-Watch/InfoGov-2013* (accessed 20 Mar. 2013).

Mobile and application flexibility

Knowledge workers who are mobile are increasingly driving computing choices, and so the information they work with must be mobile friendly. People interact with information using corporate devices that may or may not be chained to a desk; they also interact with information using personal devices. This puts corporate information outside IT management boundaries. The same is true for applications. People work where and how they want to. Many use consumer applications to create and collaborate on their content. Now more and more information sits outside the corporate firewall, and more importantly, outside Information Governance policies. Examples of this include file-sharing services that put content at risk of security and ownership breach.

The recommended path is to use mobile technology that provides consumer-like abilities but is built on an ECM system because it allows users to work with content on applications of their choice within a governed and safe environment. Information can be shared outside the firewall and the enterprise without risking ownership or security breaches. Device governance is provided such that content can be stored and utilized on mobile devices, and if the device is lost, the content can be removed remotely.

Lack of business buy-in

When there is a goal of Information Governance across an organization, it's often inconsistently applied as systems and practices vary by department and region. Some groups may involve the compliance group as they plan for governance, others may plan it themselves, and still others do not consider governance as they bring in systems. The commitment of line-of-business leaders varies as well, either because they are not clearly aware of the issues or because they do not recognize the benefits. Gaining commitment from legal/compliance, IT, and line-of-business executives is key and must be incorporated into Information Governance planning from the outset.

User adoption

Some organizations have implemented governance programs and been unsuccessful. This may be because they've not achieved strong enough user acceptance of the systems. Governance should be built into systems and processes and presented as a manual task for end users. There are several ways to achieve this, including the classification of content through process or project or by mechanisms such as auto-classification. Classification methods can be built into the environment where the user works, whether that is within their office applications, email system, Microsoft SharePoint, ERP system, web, desktop, or mobile devices, without being obtrusive to the user. The key is bringing the governance technology to the user's environment of choice and making it easy, enabling them to spend their time doing their daily activities instead of finding ways to get around using the system.

This is one of the key elements to look for with any Information Governance technology: optimal user experiences within the applications where users work.

Do costs outweigh consequences?

When it comes to mitigating risks, one of the most important questions to ask is "What's the cost of doing nothing?" No real risk can be mitigated to a zero percent likelihood of occurring, and some risks are 100 percent likely to happen. So how should an organization go about determining which risks to mitigate against and which consequences to prepare for? A key consideration is to understand the risk profile. A risk profile takes an objective look at the likelihood of identified risks to occur and their impact when they do occur.

If the organization is a litigation target, it makes very little sense to try and prevent court action (out-of-court settlements notwithstanding). Defensible deletion is a better tactic as it leads to reductions in discovery costs and legal fees. An added benefit of a defensible deletion program is that it makes organizations "info-efficient" by reducing the amount of outdated and irrelevant information that users have to sift through to get work done.

If the enterprise stores Personally Identifiable Information (PII) about stakeholders (for example, those in insurance, banking, healthcare industries) the likelihood that someone will try to compromise that information is quite high, and the impact if they succeed is considerable. Spending time and money on mitigating against unauthorized disclosure is prudent. Not only does this protect against fraud and identity theft, it also protects brand reputation.

When crafting a risk profile, it's important to look at the organization as a whole and to look at the different types of information individually. Not all information is created equally and consequently does not expose an organization to the same risk if lost or disclosed without authorization. Identifying information that is critical to continued business operations allows organizations to craft policies that result in expending resources where it provides the biggest benefit. Identifying information that, if lost or disclosed, would cause nothing more than a minor nuisance prevents organizations from expending resources where there is little appreciable gain. In other words, there's no point in buying flood insurance if your house is on a desert mountaintop.

Successful implementation of Information Governance

What does success look like? The full lifecycle of content is managed over and above merely ensuring security and privacy. Policy is consistently applied across disparate systems and content types. Governance is built into processes and strategic information sources. In the successful implementation, Information Governance is managed by more than the IT and compliance groups. It becomes part of an expansive vision, as business leaders are actively involved and engaged in the process, building Information Governance into key

Key members of the legal and compliance groups, IT, and line-of-business leaders should come together to plan and implement an Information Governance program. Many organizations form an Information Governance committee that makes key decisions on the program. A key to success is carefully choosing the members of the committee to ensure commitment and decision-making power.

When there is an overall plan in place, ensure it keeps pace with the business, with information assets being considered in project prioritization and governance planned into project requirements.

Technology implementations are well understood by most IT and business groups. The user-acceptance goal is paramount in these projects and should be taken into account during planning. Key user groups should be involved during the requirements, planning, testing, and early implementation to maximize adoption. Training is also a major component as these systems roll out, and it is often overlooked. Even when systems are very intuitive, a little training around policy, governance, and the systems can go a long way to increasing adoption and compliance to policy.

Balance matters: holistic governance, compliance, and risk management

Information Governance is about getting information to where it needs to be, faster and safer, so that maximum value can be achieved from this information with minimal risk.

Information Governance is not just about complying with regulations and minimizing risk, however, it's about maximizing the value of the information to create a good, profitable business. It applies to all enterprise information an organization is custodian of, regardless of format, function, or location. Of course Information Governance helps to minimize legal liability, secure sensitive information, and reduce unnecessary expenses, but it's really about treating information as a strategic asset. Properly and holistically applied, Information Governance improves a business. Public sector organizations are better able to assess and satisfy the needs of their constituents. Commercial enterprises are better able to understand their environments and act accordingly to become more profitable.

Governance does not have to be perfect to be effective. It merely needs to be consistently applied, and organizations need to demonstrate best effort or good faith. If organizations choose to ignore policy, they are likely to be sanctioned when investigated. Information Governance policies need to be practical so they can be implemented with adequate training and adherence monitored regularly.

It's in each enterprise's best interest to be protected from information-related risk and harm. Good Information Governance doesn't impede the enterprise's ability to do good business—it enhances it.

CHAPTER 8

INFORMATION SECURITY

CHAPTER 8

Information Security: Protecting the Power of Information

"There were 1,050 cyber-security cases reported to a Hong Kong emergency response center last year." [61]

Information Security is a very broad term and means many things to many people. It's often misunderstood as a single set of actions that prevent your information from compromise or a project that can be completed. Let's start by understanding that both of these statements are emphatically untrue.

It's only through a robust Enterprise Information Management (EIM) strategy and layered, thoughtful security practices that you can protect your organization and its data. What follows is an examination of the layers of security that surround your information and what you can do to mitigate the risk and cost associated with security breaches that are today costing enterprises just under 9 million dollars per occurrence.[62]

Information Security can be illustrated using a pyramid with Social Engineering at the top. There are many possible ways to compromise an organization's security and deny service—from extracting sales information or tracking a company's activities to any number of malicious actions. The facets of this pyramid represent the vectors by which an attack can happen—(1) Social Engineering, (2) Physical Compromise, (3) Environmental Vulnerability, and (4) Reverse Engineering—and the locations at which the CIO must mount an organization's defense of information.

---

[61] Johnny Tam and Joshua But, *"It's tough to trace hackers, says internet security expert"*, South China Morning Post, (28 Jun. 2013), *http://www. scmp.com/news/hong-kong/article/1269775/its-tough-trace-hackers-says-internet-security-expert* (accessed 5 Jul. 2013).
[62] Matthew J. Schwartz, *"Cybercrime Attacks, Costs Escalate"*, Information Week, (8 Oct. 2012), *http://www.informationweek.com/security/attacks/cybercrime-attacks-costs-escalating/240008658* (accessed 5 Mar 2013).

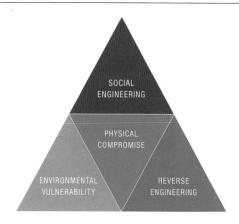

A representation of Information Security

To understand Information Security, we need to examine each of the security facets through the lens of the business, from the environment of an organization's data and the applications within that environment to its employees and the social aspects of information including corporate espionage and virtual doppelgangers, which gain access to corporate systems by exploiting human nature.

In addition to a business perspective on security, it's also important to understand more about where a compromise may occur and the motivation behind these attacks. To do so, let's analyze a breakdown of the types of attacks seen globally during the month of March 2013 (see figure).

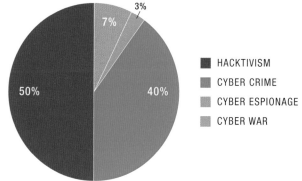

A breakdown of security breaches by type[63]

Most attacks can be attributed to cyber crime and "hacktivism". These attacks spring from many different intentions but almost always have the same manifestations: theft of or corruption to corporate information or denial of service by disrupting web facilities and application availability. In all of these cases, your organization is prevented from working by depriving it of effective information transfer.

---

[63] Hackmageddon.com, *"Cyber Attacks Timelines and Statistics"*, *http://hackmageddon.com/* (accessed 10 May 2013).

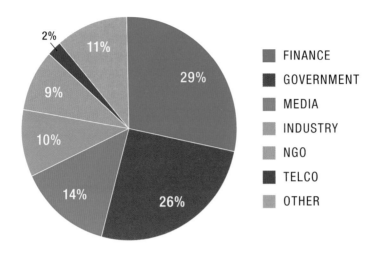

Attacks distributed by industry [64]

Security attacks don't just happen in a single trade: they can occur in every industry in every country. It's important to always be diligent in the protection of corporate information. Knowing that every organization is operating in a potential environment of risk, let's examine the facets of our Information Security pyramid as a baseline for our journey into the security of EIM.

Application security

In the context of EIM solutions, application security means securing your corporate information. This is achieved not only by properly using effective Enterprise Content Management (ECM), Business Process Management (BPM), Customer Experience Management (CEM), Information Exchange, and Discovery applications but also by ensuring that their associated environments and infrastructures are protected.

Within your EIM applications, there are a number of considerations to make that your data and processes are secured. These may include the following:

- Access Control Lists and User Permissions
- Secure Search Configuration
- Audit Controls and Administrative Logging Requirements
- Records Management and Information Compliance
- Application Patching and Maintenance

[64] *Ibid.*

- Brute Force Protection
- Network Configuration
- Obfuscation of Code and APIs
- Administrative Configuration and Separation
- Physical Security
- Environmental Security
- Infrastructure Security
- Other Application-Based Security Concerns

More than anything else, having a secure EIM platform will ensure the integrity of your data. Not only because your data resides on the platform but also because it is the interface through which your people interact with data. The application tier is where your data "comes alive".

We will uncover the specifics of securing the layers surrounding your EIM applications and platform further along in this chapter. In order to verify that your enterprise information environment is robust and secure, it's imperative that all aspects of application security are considered—from the vendor of your solution providing mechanisms by which application security can be enforced, monitored, and adjusted to ensuring that your employees have access to the right information at the right time and that ethical walls are not breached. When we look at the big picture of Information Security from a holistic perspective, application security is just a small part of a complete solution. Let's examine the four vectors of attack.

1. Social Engineering

Social Engineering describes the oldest and most popular form of cyber attack. It can be used to extract information and cause damage to information systems or even physical assets. Social Engineering is, in fact, exactly what it sounds like: the use of social mechanisms to compromise electronic systems. This type of compromise could be someone calling your IT Desk requesting that a password be reset because they are locked out of the system due to a forgotten password.

Does the administrator have a procedure in place to verify that the caller is who they claim to be? Has your organization considered possible social vectors within your processes? With access to even a single password by deceiving a helpdesk representative, an intruder could have access to the company's network or at minimum one of their systems. Social Engineering can also assist the penetration of an organization's defenses through one or many of the other facets of the pyramid. For example, an employee from your company encounters the same person every morning at the coffee shop across the street from an office campus. This is a regular stopover for many of the employees before work. The individual that the employee bumps into discusses a few of the big projects currently underway at your company, and your employee incorrectly assumes the interloper to be a colleague. After chatting a while, they walk to work together. The employee uses her RFID tag and pin code to hold the door open for the interloper, allowing the individual to gain access on the single-access verification, an act known as "tailgating". The individual is not an employee but now has physical access to your building, LAN infrastructure, potentially your data center, and any unlocked terminals they might walk by. This is an example of Social Engineering assisting in a Physical Compromise. Similar scenarios could easily be played out for Reverse Engineering and Environmental Vectors, which is why it's imperative to ensure all of the layers of your Information Security are considered and secured.

It cannot be understated how common, low cost, and relatively easy the Social Engineering vector is, making it prevalent in compromises of all varieties.

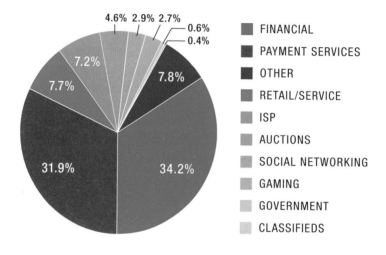

Most targeted industry sectors for social engineering[65]

2. Physical Compromise

Physical Compromise needs little explanation. Without physical security, there is no security. If a bad actor can walk into your data center, take a server from the rack, and walk out with duplicates of your data and environmental parameters or inject malicious software or hardware, you have been compromised. Physical Compromise doesn't just exist in the data center, however.

Employees with mobile devices and personal computers on your network or with access to your application environment are just as vulnerable. For example, let's consider an

---

[65] Help Net Security, *"Cybergangs embracing crimewear over social engineering"*, *http://www.net-security.org/secworld.php?id=14343* (accessed 24 Feb. 2013).

employee with an easy-to-guess PIN code or pattern on a mobile device. If this person loses this device, an unscrupulous person working for a competitor or analyst could find the device and guess the code in an attempt to figure out whose it is. If the device unlocks and the owner has chosen "remember me" on every mobile application they own, including some of those for corporate systems, access to your network can be gained. This is a physical compromise in which the device was lost with all data unprotected by a simple PIN.

Physical Compromise can occur simply and with best intentions, in the form of a smartphone left in the cab or at the airport, but is damaging nonetheless.

3. Environmental Vulnerability

With EIM, as is true in every other aspect of Information and Communications Technology (ICT) security, a large amount of operational investment is associated with achieving environmental security. This is because every environment is composed of a combination of systems, protocols, applications, and dependencies. These are the factors that surround your applications and users. Environmental vulnerability considerations include, but are not limited to

• Operating System Maintenance and Security

• Patching and Updating of

> • Applications

> • Prerequisites

> • Operating Systems

> • Monitoring and Event Software

• Administrative and Application Configurations

• Logging and Monitoring

• Performance and Security Optimization

• Security Certificate and Public Key Infrastructure Operations

• Procedures and Operating Protocol

• Security Policies and Implementation

The real challenge with enacting effective environmental security is keeping on top of it, as the applications and systems within your environment need to be constantly updated, maintained, and monitored for poor practices, rogue behavior, reverse engineering, and outdated technology or software versions.

Database and file system security

Database and file system security are pivotal in ensuring your solutions are secure and that your enterprise information is not a target of corporate espionage, rogue internal threats, cyber attacks from the broader online populace, or other malicious behavior by bad actors inside or outside of your environment.

Every information solution stores data. A datum may be documents, process metadata, search indexes, or other vital and vulnerable information. This data is almost always stored on a file system, such as the company's storage area network or network accessible storage, enterprise disk, optical drives, or other medium. When storing information and dealing with it "at rest", it's imperative to consider the sensitivity of the data and what a potential breach would represent in terms of risk to your organization. For example, trade secrets or other high-value information may need to reside in an encrypted database or file system or may be encrypted themselves. These parameters may be an option provided by an Archive Server solution, or they may be entirely reliant on the provider of the underlying technology, such as a native database's capacity to encrypt itself and provide API calls through which trusted applications can access the encrypted data. Leading database vendors often offer this capability as baseline functionality.

When formulating a secure EIM strategy, an assessment must be made as to the value and sensitivity of the data and the cost associated with implementing and maintaining additional levels of security. For example, an encrypted database will perform more slowly than a plain text variant, which means additional hardware, load balancing, and other infrastructure must be added to the environment to offset the overhead incurred by protecting the database and file system. This analysis should be made each time a system is deployed to understand which level of security is appropriate for the application and information in question. An encrypted database containing customer lists that is copied by a rogue employee is largely useless without the encryption keys, making the data and potential risk associated with leakage of that data as a complete set much lower.

User security

One of the often overlooked but most fundamental aspects of enterprise Information Security is user security. This encompasses many procedures within an enterprise, ranging from but not limited to

• Proper configuration of access control lists to grant the appropriate people access to the appropriate content. This ensures that sensitive information is not broadcast throughout your organization, diminishing the capability of the enterprise to exert control over its availability.

• Proper user training is another vital part of EIM security practices. Users have the ability to compromise your data and procedures with or without willful intent. As an example, when users have the option to export content to a local device (such as a smartphone, tablet, laptop computer) or to view the content online without generating local copies on remote devices, they should always choose the latter as a matter of practice. Assuming the environment and infrastructure is secure, this means a reduction in "orbital assets" on edge devices, which are typically where enterprise security is compromised, whether it's a lost smartphone in a taxi or a laptop left at a customer presentation, and this makes a security threat a possibility.

• Device, password, and other policy management affect user security as well. Does your organization allow end users to select "remember me" on mobile device or web applications with access to enterprise data? This is poor end-user security, which promotes insecure ease of access for employees and for bad actors as well. Other pragmatic policy options include password policies, mixes of letter case, alphanumeric and special characters, and requisite password lengths to make brute-force hacking less of a threat.

Communication protocol security

Protocol security encompasses "information in transit", which happens when your data is transmitted over myriad transport protocols to exchange information between clients, servers, or both.

There are a vast number of protocols and communication mediums in play through today's technologies and devices, including the following:

- Hyper Text Transfer Protocol (HTTP)
- Secure Hyper Text Transfer Protocol (HTTPS)
- Bluetooth
- Secure Shell
- File Transfer Protocol (FTP)
- Secure File Transfer Protocol
- Transport Layer Security
- Secure Socks Layer (SSL)
- Fiber Channel Network Protocols
- Post Office Protocol (Email)
- Wireless and Radio Protocols

Each of these protocols typically has a secure variant (as with HTTP and HTTPS/SSL). Where there is no secure variant offered, it's recommended that organizations leverage the capabilities of a secure Virtual Private Network (VPN), which will holistically encrypt all data transmitted between two nodes, regardless of whether the base protocol itself is encrypted, if the connection is between two points on the same VPN. Imagine this as a secure, unreadable envelope that can't be opened or viewed by anyone but the sender and receiver, so regardless of the contents of the envelope (a plain text letter), they cannot be intercepted and read by anyone outside of the trusted sequence.

Without appropriate protocol security, it's possible for a malicious employee, competitor, hacker, or other entity to intercept communications from your network and derive their contents from the protocol payloads (the data being transmitted) without first breaking the encryption. This is critical in ensuring your information is secure while it's at rest in the database or file system, in flight over the protocol, or in motion through the application currently in use.

Infrastructure security

Infrastructure security encompasses the other requirements associated with the network and data center at your organization. This includes the proper configuration of firewall and port controls, the maintenance of user-provisioning systems or Certificates in your Public Key Infrastructure (PKIs), and Hardware Security Modules.

Having a secure infrastructure can help by providing intrusion detection, redundancy, and administrative segmentation, as well as duplicitous firewall configurations to protect both applications from the internet and databases and file systems from applications. This provides an extra layer of electronic security to the applications using your enterprise infrastructure.

4. Reverse Engineering

Reverse Engineering is another method by which malicious actors can compromise Enterprise Security. This is usually the least-used variant of intrusion because it is the most complex and costly. Reverse Engineering happens when an engineer or team of engineers take the target (for compromise), whether it's an application, database, or protocol, and deconstruct it to understand its most basic elements and method of assembly. If a technology can be taken apart and understood at its molecular level, the malicious actors can leverage information gleaned from these basic building blocks and formulate parasitic applications, vulnerabilities, or purpose-built exploits that can then be targeted at the production system, which is the ultimate prize of their endeavors.

Reverse Engineering is less common than other vectors of compromise in that it requires a high degree of specialization and talent. Sometimes it requires access to the source code of the target application and is a lengthy and expensive undertaking. This isn't to say that it doesn't happen because it does, particularly around Intellectual Property theft in the form of building the next generation of smartphones by disassembling and innovating upon the intellectual property of a competitor, for example. Due to the complexity, cost, and requisite talent involved, however, this type of attack is seen less frequently than Social Engineering, Physical Compromise, or exploiting vulnerabilities in the ecosystem or infrastructure.

The secure CIO

What is the role of today's CIO? We see the CIO position in most large businesses, but what, fundamentally, is their charge in today's enterprise? Is the CIO a purchasing center and infrastructure provider?

In actual fact, the CIO is much more. Above and beyond effectively delivering the services and applications that keep an organization working, today's CIO is the digital guardian of the enterprise, fending off attacks, securing vital organizational data, and ensuring that end users don't become their own worst enemy.

In the context of security, CIOs are required to perform a variety of functions from securing the company's network and ensuring applications are up-to-date and fault tolerant to protecting edge devices and the organization from internal and external threats.

It's critical that today's CIO not only protects their information from a compliance perspective, but also focuses on malicious and explicit security threats. This shift to proactive protection is imperative in today's environment. There is little value in building a program to the letter of an auditor's standard and then leaving security gaps simply because they aren't mandatory to achieve compliance or regulatory requirements. This behavior is akin to locking the front door and leaving all of the windows open. Data is not location-centric. Data is dynamic—moving, shifting and changing over time. Data moves from system to system into and through repositories, process engines, and outside the company through external communications services like fax, EDI, email, file sharing, websites, and others.

Though a competent CIO can work to secure the end points and likely intrusion vectors on their network through firewall configuration, threat detection appliances, and good password and security policies, it's still extremely difficult to protect the amorphous data that composes the lifeblood of your company. This difficulty doesn't exist simply because the data itself is portable: it exists because our perception of security isn't associated with the content and processes that we use. Security, as we think about it traditionally, represents only the infrastructure and environmental components, but this perspective is no longer sufficient.

Effective EIM is designed to secure information in a process- and data-centric way by protecting information where it is used: in the application. Some mechanisms that can be applied to secure dynamic content (whether it's a document, a process, a media file, or web presence) include the following:

- Information Compliance and Records Management

- Information and Object Audit Capabilities

- Administrative Monitoring

- Access and Control Lists and Permissions

- Archive Encryption and Key Security

- Secure Information Exchange

Information compliance and Records Management

Security should be thought of as more than the protection of data from external (or internal) threats and malicious intent. Protecting your data also means protecting your organization from itself. In every industry, it's imperative to ensure that your information meets compliance and governance requirements. A failure to do so can cause a stoppage of business, revenue adjustments, lost intellectual property, or indefensible litigation. Effective Records Management and ECM solutions help CIOs and organizations to secure information through legal and records holds and sound Content Lifecycle Management, ensuring that information can't be accessed or destroyed when such an action would be contradictory to company needs.

This type of compliance-based security is critical in all businesses. Some industries are more highly regulated than others, requiring adherence to compliance standards such as DoD, VERS, MOREQ2, or other Records Management standards. However, even without these requirements as mandatory baselines, every organization is subject to tax law, financial law, and potential litigation. Holding records too long or not long enough is a critical failure of information security, which could damage your business.

We will explore information governance and compliance later in this chapter.

Information and object audit capabilities

When a compromise does occur or a suspected compromise is at hand, it's vital to be able to understand the full history of sensitive content and reconstruct its forensic trail. From who has viewed or downloaded the information to administrative actions such as changing permissions or access within a set of content, information audit capabilities are an additional layer designed to help you manage and assess threats around your information.

Security threats don't only exist to steal, leak, sell, and share your trade secrets in manufacturing and energy industries, they also exist in financial markets with potential risks associated with trading on inside information, selling data to a competitor, or any number of appalling actions that compromise the integrity and confidentiality of your information or damage the value of your brand and company.

EIM solutions offer customers the ability to understand the full lifecycle of content and all of the actions that have been performed on it, including

- When and by whom an asset is accessed,

- When it is viewed,

- When it is downloaded,

- When it is deleted or moved,

- When administrative settings or access has changed, and

- When a new version is added.

This type of audit logging ensures that if and when an incident does occur, the CIO is able to reconstruct the stream of events and implement corrections to environment, infrastructure, and procedure to ensure no repeat occurrences.

Administrative monitoring

Sometimes it's not sufficient to simply audit the trail of a document or process. In today's environment of application outsourcing and high employee turnover, a rogue administrator is an ever-present hazard. Administrative logging is valuable in disaster recovery and in cases of other major events, for which you may need to reconstruct the timeline to analyze data leakage, production impact, or other factors.

It's also good practice to separate administrative duties and look for EIM solutions that facilitate this separation. As a practical example, it's sound procedure to ensure that your database administrator is not the same person with the same credentials as your application or content/process administrators. Leaving all of the "keys to the kingdom" with a single individual is a risky proposition. Dividing administrative duties and privileges helps to mitigate this risk by ensuring that any willful, malicious act will require the involvement of two or more administrators—considerably lessening the likelihood of a breach.

Access and control lists and permissions

In addition to the intentional behaviors that may result in a security breach, physical compromise, or data leakage, we must consider the actions and behaviors of individual users. Humans are creatures of curiosity, and it's inevitable that users will consume data not intended for them if presented with it. The temptation is sometimes too great.

Effective EIM systems have access and control lists and complex permission structures to ensure users only have access to what they need and what they are permitted to see. This doesn't just apply to documents and content of a sensitive nature. It also includes processes and the ability to provide decision dispositions against them, as well as secure communications and information exchange, such as a user sharing files with a colleague or client or using secure fax to correspond with suppliers.

Most likely it is content that you want to protect. From trade secrets to blueprints and litigation matters—whatever the information is—it's imperative that the right people have easy access to the right information and the wrong people do not have access. This pertains to users searching for data, looking through folders, following a link from a colleague, or following process-flow instructions. Access and control is critical to information security, and figuring out the right balance of access is often not easy. If it is too tightly controlled, an organization runs the risk of hampering innovation and information reuse. If it is too lightly controlled, the risk is data leakage.

Archive encryption and key security

Once your organization has worked its way through provisioning a secure environment on site, in the Cloud, or as a hybrid (and done so based on a secure infrastructure), you are ready to move on to defining your information taxonomies and corresponding access and control structure.

Your organization is now ready to start managing its data effectively. You might have a couple of diligent administrators who handle segmented parts of the administrative workload, with one focusing on your environment and one maintaining your applications. Your organization now needs to consider whether or not your archived data, produced and stored in your EIM environment, needs to be protected while it is idle in the archive or at rest. Often overlooked, information at rest is vulnerable. An Archive Server solution allows your organization to encrypt their information within the archive. This ensures that with a social, physical, or environmental breach (which allows the archived data to be copied or distributed) the information contained within it is useless without the decryption keys. This adds an additional layer of security to your information.

A discussion of data security would not be complete without a review of encryption and the various methods that are used to protect your data. In simplest terms, encryption is the process of encoding a message so that it can only be decrypted and read by a trusted party. Chief among data protection methods are hashing and encryption, and while often placed under the same umbrella of data protection tools, they are very different.

Fundamental to the discussion of encryption is an understanding of the concepts surrounding the length or complexity of an encryption key or hash. The length or complexity of the key is measured in bits. The more bits used to represent the key, the longer the length. The longer the key, the tougher it is to crack. With advancements in computational power, keys that were once thought to be secure are now relatively easy to crack via brute-force techniques, where every combination of keys is tried until a match is found. A DES key, which is made up of 70 quadrillion possible combinations (56-Bit key) is now easily cracked through simple brute-force attacks. More common today is the Advancement Encryption Standard (AES), which uses 128 to 256-Bit keys. A 256-Bit key is almost impossible to crack through brute-force methods. If an individual were to try every possible key, this would entail a possible 2^{256} keys. This is an extremely large number. To put it in perspective, if every atom on earth was a computer that could try ten billion keys a second, it would still take about 2.84 billion years to find the key even if it found a match after trying half of the possible keys. A brute-force attack is simply not feasible; a flaw in the actual encryption algorithm would have to be found to crack this level of encryption.

Hashing is a one-way, irreversible mapping, which makes it technically impossible to return the original data after it has been hashed. Common hashing algorithms used today include SHA1 (Secure Hash Algorithm) and the versions that have followed it, where each subsequent version is increasingly secure as hashes are yielded with more bits. A common

> Gary Weiss

Twitter: @gary_weiss

Gary Weiss, Senior VP and General Manager of the Information Exchange Business Unit, OpenText

…On the ever-changing threats to enterprise security

The changes to the IT landscape that we have seen over the last 30 years have been quite remarkable. With this changing landscape, information security has probably been the biggest area of concern for any CIO. And this is because security—and the way we view security—has also been changing.

The traditional view of security has always been perimeter based. It has been about viruses, about protecting the perimeter. You had a firewall. You had endpoints. And for the first time in the history of IT, the endpoints are now eroding. There are no endpoints! Nobody was ready for this. Suddenly everyone was scrambling to create information management strategies to protect this flood of unsecure information. Organizations started asking questions like: "Where is my information? How do I firewall it from other folks? How do I create access control rights to make sure certain people with certain privileges enter the right IDs and get access to the right information when they need it?" These technologies exist, of course, in the form of identity and access management, information management, mobile security, and secure messaging technologies. But at the end of the day, it has to do with making sure the right people get access to the right information at the right time.

Another concern is something called "social engineering". Social engineering occurs when people are given access to information they would not otherwise be able to access on their own. This can happen in the form of passwords, IDs, or files provided by a friendly coworker. Many companies right now do not have strategies in place to actively protect themselves from social engineering and they generally do not hold their employees accountable for not protecting their passwords and IDs. However, implementing such policies would already propel them a step ahead of what the majority of the market is doing. OpenText, for one, has technologies that can support this. But for an organization to implement the right security strategy for their environment and manage this ever-changing information management landscape, it needs to be supported not just by one but by an ecosystem of vendors. In fact, an organization needs a comprehensive strategy that is vendor agnostic.

OpenText is happy to participate in that environment, but we're not alone. It will take a conglomerate, a consortium if you will, to create a strategy that will properly secure an organization. At the end of the day, if somebody really wants to break in and attack your company, the best you can do is try to detect it immediately and respond to it quickly. Unfortunately, there is no foolproof way to secure everything. Yet.

use of hashing is in the storage of passwords, where an application will apply a strong hash to your password before storing it in the application's database. Have you ever wondered why when you forget your password it can be reset but not retrieved? This is because your password has been hashed, making it almost impossible to retrieve if it has been hashed with a strong algorithm.

There are methods for bad actors to defeat this method of protection by generating an encrypted representation of the data. This is where "salting" a hash comes into play, especially when storing passwords. A "salt" is a random string of data that is used as additional input when running a password through a hashing algorithm. For example, if you set your password to "OpenText", this might be salted with the word "enterprise" through a concatenation of the two strings. The original password along with the salt would then be stored in the application database.

Encryption is a two-way function, with the two most common methods being symmetric (also known as shared-key) and asymmetric (known as public-key) encryption.

Symmetric encryption
With symmetric encryption the encryption keys are the same, meaning the data is encrypted and decrypted using the same key. Both the sender and receiver use the same private key to encrypt and decrypt messages. Some examples of public-key encryption include TripleDES and AES.

Asymmetric encryption
Asymmetric or public-key encryption makes use of two keys: a private key and a public key. As the name implies, a public key is freely available and can be used by anyone who wants to send a secure message to the owner of the private key. The public key is used to encrypt the message, and the private key is used to decrypt it. An example of an asymmetric encryption system is RSA.

Secure Information Exchange
Secure Information Exchange allows organizations to communicate and trade information securely. It doesn't follow all of the same principles as the other areas of EIM such as ECM, BPM, CEM, or Discovery. This is because Information Exchange isn't about managing repositories of unstructured or process-based data: it's about communications and exchanging data. Whether it's sending a fax or managed file transfer of digital assets, secure Information Exchange sets the bar for secured communications. The following capabilities make secure Information Exchange unique:

• Encrypted data at all times during file transfer and information exchanges—both inside and outside the enterprise—providing superior protection of sensitive data.

• Collaboration via threaded messages, which include file uploads that enable users to connect with a high degree of transparency and allow for more intuitive organization of content.

- Notifications that are date- and time-stamped when messages are received and files are downloaded, allowing for easier tracking and more efficient workflow management.

- Full control over file/data download availability.

Information governance and compliance

Information governance and compliance are not considered a critical aspect of information security often enough. Typically, when we think of security, we think mostly of external or internal threats, which require an explicit or inadvertent action to compromise the integrity of an organization's information. In the context of information governance and compliance, we need to flip this perspective and consider the information itself to be the object, which may catalyze a security event. When information needs to be retained for litigious or compliance reasons, it's imperative to ensure that the information remains intact, pristine, and not only defensible but discoverable and unmodified. Information that isn't in this condition with the requisite controls and discovery mechanisms becomes a threat to the organization. Whether it's the defense of a lawsuit or the data needed for submission to bring a new drug to market, losing or damaging information represents a financial and competitive risk to the organization in question.

Regardless of which industry you're in, promoting good governance requires moving beyond mitigating risk and ensuring the security of your data to encompass the continuity and foundations of your business.

Equally important to the good retention, categorization, and discovery of your records is the ability to dispose of them when they are no longer needed. The ability to effectively implement compliance and corporate governance doesn't end with the retention and management of your records. There are a number of benefits to the proper destruction of unneeded historical records, from the mitigation of risk associated with old content exposed to data leakage, theft, or poor long-term management to the reduced storage costs garnered from good electronic housekeeping and the destruction of data that is no longer of use or value.

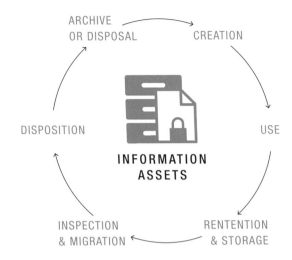

ARCHIVE OR DISPOSAL → CREATION

DISPOSITION

INFORMATION ASSETS

USE

INSPECTION & MIGRATION ← RENTENTION & STORAGE

Good governance ensures security, compliance, and business continuity

Specific geographies have specific requirements for Records Management standards, often based on very lengthy and complex implementation and feature requirement specifications. Records Management and Information Governance solutions have been designed to address legislated Records Management requirements in addition to industry standard and compliance requirements such as MoReq2, VERS, DoD 5015.02, 21 CFR Part 11, Sarbanes-Oxley, and others.

The secure path forward

CIOs need to think about security as a layered defense. According to an often-used metaphor, security is like an onion with data at its core. It's imperative not to rely on any one layer of the onion as a perfect defense from every type of threat.

Security starts at the outer layer, where Social Engineering and the policies, people, and culture of security will be your most effective defense. It's essential to make sure that your security practices are implemented in a way that encourages your people to think about security first. This may involve sound mobile-device management, secure facilities, and protocols for the use of company networks and external storage devices. Be comprehensive in your approach to security; think holistically about everything that surrounds your infrastructure, environment, and applications. Don't limit your solution to technology as the singular safeguard of your data.

Once you're confident that the procedural, cultural, and social policies surrounding your environment are secured in proportion to the value of the data and need for openness required, you have found the right balance and it's time to implement the technological safeguard layers representing your secure environment.

First and foremost is application security. The ability to protect your information in a multi-tiered application environment delivered by effective EIM is extremely important when deciding how to manage your enterprise information. EIM provides the following mechanisms to help ensure the integrity of your business:

- Data Archiving and Long-Term Retention

- Archive Encryption and Storage Management

- Records Management and Information Governance

- User and Administrator Access and Controls Management

- Secure Content and Process Audit Capabilities

- Version Management

- Content Categorization and Semantic Auto-Classification

- Secure, Encrypted Information Exchange

- Directory Server Synchronization

- Information Discovery Capabilities

- Permission Inheritance

- Encrypted Protocol Support

- Process Management

Configuring your EIM suite and implementing the right level of balance between the free and open flow of information and the rigid control of your content and processes is an extraordinarily important one—and one that the CIO must make in concert with the CEO, CLO, and other stakeholders. Striking the right equilibrium can mean a secure and successful future for your data and improved innovation, efficiency, and peace of mind.

Once your application environment is properly configured and secured to match the needs of your business and the sensitivity of your information, it's time to consider the environment and infrastructure on which everything is run.

Securing the application environment means protecting the machines and operating systems on which the application layer exists. It also includes the configuration and fortification of the protocols that interact with your application environment. This involves implementing Secure HTTP instead of plain text, managing secure certificates for your environment, and leveling your administrative procedures to ensure no single administrator has unadulterated access to your environment in its entirety.

Environmental security also includes basic operational security tasks like making sure that applications are patched to the most recent version of application and platform software, and continuously monitoring logs and event notifications generated by applications, operating systems, and security monitoring suites. Once you are content that your environment (including its applications, operating systems, dependencies, protocols, and administrators) is operating at the requisite levels of confidence, your infrastructure must be considered.

Your information infrastructure includes the physical protection of your data center from threats such as power loss, physical breach, cooling failure, natural disaster, and other factors. It also includes the peripherals of your application environment, such as load balancers, firewalls, network segmentation, LAN protection, threat-monitoring devices, DMZ configuration, database protections, and your broader infrastructure.

In today's environment it's just as important to understand the application, environmental, and infrastructural considerations of your Cloud, SaaS, PaaS, and hosted and managed providers. Whether you are operating in a public Cloud, such as Salesforce.com or DropBox®, or have chosen to implement your environment and infrastructure as a private or hybrid Cloud, such as with OpenText Tempo Box and Tempo Social, you must ensure your partner's security is sufficient at all layers to meet the requirements of your business. These requirements cause many to select private and hybrid Cloud configurations, which give you strict control over the levels of security implemented and managed by vendors to find the right balance for your needs.

Protecting the power of information

Now having considered and thoughtfully implemented an effective EIM suite, bolstered by the appropriate social-, physical-, environmental-, and infrastructure-based security protocols and technologies, you're ready to get to work.

The CIOs job is ceaseless. However, a comprehensive EIM platform along with continuing diligence in the monitoring and updating of your systems and security strategy to adapt to emerging threats is your best defense against security compromise.

CHAPTER 9

THE SOCIAL ENTERPRISE

CHAPTER 9

The Social Enterprise: Unlocking Social Value

"Not everything that can be counted counts. Not everything that counts can be counted." [66]

There's been a lot of talk about the Social Enterprise and how a digital social interaction can help organizations engage with their employees, customers, partners, and broader networks on a variety of topics. The promise of the social enterprise has evolved over the past few years to encompass everything from the reduction of travel expenses, training and enablement costs, risk reduction, email traffic replacement, and the minimization of duplicate attachments to the more pertinent assertions surrounding the capture, retention, and farming of corporate social data containing untold value.

There are many facets of the social enterprise to explore: how this technology affects commercial operations and returns value to end users and companies alike, the understated effects of enterprise social software, and how the data it generates is critical to your corporate memory, employee efficiency, information yield, and a number of other aspects of "socializing" your organization.

Social networks

Social networks have only been around in their contemporary format for the past ten years or so, coming into our collective consciousness as powerful, transformative technologies with the advent and release of Myspace® and Facebook in 2003 and 2004, respectively. These online consumer social giants were the logical progression of more primitive predecessors, which ranged from modem-based Bill-Board Systems (BBS) to online forums and chat facilities in the early internet. Social networking has been around longer than many of us suspect, however broad awareness of the value that these technologies garner has only started to proliferate in last few years. Their reach has extended beyond the generation of digital natives (those born between 1980 and today) to become commonplace in most users' lives through the popularity of sites like Facebook and Twitter and easily accessible interaction models leveraging mobile devices, tablets, and web user interfaces.

The commercial model for these consumer sites is based almost exclusively on the volume of traffic and the number of ads successfully positioned in front of appropriate

---

[66] William Bruce Cameron, *"Informal Sociology: A Casual Introduction to Sociological Thinking"* (New York: Random House, 1966).

users. Additionally, usage patterns, preferences, and other personal user data collected by these consumer social platform providers are for sale to the highest bidder. Consumer social users are demographic models and advertising targets to the social sites that host them. Consumer social sites are designed to collect as much usage and demographic data as possible from visitors, while positioning the largest possible volume of apropos advertising. This is where the social network and the social enterprise diverge. Enterprise social software is designed to securely generate value based on its content, context, and the power of the actual human network contained within the social infrastructure itself. Let's take a look at the dichotomy of consumer and enterprise social technologies and explore why the social enterprise is so vastly different than the social network and how it represents true value to your organization.

Expectations

The consumer web has shaped the expectations of a generation of end users. Shaped by offering "free" social capabilities in the Cloud and an almost unlimited number of connections, Facebook has more than one billion end users—a truly staggering statistic. To understand what these one billion consumer end users expect and need from a social technology, we need to understand their motivations for using these sites and how those may differ significantly from a social enterprise platform like OpenText Tempo™ Social. Many of the same idioms and concepts exist as consumer technologies but serve a different type of user looking to accomplish a different set of objectives. The social enterprise is a value engine rather than an advertising engine.

The range of impetus driving users to consumer social sites are many; some altruistic and beneficial; some not. Let's consider some of the primary motivations for users of both types of platforms and how and why they are so distinctive.

Consumer social platforms

A social network is a social structure made up of individuals (or organizations) called "nodes", which are connected by one or more specific types of interdependency, such as friendship, kinship, common interest, financial exchange, dislike, or relationships of beliefs, knowledge, or prestige.

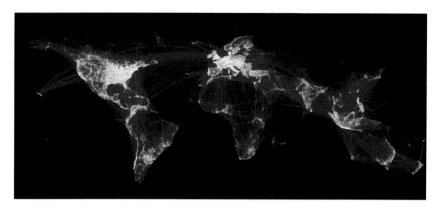

Social graph representing worldwide Facebook relationships and connections

Stay connected

Probably the single most popular motivator for the use of consumer social sites like Facebook or even LinkedIn—the latter arguably positioned as an "enterprise" social tool, but existing in the public domain—is the ability to stay connected with your network, easily.

Users of consumer social sites see the capabilities delivered for contact management, network analysis, and other related functionality as a boon to their digital Rolodex®. Being able to keep a complete list of every contact you have ever made is an invaluable tool for any person—better yet if the contact information for every member of your personal network is maintained and updated by those people (as is the model in today's consumer social networks). This capacity allows people to reach out to old contacts, present contacts, or to source new contacts through their already established and always up-to-date network, furnished by the social network provider.

This capability to always stay connected is remarkable. The fundamental concept of crowdsourcing the maintenance of your digital Rolodex to all of its individual members is extremely appealing. Recommendation engines and other analysis agents make the task of finding and building the digital representation of your social network easier and more appealing. The value to end users of staying connected with consumer social networks is obvious and one of the primary drivers for the success of tools such as Facebook and LinkedIn.

Establishing and maintaining contacts is the first activity any consumer social network user will undertake after creating an account. Who do I know? Who can I connect with now that I'm online? The simplicity of socially crowdsourcing the maintenance of your personal network is a fundamental revolution in the way we connect.

The quest for popularity

Humans are social animals. We thrive, learn, and adjust based on the feedback of our peer groups. People typically distain isolation, and the digitization of social computing has allowed us to always be connected, social, and up to date. A good social platform is only as beneficial as the quality and crispness of its content and its capacity to facilitate the expansion of its members' networks and the proliferation of the platform's value within its user base. To this end, consumer social networks rely heavily on recommendation engines, which position likely connections within the network to users and ease the manual component of the network development process for the end user. As each user is added another node on the social graph is plotted and the platform's relative value to both the end user and to the platform provider increases.

Users are constantly motivated by "popularity" or perhaps more appropriately "esteem needs" as outlined in Maslow's hierarchy of needs.[67] Social networks facilitate this need, making it easy for users to build their online reputation and reinforce their social position through capabilities provided in the social platform, such as "liking" or "up-voting" as seen on the consumer web. It's with fascination that we see human behavioral models being mapped to data object models and then plotted against the interaction and network graphs of significant amounts of the human population—in the case of Facebook, more than a billion users. In the future, the social platform provides us with the data set necessary to understand people's interaction and thought models and how those are associated with the data in the platform itself.

Fun and entertainment

New, relevant content is the water in the well of the social platform and one of the major requirements of repeat visitors. As such, consumer social networks rely heavily on recommendation engines and semantic agents to generate fresh, relevant content without human intervention. Content is tailored to the specific user visiting that site and based on their interactions with the system and those of their network, ensuring that the user always has something of interest to check out.

And don't forget that social networks are fun! They let us build and develop relationships and keep up to date with loved ones, friends, colleagues, and customers. Social networks are gaming platforms, content repositories, and media management experiences. People use social technologies to accomplish many things. We're drawn to social media and the ability to interact around content and experiences—digitizing our social interactions traverses geographies virtually, spans any distance, is instant, engaging, and creates a sense of community. It's the electronic representation of people bonding, learning, sharing, building, selling, and being. We've only begun to understand the value that social data sets provide and the extent to which that social experience can help shape organizations, all while providing a compelling, fun, and rewarding experience for customers and users.

---

[67] Saul McLeod, *"Maslow's Hierarchy of Needs", Simply Psychology", http://www.simplypsychology.org/maslow.html* (accessed 7 Apr. 2013).

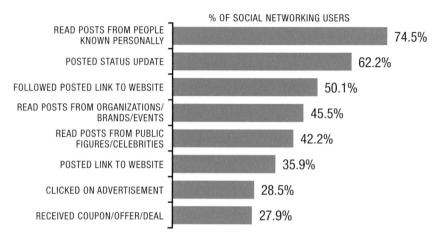

Social networking activities

Enterprise social platforms

Developing a business network

Much like the "digital Rolodex" of the consumer web, the social enterprise has the capacity through its social platform to build, maintain, suggest, and position network connections for its users. Where enterprise social platforms differ is in tracking the skills, abilities, certifications, and other data surrounding the users within the social enterprise platform. This allows employees to find subject matter experts quickly and easily, making new employees more efficient by giving them access to the corporate memory of their colleagues instantly, without the requirement to be geographically in the same place.

The networks maintained within the social enterprise allow users to connect with each other based on their mandates and interests, by joining communities of people working on similar projects and sharing relevant experience and assets. Communities can be used to organize the interactions of the social enterprise and ensure that the conversation, innovation, and other social data surrounding the work is captured, made safe, and is reusable and searchable.

Extract the conversation

There are two types of data generated socially by end users: artifacts and conversation.

1. Artifacts - Artifacts are the items we create as work products. The resolved claim, completed workflow, the happy customer, the presentation. These artifacts could be a document, completed process, handled exception, presentation or PDF file, and will ultimately be stored in the enterprise social platform or in the organization's Enterprise Content Management (ECM) system. The management of enterprise artifacts has been discussed in previous chapters in this book.

2. Conversation - The other type of data that social users generate, which is perhaps more important, is the conversational or contextual data that surrounds the artifacts. This is the chat with the subject matter expert, the discussion surrounding a point of litigation, the detail around a claim exception process—the contextual data about why a decision is made, how it is made, and why any of the previously discussed artifacts are what they are. The context is what makes the data germane.

Until recently, with the advent of enterprise social computing, it was not possible to capture this context. Social platforms have enabled organizations to make their employees more effective and to help the organization remember when those employees move on, representing true value for the social enterprise.

Secure collaboration

Social interaction can be risky—for more than just the enterprise. Online social computing is comparable to having a virtual tattoo parlor on every corner. The Internet never forgets— one errant post or photo can cause a world of strife for an unwitting social user, and this is even more relevant for social enterprises. The requirement to maintain control over the platform and ensure the content generated within it and the employees using it for their work are safe is paramount. The proper management of an enterprise social platform ensures the security of the data generated and contained within the system itself, as well as the ability for an organization to moderate the content and interaction of its users, from employees, partners, or customers to the public. These interactions should be protected from the broader Internet and safely metered and managed by the organization providing the platform and capturing the data.

Big data set collection and analysis

As we enter the era of big data and the ability to analyze extremely large data sets for trends, patterns, and unexpected interactions, it's becoming more and more important that today's enterprises have the enterprise information architecture in place to capitalize on big data.

From the first chapter in this book, we know there are two principal types of data: structured and unstructured. Unstructured data makes up some 80-90 percent of the data in any given organization and includes everything from messaging and communication systems data, through to enterprise content and Business Process Management (BPM) assets. The social interactions of your employees, customers, and other members of your social enterprise represent a wealth of value for your company and customers. A social platform enables the enterprise to construct and capture the discussions that surround its projects, products and services. It's possible to analyze and understand the sentiment of conversation, to know who speaks with whom and on which subjects, to understand the propensity of customers or users to purchase or conduct a transaction with your enterprise, and the context in which they are most likely to do so.

Taking advantage of big data starts with collecting rich, secure data sets pertaining to the area of study and ensuring that the data collected is accessible, current, and constantly refreshed. The best mechanism through which to do this is by becoming a social enterprise and deploying the capacity for your users to interact within social communities: collaborating, problem solving, locating experts, managing customer interactions, finding information, learning, and teaching.

Customer, employee, and audience engagement

There is no more convenient, cost-effective, instantaneous, or generally better mechanism through which to engage your audience than within a social enterprise. Social communities are used today in place of the corporate intranet, knowledge base, bulletin board, expert identification, peer review, customer support site, and myriad other traditional forums for exchange and engagement. Having a robust social platform alleviates the need for a multitude of disparate, fragmented systems and gives users the ability to build their community to suit their needs. It lowers costs through the efficiencies of a more malleable platform, which can be deployed to solve a number of use cases all while keeping a single, concise, and secure social data set available for the company to serve as a digital corporate memory.

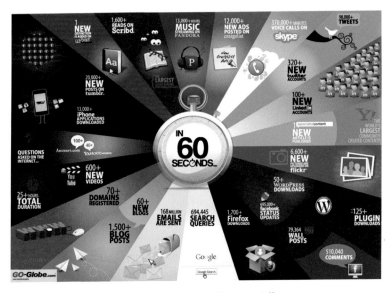

The internet every 60 seconds[68]

[68] Go-Globe, *"60 Seconds - Things that Happen on Internet Every Sixty Seconds [Infographic]"* (1 Jun. 2011), Blog, Go-Gulf.com, *http://www. go-gulf.com/blog/60-seconds/* (accessed 7 Oct. 2013).

Similar to consumer social networks, an enterprise social platform allows users to engage with vendors directly, take part in the conversation, help shape product and service development, and be a part of things. By offering customers the ability to access information via an enterprise social platform, they can contribute in a structured, controlled dialogue that is effective for both the organization and the client.

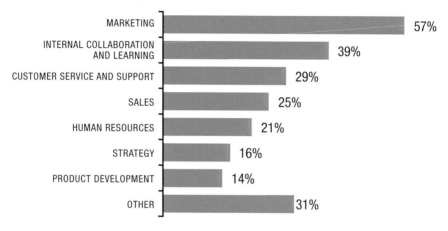

Business uses of social media

Put social to work

Social media is an important element of any online or knowledge management strategy, but more importantly, it's fundamentally changing the way people connect with each other and the way organizations interact with people: customers, partners, stakeholders, and employees.

Not your whole strategy
Social media promises to break down walls and open communication channels, but for many organizations this promise falls short. Social media isn't a strategy: it supports your strategy. Social media can deliver value once it becomes part of a larger initiative that recognizes other factors at play such as business processes, change management, employee education, and adoption.

Business-centric and purpose-driven social features
A good social solution enhances the users web experience by providing easy-to-use social apps that can socially charge current business processes in a safe and compliant fashion to help fuel a more immersive user experience both for the social workplace and the social web. When adopted, end users can

• **Create a Social Workplace:** Organizations can work more efficiently and connect more easily simply by leveraging social features such as blogs, wikis, or forums.

• **Augment Social Marketing:** Enabling an online dialogue between your users and customers—whether it's B2B, B2C, or B2E—can help create and retain customers, increase wallet-share with existing customers, and transform fans into evangelists to increase your brand reputation.

• **Build a More Social Intranet:** Encouraging employees, customers, and partners to collaborate on a platform that enables two-way communication can help increase bottom-up conversations so all users can discuss their ideas in social forums and communities.

Network effects

Metcalfe's Law states that the value of a telecommunications network is proportional to the square of the number of connected users of the system. What Metcalfe couldn't have predicted is by which proportion the value would increase with the addition of semantic navigation, recommendation engines, analytics, big data analyses, and authoring agents. Today's social enterprise offers a number of benefits for the network it serves, whether it's internal or external. These benefits are made up of both hard-cost savings and intangible benefits realized from the human and data-centric connections that an enterprise social platform supports through reduced travel and training costs. Just a few are listed below:

Cost savings

- Reduced travel
- Inexpensive customer engagement
- Increased efficiency from easy, quick access to information
- Corporate memory retention, reduced training
- Skills optimization

Intangibles

- Correlative big data analysis
- Employee knowledge transfer
- Reduced risk versus external social sites
- Direct customer engagement
- Improved communication
- Records retention

The digital water cooler

As organizations scale, it becomes more and more challenging to foster the proverbial conversation across departments and geographies. This silo effect, where each department is capable of communicating within itself but relatively ineffective at engaging the other areas of the business, results in a poor cross-functional alignment and an even poorer use of resources.

"Many hands make light work," they say, and as such, the social enterprise enables multiple departments to communicate openly in a forum where the volume of data exchanged doesn't become overwhelming. Social platforms can be used to execute on large projects spanning many departments effectively and inexpensively.

Being able to engage with the members of the organization located across geographies and functions is a critical tool for any employee and prevents the same investments from being made multiple times within the organization or "solving the same problem twice". A clear, effective, and secure social platform is the key to keeping the conversation going.

Transfer corporate memory

Another aspect of the social enterprise is the way in which employees choose to exchange information or transfer corporate memory. A subject matter expert in sales, for example, is unlikely to share her tactics and knowledge with colleagues unless she is required to. In many organizations sales territories are dispersed, which means that the experienced and new staff are seldom together to facilitate knowledge transfer. A social platform removes those geographical limitations and also provides a safe forum in which to ask questions. If prompted simply through an enterprise social platform to provide some strategy tips to a new salesperson, this rep can respond at her convenience through the social platform—making it much more likely that the knowledge transfer will take place. This means reduced training requirements, more effective employees, shorter times to productivity, and maximum utilization of subject matter experts, which the organization has invested in substantially over the years to accumulate that wealth of expertise.

A safe place to share information

Efficiency aside, let's look a little more closely at human nature: introverts, extroverts, and the nontrivial proportion of any workforce who would prefer not to engage socially in person if given the option. Every workforce is composed of a broad spectrum of individuals, from those who openly and freely share and exchange information, communicate, and are engaged socially to those who retain their information either by preference or personality or are anxious of social interactions and sharing their knowledge openly. A good social enterprise platform can help engage this broad spectrum of personality types by offering an electronic medium by which the information can be exchanged. By putting a range of personality types in contact that wouldn't normally engage, the social enterprise becomes a digitized safeguard and a sheltered environment to foster information trading between any

Twitter: @muhismajzoub

Muhi Majzoub, SVP Engineering, OpenText

…On social exchanges and the social enterprise

Technology has changed how we interact. When I started my career 20 years ago, we didn't have anything like the devices we have today. For example, my current cellphone has 100 times the power of the computer I used in college, and the way I used my computer was very different from the way I use my computer—or my cellphone—today. I can work on a document with someone on the other side of the world in real time and receive comments via secure texts from team members who are watching on their tablets on a train or on their mobiles at home. Watching technology evolve to enhance our lives and drive business processes is truly amazing.

But there is always room for improvement. Today, we are working on improving the user interface, tightening up integration capabilities, and designing new functionality and features—all this to create a compelling user experience. In this social era, it is more important than ever to quickly respond to the needs of the customer and to attract repeat customers. To accomplish this, we need to know what customers want. If your customer visits your website, and they can't find what they're looking for, they won't go back. Even worse, you may have driven them to another website. But how will you know? Gone are the days of customers filling out a feedback forms and mailing them in. It's now about engagement and conversation and exchanging ideas with customers. And we get there by using communities, social media, and instant feedback—these are tools customers can use to take control of their buying process and walk away a truly happy and repeat customer.

Communities aren't just for consumers, either. The enterprise is social too, and we need secure places where knowledge workers can foster collaboration and communication in a global enterprise. Collaboration is key for information to flow throughout the enterprise, and a social community, used behind the firewall, allows employees to freely promote enhancement and innovation. They can help each other and share answers in a way that is easier, quicker, and more dynamic than in the past. If someone has a question, they don't have to seek out a manager or call IT—they can ask their peers in a low-pressure environment. The impact of this uncensored, cooperative space is a happier, more empowered workforce.

constituency of your organization or customer base. Removing these social barriers means that a significant proportion of your user or customer base is able to provide input for the first time in an environment that works for them, changing the nature of the exchange and offering a more representative and comprehensive data set for the enterprise to make decisions.

Internal and external

The social enterprise facilitates open communication between its employees and its customers, partners, and external nodes. The value of communicating with your customers, employees, and other audiences on a single, secure social platform means that all of the communication can be stored, managed, and analyzed over time. This is especially important for customer data, which can be used to understand how you can optimize your business based directly on the feedback of your clients. Employees at any level can also see this information and use it to guide their day-to-day activities, whether their customers are internal or external to the organization.

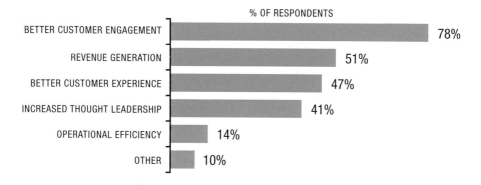

Top business objectives for social media in 2012

Coupling your social platform with your Customer Experience Management (CEM) infrastructure such as your Web Content Management (WCM), Portal, and other capabilities means that a seamless, integrated experience can be provided from the first time a customer hits your website to the time an engineer is designing the next-generation product. Every step from conception to fruition and support can be managed on your enterprise social platform, and every department can be engaged in the conversation. Marketing can begin their work and interact directly with product teams as new offerings are brought to market. Sales can watch, listen, and learn from the customers and what they discuss.

Mobilization

With the advent of smartphones and tablets, the mobilization of the modern social enterprise has only just begun. These technologies mean that the social platform is no longer only accessible to office workers who have access to a computer but to every employee. Whether it's environmental inspectors in the field, engineers at an energy company, assembly line workers in manufacturing, or a marketing division for a consumer packaged-goods company. Mobility means that everyone can join in on the social exchange.

The era of "Bring Your Own Device" (BYOD) is now well underway, with companies and employees preferring to allow people to make their own choices on mobile devices supported for work. This is important to the employee base: mobile phones are very personal devices. They represent our personalities, have specifications to meet our usage demands, and carry our life's data around with us everywhere we go. This freedom also comes with a challenge. Being able to support an almost infinite number of mobile devices, operating systems, and device hardware permutations has companies scrambling to keep up. Whether your organization provides a predetermined selection of devices or whether you're a BYOD shop, one thing is clear: mobile access makes today's enterprise more social. It's the omnipresent portal, the personal lifeline, the common denominator; the mechanism through which you and your social platform can reach the furthest points on your social enterprise graph.

Enterprise social platforms offer an additional layer of security over consumer social applications in that they only do what the deploying enterprise allows them to do. For example, an enterprise social application installed on an employee's smartphone will serve as a secure gateway to the company's enterprise social platform—and only that. A consumer social application used to host a customer forum for a company will extract the phonebook and contents of the smartphone and convert them to a data set, which is usable and sellable by the social platform provider. This is a very large risk for an enterprise to take; allowing that data to be exposed through the use of free consumer social technologies. Such risks can be simply avoided with the use of a robust social enterprise platform.

Social in the Cloud

The social enterprise may choose to deploy its capabilities on premises or in the Cloud. The benefits of social Cloud solutions are many, including the lack of capital investment for infrastructure or the ability to spin up many smaller social sites quickly and cost effectively to manage the needs of specific campaigns or child organizations. The former is known as cap-ex free computing. The next benefit to having a secure enterprise social platform in the Cloud is the ability to deploy projects much faster, making the organization more competitive and innovative.

WHAT DOES THE SOCIAL ENTERPRISE BRING TO BUSINESS?

- Makes Business Personal
- Streamlines Process
- Avoids Duplication
- Gives Employees a Voice
- Increases Engagement

- Two-Way Dialogue
- Transfers Knowledge
- Connects Us Globally
- Identifies Expertise
- Brings Ousiders In

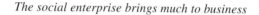

The social enterprise brings much to business

From an end user's perspective, these social solutions are always in the Cloud: they do not reside locally on their machines. For the enterprise, a decision has to be made about the right approach for deploying a social enterprise platform. Cloud solutions can scale as needed without the planning, investment, and downtime required by IT departments to migrate systems to larger infrastructure. The ongoing cost of operations is also lower as Cloud vendors drive to economies of scale in their environments and pass those savings on to customers.

Resiliency and redundancy is another benefit of a Cloud-based social enterprise. Cloud providers specialize in "keeping the lights on" and making sure that their customer's data is safe and that their service is perpetually available. It's possible to negotiate a wide variety of service level agreements with Cloud providers to ensure your social platform has the infrastructure it needs to best support the operations of your business.

Unlocking social value

There are several tangible values brought forth by the social enterprise. For example, the ability for employees to connect on a given topic, to hold training, to execute on a project, and to innovate without having to physically co-locate delivers a huge savings in travel costs to organizations and is simply measured. After deploying your enterprise social platform, start holding your meetings, enablement sessions, and project team meetings virtually and socially online instead of in person. Measure the savings over time through reduced travel—this is one simple metric for understanding some of the quantifiable, monetary benefits of an enterprise social platform. In addition to reduced travel costs, consider the cost of bringing a new employee up to full productivity within any given discipline in your organization.

Employees gather the information they need to do their jobs by interacting with their peers, asking questions, attending training, and otherwise sharing information. This can often be a lengthy process, but an enterprise social platform allows users to engage more easily with the rest of their colleagues, it helps them to find experts, and it makes them more effective, more quickly. This accelerated learning curve through a more effective proliferation of information and more easily facilitated social and expert exchange means actual dollars saved. A good social platform can get employees up to speed more quickly and reduce the time lost to training by immediately giving your staff access to the information they require.

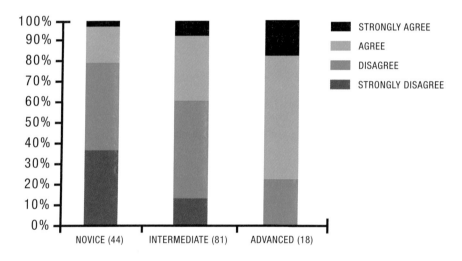

Social media business programs cross-functional silos

There is a number of other hard value and cost reduction elements to the social enterprise, but perhaps most valuable of all are the intangible benefits wrought by the use of social communities. The enterprise benefits from the formation of a social big data set and the reduced risk in having employees use a moderated, safe social platform, instead of consumer platforms that sell demographic and usage information to the highest bidder.

Organizations should strive for a social platform that can be integrated with other unstructured data sources in its infrastructure to provide unprecedented access to information and value to its customers. The social enterprise is here to stay and represents true value to organizations that are ready to take advantage of it.

CHAPTER 10

MOBILE COMPUTING AND THE CLOUD

Mobile Computing and the Cloud: The Impact of Disruptive Innovation on EIM

"More than 75 percent of organizations globally have decided on a strategy for adopting Cloud." [69]

Mobile computing and the Cloud are two of the most important new trends in IT to challenge the enterprise. A typical IT reaction to the emergence of new technologies is to determine which applications can be moved into the Cloud and which can be modified for mobile. But more lofty implications can be made. In his article for the Harvard Business Review, Clayton Christensen defines the term "disruptive technology", now more commonly referred to as "disruptive innovation", as "an innovation that helps create a new market and value network and eventually goes on to disrupt an existing market and value network (over a few years or decades), displacing an earlier technology."

As disruptive innovations, mobile and Cloud fit this definition to a fault. Moreover, the emergence of these two technologies at roughly the same time and the extent that each one helps fuel the growth of the other makes the disruptive impact all the more powerful.

Both phenomena represent a tremendous opportunity for a progressive enterprise to think differently about how they work with their customers—more specifically, how they provide better products or services to them.

The enterprise should not only be trying to figure out what legacy systems they can adapt to this new environment but should also determine the value of these new disruptive innovations and how they will expand the ability of the enterprise to compete successfully in its marketplace.

First, let's examine mobile as the new user delivery mechanism of choice and its impact on how organizations need to rethink their infrastructure and application platform. Then we will discuss why the Cloud is changing the role of IT from an infrastructure-delivery organization to a business-value-delivery organization. Finally, let's look at how both Cloud and mobile are transforming EIM.

---

[69] Sam Shead, *"Cloud decisions are no longer in the IT department's hands - the suits have taken over"*, ZDNet.com, *http://www.zdnet.com/uk/ Cloud-decisions-are-no-longer-in-the-it-departments-hands-the-suits-have-taken-over-7000008141/* (accessed 6 Jul. 2013).

Mobile: extending the information

The mobile market recently passed an important milestone. In 2011, mobile data revenues eclipsed $300 billion for the first time ever. More importantly, it's also the first year ever that non-messaging data revenues made up the majority of overall global data revenues at 53 percent. The mobile industry is characterized as the most vibrant and fastest growing industry on the planet. The same report suggested that data is on pace to make up 95 percent of global mobile revenues by 2015.[70] If there was ever any lingering doubt that the world is going mobile, these numbers put those concerns to rest.

Mobile communications is an essential part of the global fabric. With almost 70 percent global subscription penetration as of 2010, mobility is everywhere.[71] Mobile represents a singular opportunity to build an entirely new model for how organizations do business. The ability to extend and manage enterprise information and business processes for both their internal users and their customers will be impacted.

Because of its ability to bring together remote location and preferences in a time-relevant manner, mobile is creating new, highly targeted decision-making opportunities and making them available to a much larger set of users than ever before possible with a PC or laptop.

Fueled in part at least by mobile, modern enterprises are generating exponentially more data today than they have in the past. More access points mean more data. The volume of data and the velocity at which it's being created is staggering. Every day we are creating 2.5 quintillion (2.5 X 10^{18}) bytes of data. That means that 90 percent of the data in the world today was created in the last 2 years.[72] Traditional databases and information management systems simply do not keep up with the velocity and growth any longer.

Collectively this data surge has been referred to as big data, the latest buzzword for a growing problem that has been around for a while. It has also been clearly identified as a top concern by mobile IT industry professionals.

Chetan Sharma Consulting is a leading consultancy in the mobile market space. They undertake their *Mobile Industry Predictions Survey* each year, and their 2013 results garnered from mobile IT industry professionals are highly instructive and represent insight into how internal users see mobile impacting their organizations.

The top six categories in the survey are all data related and all represent significant growth potential for carriers in the enterprise or B2B market as their traditional fixed-line businesses continue to dwindle. The categories include the following:

- Mobile Payments
- Mobile Cloud Services

---

[70] Mobile Marketing Watch, *"Major Mobile Trends Show Global Mobile Industry Is Now the Fastest Growing Market in the World"*, MobileMarketingWatch.com, *http://www.mobilemarketingwatch.com/major-mobile-trends-show-global-mobile-industry-is-now-the-fastest-growing-market-in-the-world-16840/* (accessed 3 Jun. 2013).

[71] Chetan Sharma, *"Competition and the Evolution of Mobile Markets – A Study of Competition in Global Mobile Markets, A Working Paper"*, Chetan Sharma Consulting (2011), *http://chetansharma.com/mobilecompetition.htm* (accessed 7 Feb. 2012).

[72] IBM, *"Big Data at the Speed of Business"*, Big Data Hub, *http://www.ibmbigdatahub.com/video/big-data-speed-business* (accessed 8 Jul. 2013).

- Mobile Commerce
- Big Data
- Connected Devices
- Mobile Enterprise

The consumer-facing or B2C markets continue strong with messaging, mobile payments, and social media as areas of strength in both the developed and developing worlds. Mobile is not just about smartphones. Both tablets and smartphones in the Chetan survey are viewed as "taking over computing" at the expense of the PC, which is perceived as "falling off the cliff".[73]

More importantly for the enterprise markets, mobile moves decision making to the frontlines with teams in the field—both internal and with your supply chain. There is no doubt that globally there has been a continuing slowdown of PC shipments.[74]

The proliferation of mobile is making its mark on the enterprise. Often defined as a consumerization of the office environment, the BYOD trend has created new headaches for IT departments. Exponentially more data is coming in to enterprise assets from an array of mobile platforms in different formats—opening the door to dramatic increase in governance, security, and integration challenges across the entire EIM spectrum. Unfortunately for IT departments, closing the doors on mobile is not going to do any good: the horse has already left the barn. Studies have shown that 73 percent of enterprises have non-IT managed devices accessing corporate resources.[75] As illustrated in the graph below, the system data types being accessed are fairly typical across industries:[76]

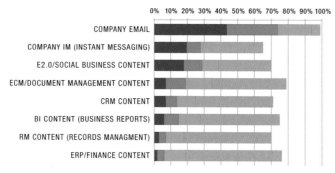

System data types accessed on mobile devices in the typical organization

The impact on EIM is profound, and the race is on. The good news is that it's still early.

[73] Chetan Sharma, *"2013 Mobile Industry Predictions Survey"*, Chetan Sharma Consulting (Jan. 2013), *http://www.chetansharma.com/MobilePredictions2013.htm* (accessed 7 May 2013).
[74] Mikako Kitagawa, Principal Analyst Gartner, Gartner Inc., *http://www.gartner.com/AnalystBiography?authorId=17156* (accessed 14 Jun. 2013).
[75] Hendrikse, Rene, *"How to Introduce Bring-Your-Own-Device Schemes in the Enterprise Computer Weekly UK, 2013"*, *http://www.computerweekly.com/opinion/Bring-Your-Own-Device-in-the-Enterprise* (accessed 14 Jun. 2013).
[76] AIIM White Paper, *"Making the Most of Mobile – Content on the Move 2011"* *http://campaigns.opentext.com/forms/FY12-Q3-AM-ALL-ECMC-IG-Mobility* (accessed 19 Nov. 2012).

Twitter: @adamhowatson

Adam Howatson, Vice President, Products, OpenText

…On the future of enterprise mobility

Mobility in the context of EIM has evolved a lot over the past couple of years, and we are continuing to make great strides. Organizations are implementing platform standardization. OpenText has a unique technology in our AppWorks platform that allows us to author an app once using simple and broadly adopted technologies like HTML, CSS, and JavaScript, and then push apps out to all web browsers, desktop users, and mobile devices simultaneously and instantaneously (including smartphones, tablets, and even kiosks and display panels), without additional work for developers or costs incurred by the customer. You create the app once, and then it is available everywhere, and it's integrated with your enterprise directory server, security policies, and corporate systems. Additionally, we are now seeing the features that have made consumer apps so popular and successful work their way into the enterprise. We are seeing a demand to have simple, pleasing enterprise apps for business functions such as onboarding, managing vendor relations, employee files, business processes, etc. These apps eliminate the need to send users to multiple, complex, back-office interfaces and deliver an integrated, more secure user experience that's easy for IT to manage and extraordinarily simple and compelling for end users.

Enterprise mobile application management and mobile device management are becoming a larger part of the enterprise mandate, as well. Mobile app management enables the management of the audience to which your enterprise apps are deployed, being able to update apps seamlessly and install and deploy new apps simply in seconds without any user intervention. Mobile device management enables the ability to manage and secure all enterprise devices effectively. Such as being able to wipe a device remotely in the event of loss or theft and the ability to generate reports and gather metrics on which systems are being used the most.

The future of enterprise mobility is bright. It's a world where compelling, effective, and ubiquitous apps are made available to your audience in a secure, managed, and integrated way. The future is here, and it allows you to transform your business by providing a more efficient, adoptable, integrated, and secure experience for users, while making it easy and fast for developers to build the apps that drive your business, unleashing the power of information.

Business challenges

One of the core challenges that any enterprise needs to confront is how to efficiently manage content and its underlying business processes. This is fundamental to any business. How does it reach out and communicate with the consumers of its products or services? Mobile technology is making this exponentially more difficult.

There is a veritable cascade of mobile devices entering the enterprise, and typically, there is no coherent enterprise mobility strategy. The presence of these devices can throw IT departments into utter turmoil. Departments frequently lack the right tools to manage these devices, which results in increased cost. Risks of data loss, data breach, and non-compliance also increase significantly.

Mobile's entry to the enterprise is unusual in that it started from the bottom up. Over the last few years, more and more individuals have acquired smartphones and personal tablet devices like the iPad® have been appearing on the radar of corporate IT. It's the BYOD trend. A pro-active mobility strategy is crucial if the enterprise is to avoid these potential risks and additional costs.

All too often enterprise reaction is reactive and in response to some type of an incident—a data breach or data loss being the most common. Change is slow, but it is happening.

Enterprise concerns in a BYOD world

There are major challenges with having enterprise assets on a proliferation of unknown devices that the business does not have the ability to secure. Security has always been a major concern for corporate IT, but with mobile it is not only the level of security inherent in the mobile device itself (or the relative lack thereof) but also the fact that mobile means you are taking data with you wherever you go.

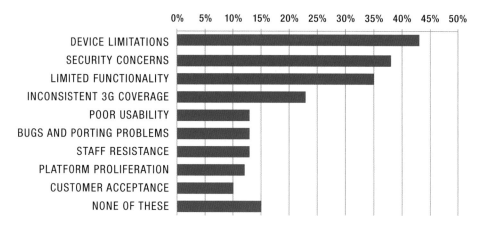

Common issues with mobile-specific applications

Add to this the multitude of heterogeneous platforms with varying levels of interoperability within the enterprise infrastructure and corporate IT is finding the need to shift their focus from their traditional mode of security via infrastructure to security for applications and information squarely into the realm of EIM.

Other issues for the enterprise:

- More people using your systems means increased cost.
- Service issues: If there is a problem, who is notified and who deals with it—corporate IT, the user, the carrier, the device manufacturer?

Some BYOD solutions
Coordination of corporate assets - onboarding

BYOD is about building a secure virtual container for enterprise applications and information. Access policies need to be managed to ensure compliance with all existing security policies. Recent survey responses suggest that results have been mixed.[77]

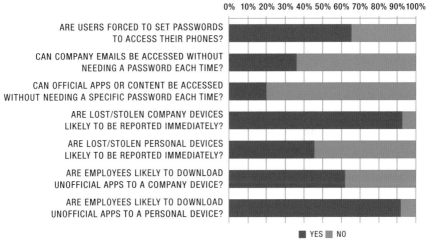

Compliance and security issues with mobile devices

Employee responses to their relative willingness to download unofficial apps to company and personal devices are particularly troubling.

The device itself is not the point of control moving forward. An important first step in this process however is the registration and onboarding of new devices, preferably from a single point of control. Registration allows these devices to be identified and user credentials to be validated, otherwise IT will have no way to differentiate and control network and data access privileges. This is a crucial step.

It should come as no surprise that security and scalability rule the roost in mobile application development. The sector is also relying heavily on well-designed Service-Oriented

[77] *Ibid.*

Architecture (SOA) to make this happen. To quote Michael Facemire, senior analyst at Forrester Research: "Mobile demands scale. If SOA is done properly, you have a much higher level of engagement with mobile users."[78]

Cost control

There is little doubt that mobility costs are going to continue to rise. A few key statistics make the case. Average smartphone usage nearly tripled in 2011 and each tablet device generates 3.4 times as much data as the typical smartphone. The typical mobile employee currently uses an average of 3.5 devices ranging from smartphones and laptops, to notebooks and tablets.[79] Corporate IT needs to ensure that they can handle all this without dramatic increases in costs, with minimal impact to bottom line profitability. Additional costs without additional revenues are never a winning combination.

Controlling these costs is crucial, but needs to happen within the context of a corporate IT strategy. Efforts to date have too frequently consisted of *ad hoc*, knee-jerk efforts at frugality, without a view towards the potentially negative impact of that frugality.

Mobile opportunities

One of the key benefits of mobility is its ability to enrich remote interactions and make them more effective. Defining remote is a straightforward exercise: it's any interaction that doesn't occur behind a desk. It doesn't matter if it's a sales executive, a worker on a factory floor, a physician, or a police officer. If you are providing them with real-time information, you are significantly improving their efficiency and the odds of their being successful at whatever it is that they are doing.

Enriching remote interactions with a given mobile device is certainly important, but how you accomplish this, in other words making available the applications that facilitate these interactions, is equally important. Mobile provides a new universe of opportunities to rethink how we structure the information that flows out to the remote user.

Rethinking mobile applications

The need to make information accessible to your customers has not changed. The explosion of access points to enterprise information that mobile introduces complicates information delivery considerably. Corporate IT can no longer only concern itself with managing resource flows from laptops and on-premise workstations. Organizations must consider fundamental changes to the nature of the applications that deliver information to their users and customers. This proliferation of hits on corporate IT assets really demands it.

Traditional software development in the enterprise has always been complex. Add mobile into the equation and complexity increases one more step. It is simply not realistic to think that the enterprise can continue to develop applications the same way they always have.

---

[78] Mann, Stephanie, *"Mobile App Development Trends in 2012 and beyond"*, http://searchsoa.techtarget.com/feature/Mobile-app-development-trends-in-2012-and-beyond (accessed 8 Feb. 2013).
[79] *Ibid.*

The issue is not just about establishing information management controls for the way you used to do business. You need to rethink your applications in order to take advantage of the new capabilities that mobile makes available to you as a business. Do it right, and you will gain a significant competitive edge for your enterprise. If you don't, your ability to compete will be severely impacted in a negative way.

Consumerization of the marketplace

There are literally thousands of mobile applications available for the consumer market—everything from games, social networks, newsreaders, travel booking apps, etc. Users have become comfortable with how the User Interface (UI) is built and interacting with their device. Not everyone is an engineer, and gone are the days of 100+ page "quick start" guides and extensive training sessions to learn an application.

As the demand for platform-to-platform and application-to-application integration continues to grow, there has also been a significant acceleration in the development and sophistication of open APIs. This is all part of a larger shift towards consumer-centric development strategies. Proliferation of access devices means more and more people have access to enterprise systems.

It is inevitable that the general level of technology expertise is going to decrease. This is what fuels that consumer-centric approach. The more simplicity on the UI side of the equation equates to more complexity and flexibility in the backend and application coding. When you have exponential increases in the numbers of users across a broader spectrum of sophistication, this also means orders of magnitude increases in how that information is both managed and presented—a significant EIM challenge. This applies equally across a broad range of technologies—Cloud included—as well as the types of data structures being managed and used. These are the traditional structured data sets that corporate IT has long experience in dealing with, typically in a relational Database Management System (DBMS) environment, as well as unstructured data where corporate IT has relatively little experience. Web click streams, data log files, and assorted social media data feeds are the primary culprits for unstructured data.

This has clear implications to application architectures, which must evolve to accommodate these developments. This trend began with the earliest public Cloud environments and has only accelerated with mobile. It is also fueling changes in traditional enterprise application environments. User expectations are changing and developers are slowly but surely accommodating these changes.

A good example is a feature like touchscreens. Originally developed as a means of making digital assets accessible to smaller mobile devices, we are already seeing it incorporated into tablets and laptop-size devices. As recently as 10-12 years ago
- An enterprise software application would have been targeted almost exclusively to a highly technical consumer of the application—more often than not, an engineer.

- A typical reaction to some issue in the user experience of that enterprise software would have been: "Don't worry; we'll fix it next time".

This approach is simply no longer possible. It would not be commercially viable in today's marketplace. Companies are consuming information today from a much broader range of inputs as a result of mobile devices. The range of technical sophistication of the users providing this input is also much wider. The nature of information production is changing and by extension, the way it is consumed and managed is also changing. Information management must be ready to meet this challenge.

The enterprise UI

The clear implication of consumerization is that your enterprise applications need to be offering an experience that is comparable to consumer-grade applications. It's about better use of information via greater personalization and use of context, like geography.

The mobile UI experience is different from the desktop. It's simpler and of necessity much smaller to accommodate the limitations imposed by a significantly smaller display. Integration of technologies like GPS for geographically based interactions and cameras for image capture were never even imagined for the desktop, yet each of these operate on very different platforms that now need to be accommodated by corporate IT. Add to this mix the sheer number of mobile device models, operating system environments, and screen sizes, and you only just begin to understand the complexity of the problems presented here.

Backend architecture implications

Organizations need to build applications differently. With a multitude of devices on the network, applications need to scale considerably more. Enterprise systems should offer the right API to enable data brokerage from a variety of user experiences; in other words, they have to be able to write once and reuse many, many times. It's essential that application architecture include composite applications that are delivered through Cloud-based integration brokerage services. Finally, security challenges directly impact the way the system backend is architected. Since applications are going to be accessed by mobile devices, these devices will often be outside of the network. How does the enterprise architect their applications to cope with this new model?

To this end, new kinds of middleware are evolving to deal with mobile diversity, most commonly referred to as Platform as a Service (PaaS). Traditional middleware for both mobile and conventional environments federates services through a physical server; PaaS does so through the Cloud for mobile environments.

Early responses to all these concerns represent the first wave of what Forrester refers to as Smart Process Applications, which will be discussed in more detail later. These applications will largely be Cloud based, making them easier to deploy, support, and continuously improve. Software as a Service (SaaS) will be the dominant delivery platform, providing applets for mobile users to add their opinions or approvals to options or decisions under consideration. It will, in fact, be the combination of the two—mobile and Cloud—that represent a clear competitive differentiation.

The Cloud is the future

A recent KPMG study found that 81 percent of businesses were either evaluating Cloud services, planned a Cloud implementation, or already had a Cloud implementation in place.[80] How business moves to the Cloud may be in doubt, but they are moving there. The benefits to business are real. The Cloud provides agility, flexibility, and scalability while helping to control costs—a major concern in an era of seemingly ever-shrinking IT budgets. As always, the devil is in the details. The enterprise must figure out how to do this efficiently and cost effectively.

As with any relatively new technology, mistakes are going to be made.

Public vs. private vs. hybrid

When it comes to Cloud computing, there is no "one size fits all". Companies are faced with a strategic choice among the different models of Cloud computing available to them.

- **Public** – Services are provided over the Internet. A Cloud service provider on the service provider's premises hosts the customer's infrastructure and or applications. It is generally inexpensive and hassle-free for the customer, since the service provider is managing all aspects of the environment.

    - The downsides for the customer include lack of control, frequent slow speeds due to the connection being over the internet, and a perceived lack of security. Public services do offer security, but since companies have relinquished control of their data assets in this scenario, the perception that security could not possibly be as good as what the company could provide for itself is very real.

- **Private** – Services are hosted on a private platform in the customer's data center. This offers greater control, more security, higher performance (since it's inside the customer's intranet), tighter regulatory compliance, and it is customizable.

    - The main downside for the customer is the costs are almost always higher. They require investment in the hardware, the software, and maintenance costs, as well as the cost of labor required to manage these assets. With a public Cloud service, all these cost are borne by the provider. There is also the issue of a capacity cap. If you run out of storage or compute capacity, the customer must bear the cost of adding it, which typically means additional capital expenditure. A public Cloud provider can readily add capacity for modest additional operational expenditure.

---

[80] Business implication of Cloud, *KPMG http://www.kpmg.com/global/en/topics/cloud-computing/pages/default.aspx* (accessed 16 May 2013).

Fundamentally these two options come down to a choice between cost and control. This is why so many organizations choose a hybrid solution.

- **Hybrid** – Just as the name implies, this a combination of public and private Clouds, and this is proving to be an extremely popular model. It's an easy way, for example, for companies to segregate sensitive versus non-sensitive applications. The sensitive material stays in-house and non-sensitive content is available to the public environment. A transitional platform, hybrid Cloud environments will be the enterprise platform of choice through 2016, *en route* to a future dominated by public and private Clouds.[81]

CLOUD COMPUTING TYPES

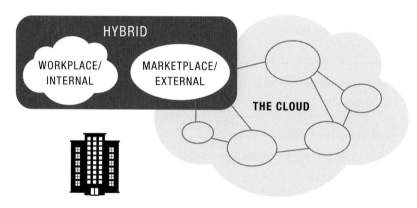

Types of Cloud services

Now what?

No matter what kind of Cloud service you select, the fundamental question remains about what business value the Cloud brings to your organization. How does the Cloud impact your organization's ability to manage key enterprise applications and functionality in order to fulfill your mission? What additional functionality or capabilities does the Cloud provide that allows you to expand or improve your business and maintain a competitive edge?

[81] Bill Guptill and Alex Bakker et al., Saugatuck Technology, *"2012 Cloud Business Solution Survey Global N=228"* (February 2012) *http:// saugatucktechnology.com/research/browse-research-library-by-category/1041ssr-2012-cloud-business-solution-survey-summary-data-report.html* (accessed 3 Mar. 2012).

Gartner Inc. views the architecture of Cloud computing as three foundation layers:[82]

1. The application service layer (mostly known as SaaS), delivering user application functionalities, such as Enterprise Content Management (ECM), Customer Experience Management (CEM), Discovery, Enterprise Resource Planning (ERP), Customer Relationship Management (CRM), human capital management, collaboration, web conferencing, email, and a myriad of other scenarios, including those for specific vertical markets

2. The application infrastructure service layer (usually called PaaS), implementing DBMS, application server, messaging, Information Exchange, Business Process Management (BPM), Master File Table (MFT), B2B integration, data and application integration, SOA governance, and a variety of other "middle-tier" application services

3. The system infrastructure service layer (commonly referred to as Infrastructure as a Service [IaaS]), providing core computing, networking, and storage services

Cloud services: A detailed overview

The best way to think about these architectures is as a continuum: distinct layers within an integrated whole that function as integral components of a business process that facilitate the exchange of information. The pyramid below provides a helpful visual reference to these concepts.

Managed hosting services, or IaaS, provides the foundation layer and is frequently referred to as the raw infrastructure. Starting with the networked, hardware infrastructure resident within a data center is the physical basis for the software stack that will reside on an organization's Cloud. This is typically the first step taken by most enterprises. They give up a bit of control in exchange for maintaining the ability to architect and manage applications.

The operating system layer is next, where the enterprise elects to follow the Microsoft Windows® or Linux path.

Next is the middleware piece, depicted here as Microsoft SQL Server® or Oracle databases. These are representative selections but by no means the only options. Not only can this layer include any database solution, it will also frequently include web servers, application servers, and a myriad of other tools intended to optimize performance and ensure and maintain data security and integrity. Collectively this constitutes a comprehensive application infrastructure (PaaS).

[82] Fabrizio Biscotti and Yefim V. Natis et al., *"Gartner Forecast: Platform as a Service, Worldwide, 2010-2015, 3Q11 Update"*, 14 September 2011, *Gartner Inc., http://www.gartner.com/id=1792219* (accessed 29 Oct. 2011).

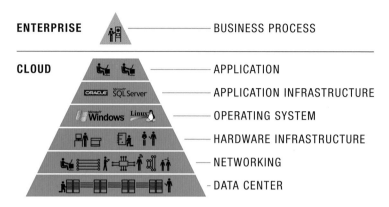

An integrated Cloud platform

Taken as a whole, this continuum represents an integrated Cloud platform, whether on premise or in a public environment. Business applications reside at the top of the stack, and will typically be a part of an on-premise environment. Information flows freely both within and between each of the layers.

SOA and Cloud: reinforcing each other

Cloud can provide enormous advantages to the enterprise in terms of self-service, scalability, flexibility, pay-as-you-go, and improved time to value. Making the move to the Cloud successfully requires an architecture that will support all of the new capabilities. There is general agreement among business leaders and analysts that the move to a Cloud environment requires a solid SOA to provide the infrastructure required for an implementation.[83]

> *"Cloud computing is a deployment architecture, not an architectural approach for how (to) architect your enterprise IT (as SOA is)."*[84]

---

[83] IBM, *"How SOA can ease your move to Cloud Computing"*, IBM.com, *http://www-01.ibm.com/software/solutions/soa/newsletter/nov09/article_ soaandcloud.html* (accessed 14 Apr. 2013).

[84] IBM, *"How SOA can ease your move to cloud computing"*, The Smart SOA Approach, IBM.com, *http://www-01.ibm.com/software/solutions/soa/ newsletter/nov09/article_soaandcloud.html* (accessed 15 May 2013).

Cloud as a business service

The role of the Cloud has changed significantly[85] for the enterprise in a relatively short period of time. Early incarnations were almost always limited to IaaS offerings. This was particularly evident with the public Cloud providers like Amazon® Web Services, RackSpace® and Savvis®. Each of them had offered managed, hosted environments to their customers for some time, so it was relatively easy for them to adapt that to the Cloud—particularly a public Cloud where the advantages of scale came into play—one environment to manage, with multiple tenants in that environment.

It quickly became apparent that the Cloud is an ideal platform for providing value-added services. The earliest Cloud instances in the marketplace were IaaS. Their earliest customers, in turn, were companies looking to provide an application infrastructure layer or PaaS. The economic advantages of this are clear. If you have one stable, managed foundation that you can make available to multiple users, as the architect of that foundation you are going to minimize costs and maximize your potential ROI. As a consumer of the platform you are accomplishing two things immediately. First of all, you are trading the high cost of capital investment and management of the environment for a typically modest monthly fee. Second of all, the enterprise can focus core IT resources on their core business, not on managing a data center.

An enormous amount of data can flow into any Cloud environment. That data only flows out as information, i.e. data that has value as an asset to the business if it can move freely throughout the enterprise. Being able to facilitate information exchange is an important growth area for IT. Gartner estimates that growth in information exchange will represent roughly $2.5 billion in revenues by 2015.[86] This is crucial piece of the EIM equation.

Let's look at a simple example to illustrate: a standard order placement for a product. This initiates a business process to generate an order form, create a pick to pull the product from inventory, create a packing list, package the product, ship it to the customer, and generate an invoice based upon financial terms on file. What happens if the customer reports that a critical component of the product is defective or worse yet, it was known that this component was defective before the customer's order was shipped but there was no process in place to flag the defective piece in a systematic fashion and change it? This is precisely the kind of new capability that information exchange can make available for the enterprise.

This kind of error can be incredibly costly, generating not only ill will with customers, but additional costs to fill the same orders more than once, and in some extreme cases, claims for liability and damages from customers. The key elements here are the efficient and

---

[85] Paul Krill, *"The Cloud-SOA Connection"*, InfoWorld *http://www.infoworld.com/d/cloud-computing/cloud-soa-connection-724* (accessed 8 Jul. 2013).
[86] Fabrizio Biscotti and Paolo Malinverno et al., *"Market Trends: Multi-enterprise/B2B Infrastructure Market, Worldwide, 2010-2015, 1Q11 Update"*, Gartner Inc., February 2011, *http://www.gartner.com/id=1545115* (accessed 23 Mar. 2011).

precise management of processes, as well as the transparent brokerage of information throughout all facets of the enterprise and all the affected business processes.

New opportunities for Cloud services

The new data and services brokering capabilities of the Cloud offer a lot of opportunities for unleashing the value of EIM across the enterprise. Thanks to the Cloud's brokering capabilities, organizations can now more quickly realize the EIM vision: a truly integrated way of managing, governing, integrating, and extracting value from enterprise Information.

What this means for EIM

Integration brokerage: a core element of an integrated EIM Cloud strategy

A lesson to draw from the example above is that the elements of EIM are not implemented in isolation. At the beginning of this discussion, mobile and Cloud environments were introduced as disruptive innovations. Each helps fuel the grown of the other. This technological synergy makes the disruptive impact all the more powerful.

Integration Brokerage (IB), as Gartner defines this space, is a category of discrete IT outsourcing for integration projects, such as those involving Cloud services integration and supply chain integration. IB is one of three primary Cloud service broker roles and combines Cloud-based B2B integration infrastructures with people and processes to help companies with initial implementation and ongoing project management for a wide range of Cloud and B2B integration projects.[87]

Smart Process Applications: the face of integration brokerage

Applications represent the customer-facing component of EIM. Terminology in this area varies. Forrester defines this area as Smart Process Applications, delivered largely in the Cloud. The focus here is predominantly on the automation of business processes for unstructured data. This is the next step beyond ERP systems, which typically handle structured data well. This is truly the last mile of business process automation. Forrester describes Smart Process Applications as follows:

- **Imported or embedded awareness data relevant to the business activity**. All collaborative business activity starts with a set of data that provides the trigger or backdrop or framework for that activity. In the creation and management of contracts, that data set will be the repository of existing contracts and standard contract terms and conditions.

- **Document capture for incoming documents, forms, and faxes relevant to the business activity.** Many, but not all, collaborative processes still start with a mound of incoming paper documents and faxes that require manual work to process. Examples include customer forms for new account opening, invoice documents for

---

[87] *Ibid.*

invoice processing, customer requests and feedback forms in retail, sales orders in manufacturing, and applicant information in recruiting and hiring. To tackle this paper burden, smart process applications support an integrated document capture solution for scanning and indexing incoming paper, managing incoming faxes, and supporting electronic signatures for high volumes of documents in the 30,000 to 50,000 per year range. This document capture solution will be integrated with BPM and ECM capabilities.

- **Embedded analytical tools designed for a business activity.** The people engaged in a business activity will need analytical tools designed for the task at hand, not a generic set of Business Intelligence (BI) reports and query tools. Those responsible for corporate risk management will need predictive analytical tools that can highlight potential threats to business operations or assets. Those engaged in preparing a new marketing campaign will want descriptive analytics that show historic results from past campaigns and current information on the demographics of the target audience. People in a social services organization managing client cases will need diagnostic analytics to understand the causes of the problems the client is facing. A sourcing team will need analytics that identify the best spend categories for strategic sourcing negotiations.

- **Collaboration platform for people to create content needed for the activity.** The people in the activity are meant to accomplish something, not just sit there in analysis paralysis. They need to work together to create a deliverable, whether it is a report, a plan, a problem resolution, a recommendation for action, or any other kind of work object. Those people may be employees in an office, but they may equally be employees on the road, contractors or consultants, customers, suppliers, or other partners. They will need to share ideas, submit their own solutions, critique and comment on the contributions of others, and work and rework the deliverable that will define what should be done next.

- **BPM tools for executing the steps involved in the activity**. Having identified and created a solution, a remedy, or a call for action through collaboration, people then need to execute the steps needed to turn planning into action. This is where BPM elements of workflow, rules engines, enterprise application integration, process modeling, process monitoring, and dynamic case management come into play.

SaaS is the dominant delivery platform for Smart Process Apps. In addition to these core features, they will largely be Cloud-based, making it easier to deploy, support, and continuously improve them. Indeed, much of the growth in SaaS applications will be Smart Process Apps that complement core transactional applications, rather than in SaaS apps that replace those transactional apps.[88]

---

[88] Andrew Bartels and Connie Moore, *"Smart Process Applications Fill A Big Business Gap"*, Forrester, November 5, 2012 *http://bps.opentext.com/ resources/Smart_Process_Application.pdf* (accessed 2 Sep. 2013).

Information needs to flow between organizations, partners, and customers. This ability to exchange information in any format between any senders and receivers interconnects Smart Process Application elements to address business process needs.

Smart processes will also require access from mobile users using smartphones and tablets. They will involve applets for these mobile workers to add their opinions or approvals to options and decisions under consideration. However, neither one of these capabilities individually, is differentiating for smart process applications. Many categories of software are adding both mobility and Cloud, which will quickly become table stakes for smart process applications—vendors must add them to be competitive.

Information Exchange and BPM

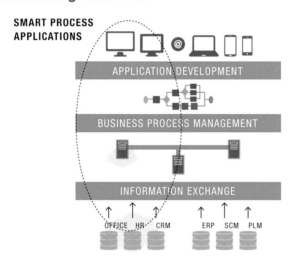

BPM + Information Exchange = Smart Process Applications

The figure above provides a good visual within the context of an information exchange. At the foundational level is B2B Managed Services deployed in the Cloud or as components within a hybrid model. Customers consume BPM and Information Exchange services as a Cloud service or in a hybrid model. Information Exchange uses web-based messaging services for delivery of content to users from the Cloud and on premise. A BPM suite provides process automation and management, including case management, BPM, rules, and business activity monitoring.

Finally, an application framework creates packaged, composite web UI and business applications—both fixed and mobile that leverage BPM and IX. This is a Smart Process Application.

Information Exchange facilitates the efficient secure and compliant exchange of information, both inside and outside the enterprise. Documents and associated data must routinely be brought together for use in processes and case management to make this a reality.

Information Exchange is a critical component of EIM. The vision for Information Exchange is clear: it is the ability to exchange any information in any format between any devices. Enterprise users should be able send and receive any information to anyone regardless of format and device involved in the exchange. Effective Information Exchange technology allows people to receive a fax, for example, and have it automatically transformed into an email and delivered to the device of choice. This is only the beginning. If you extend this concept to a global address book, its potential is clear: the ability to exchange messages with anyone quickly and securely, wherever they are, in any format, on any device.

Business-to-business interaction also needs to be transformed. Businesses today are struggling to exchange information for a whole host of reasons. A frequent challenge is the internal exchange of information. Providing business with the services they need to empower communication and information exchange with all internal divisions (for the large enterprise), as well as with other businesses will represent an incredibly compelling enterprise asset. These types of B2B managed and integrated services can easily be tailored for specific use cases in vertical industries.

Like any other application, mobile devices provide a UI to consume and interact with information. The key differentiator is that a mobile application tends to happen in real time, as well as being more focused on just the information needed in context. The Cloud provides organizations with the services required for that information to be produced and processed. Mobile delivers the information to customers. Cloud is the broker that supports and provides all the required information services. The combination of the two is incredibly powerful and allows customers and users make those last mile decisions—approve that purchase order, validate that contract, and more. Both these technologies are capable of bringing exciting new capabilities to the enterprise.

To provide this type of integration on premise requires that the enterprise become an integrator—likely not its core business! A much better approach to leveraging Cloud and mobile is to work with an organization that has these kinds of integration skills built into their corporate DNA.

ECM

Virtually every application and every business process contain some content. This content needs to be managed and stored. The core requirement has not changed. What is different is where that content is coming from, where it is being stored, and how it is being accessed.

Data sovereignty is also a huge issue. Any information that has been converted into a digital format is subject to the laws of the country in which it is stored. It is common for companies or governments to require that content be managed in such a way that it does not leave their borders or does not enter certain other countries. One of the most visible examples here is the EU Data Protection Directive. The US Department of Defense (DoD) Unique Identification (UID) and Radio Frequency Identification (RFID) regulations also apply—not just to the DoD but to anyone who hopes to do business with the DoD.

Any Cloud-enabled ECM governance framework needs to provide the ability for content to be tied to a specific geographical set of rules. EIM delivers these capabilities within an information governance framework that is expanding rapidly to accommodate mobile and Cloud computing.

CEM

Effectively managing the customer experience is critical to any successful business. The extent to which an enterprise exceeds their customer expectations and provides a superior experience across all touch points is what makes an organization stand out from its competition. One of the most important implications of both mobile and Cloud technologies is the consumerization trend discussed earlier, or the extent to which both have dramatically expanded, the number and nature of customer touch points.

The need for a comprehensive EIM framework that accommodates CEM is of critical importance. EIM products like Mobile Wave are already reducing the cost and complexity of creating, developing, and delivering a rich universe of mobile applications, reaching the broadest audience possible, providing customers with high-quality mobile experiences.

Discovery

The nature of Discovery is providing rich search capabilities and content analytics that function throughout the range of the EIM environment. The introduction of mobile and Cloud environments complicate Discovery by several orders of magnitude with the introduction of additional data formats, operating systems, and applications.

Discovery technologies are being developed to incorporate an ever-expanding range of mobile and Cloud platforms.

The impact of disruptive innovation on EIM

This chapter opened with a reference to Clayton Christensen and his landmark discussions in 1995 about disruptive innovations in the marketplace. Professor Christensen followed up his original article with a book, *The Innovator's Dilemma: When New Technologies Cause Great Firms to Fail*, in 1997. The title summarizes the key point he wanted to drive home—great companies can fail even if they do everything right. The key distinction here being that "right" is defined as doing things the way they have always done them. Mobile computing and the Cloud represent precisely the kinds of disruptive innovation he was talking about.

The good news is that organizations that pay attention to disruptive trends and successfully leverage the new capabilities that these technologies bring to the marketplace will thrive and dominate in their respective market segments.

Mobile computing and the Cloud are important architectures that provide a framework for the enterprise to extend and expand its ability to serve its customers. Both disruptive innovations should be evaluated within the framework of a coherent strategy that takes into account all aspects of an enterprise business strategy. To examine them in isolation would be missing the enormous potential they bring to the table to expand the capabilities and services organizations provide for their customers.

Mobile computing and the Cloud are disruptive technologies that affect every aspect of a business—and each of the EIM pillars (ECM, BPM, CEM, Discovery, and Information Exchange). The ubiquitous nature of their impact, coupled with a seamless user experience will allow the enterprise to unleash the full power of information. Disruptive technologies, by their very nature, shake up the status quo. At the early stage of adoption and implementation, the full scope of their impact is difficult to predict. Mobile computing and the Cloud are no exceptions, particularly in view of their influence across the entire EIM spectrum.

CHAPTER 11

FOCUSED ON THE VALUE

Interaction among value drivers is the big opportunity

It is important to understand and cultivate the impact that each of these five key value drivers has on the others. Customer relationships impact revenue, efficiency effects margins, governance influences efficiency, and so on. And the interaction among the value drivers is a great opportunity. Information is the common denominator that each driver shares, and when we create flows that effectively drive information and processes throughout an organization, each positive investment we make amplifies the benefit of every other. It's all connected.

An EIM strategy is a fundamental part of a value strategy. Strategic investments in information can have a very significant effect not only on each value driver but also on how well each driver influences the others.

How EIM enhances value drivers

It's not difficult to create a rough approximation of how EIM can impact your revenue. If we take a look at each of the five value drivers and how information impacts them, the ability to enable information flow and process efficiency jumps off the page.

EIM improves revenue

First and foremost, profitability depends on generating revenue. Increasing revenue is an obvious place to look for increased profitability. Your business will generate revenue in its own way, but generally it is about making products or services and marketing and selling them.

A sketch of your revenue model might look roughly like this:

A basic revenue model

More effective product development

As a part of your basic revenue model, let's consider product development. To fully understand how EIM can impact your revenue cycle, you might choose to break it down and chart your product development cycle. This cycle will include aspects of development like customer research or perhaps other types of research or experimentation, a development and testing process, possibly a supply chain, and some distribution channels. Ask yourself what types of information are critical to each of these elements. Across the entire product development cycle EIM facilitates more effective product development by enabling secure information management, fluid collaboration among the people working to solve challenges and innovate opportunities, Business Process Management (BPM) for efficient execution and quality control, and media management to support technical drawings or other rich media that is part of your product or its development.

Enrich marketing throughput, reach, and efficacy

Marketing builds revenue by finding new customers and growing the value of existing customers. Marketing encompasses market research, outreach, and relationship management, along with a constant measurement and monitoring of each for refinement and improvement. EIM Customer Experience Management (CEM) technologies support your marketing team by making it easier to understand the market and enabling them to send more personalized marketing messages using more effective channels to deliver exceptional brand experiences.

How much of your marketing is digital? How can you increase marketing efficiency, reach, and effectiveness? The answers to these questions depend on the quality of the market information you have, your presence in each channel, how many channels you participate in—digital, partner, mobile, print, retail, etc.

EIM equips today's marketing departments with solutions in the following:

- Planning and collaboration
- Media creation, publishing, and distribution
- Digital experiences, such as websites and mobile apps
- Multichannel experiences, including web, mobile, and print
- Personalization capabilities in all channels based on customer information
- Process management
- Analytics

Improving any of these will improve your marketing value, with each compounding the overall impact of your marketing programs.

Increase sales

A sale is the act of capturing revenue. Sales are based on information: information about prospects: what they need and how you can meet those needs. Sales is about finding opportunities, tracking them, and providing prospects with the right information at the right time. It is about projections, strategy, and execution. Effective sales meet customer needs efficiently—often through smart processes, which ensure that every customer has a great sales experience. Creating a positive sales experience is based on accurate, up-to-date, and easily accessible customer information—who has purchased what, billing, account status, special needs, and more to ensure satisfaction and realization of revenue. EIM helps you manage all customer information, in any format, across the entire lifecycle of the customer.

EIM gives your sales team secure access to the following:
- Customer information
- Market information
- Product information
- Account planning and tracking
- Smart sales processes
- Integration with billing and commissioning systems

An EIM system and strategy allows information and processes to flow among departments—product development, marketing, sales, and customer support—and can mean the difference between good growth and outstanding growth. Does your marketing department have consistent, real-time information on how the sales process is working? Does your development organization have visibility into both sales and customer service?

What would happen to your revenue if you could reduce the time it takes for the sales cycle by ten percent because your representatives were given better access to product information and more efficient Customer Relationship Management (CRM) processes? What if you could increase the average purchase size by five percent because sales had better insight into what your customers wanted and what research and development delivered against?

EIM deepens customer relationships

Customer relationships are a core driver of profitability. The better your customer relationships are, or the more satisfied your customers are, the more loyal they will be. When customers are loyal, their lifetime value increases. This has always been a commonly held view, and is now well substantiated by data.[91]

---

[91] Temkin Group Research, *"The ROI of Customer Experience"*, Temkin Group (Mar. 2012).

When we examine each stage in optimizing customer relationships (as illustrated in the figure below) we can see that enterprise information drives a flow of value and information from customer insight through retention, repeat sales, and referrals.

EIM creates value through improved customer relationships

Increase customer insight

Customer insight comes from sales, customer support, web analytics, customer advisory boards, surveys, conversations, social media, and more. An excellent EIM strategy can ensure that these insights are available to the right people at the right time. An example is ensuring that customer services insights are included in product development and R&D discussions and product roadmaps are available to customer service representatives. Equally important is ensuring that web analytics for a page or campaign informs the design of the next. Customer service and quality control information can also improve manufacturing processes, documentation, design sales processes, and loyalty programs. EIM allows the collection, creation, management, and appropriate use of the following:

- Customer information
- Collaboration and cooperation support to circulate and act on information
- Design processes
- Analytics

- Surveys

- Complaints

When these facets of customer information are combined, they produce richer insights about your customers. Generating this information, ensuring that it respects the privacy and security of the customer and the enterprise, while still informing the many adjacent components can only be achieved with a robust EIM strategy.

Build customer experience

Customer experience is the experience a person has when they interact with your organization and its brand(s). The journey begins with awareness, moves through some kind of interest or engagement, may lead to a sale, and hopefully continues from there to include elements like the product itself, its packaging or delivery, the service around the sale, billing, and future needs. In other words, any interaction a person may have with your brands or products is part of a customer experience.

Customer experience is defined wherever your brand has any kind of presence—across myriad devices, channels, and formats. For example, this experience may take place on your website, during an online transaction or purchase of a product, on the phone with a customer support representative, or at the point-of-sale in a department store. Based on the number of interactions available and the channels involved, delivering exceptional customer experiences is a significant information challenge for organizations.

Creating successful customer experiences can only be meaningfully achieved with a strong EIM strategy. You want your experiences to be cohesive, personalized to the needs of each user, and optimized to deliver satisfaction and revenue while maintaining costs.

Enhance customer service

Extraordinary customer service is critical in the retention of existing customers and the acquisition of new customers. EIM helps you deliver new and innovative process improvements and services to your customers, while increasing the productivity and efficiency of your customer service organization. Using EIM Business Process Management (BPM) solutions, you can

- Deliver extraordinary customer service at an enterprise scale by responding to customers faster and across multiple channels.

- Increase visibility with a 360-degree view of the customer service experience.

- Accelerate decision-making by applying metric-driven justification for process improvements.

- Quickly design, deploy, and deliver new products and services to meet changing business requirements.

Increase customer satisfaction

Customer satisfaction has a direct influence on revenue. Satisfaction is determined by the quality and nature of your brand, your product, your digital presence, your physical presence, and the people, processes, and assets your customers deal with. Most of these are improved with information. Through its CEM portfolio, EIM helps streamline the customer experience, which in turn increases customer satisfaction and the promise of repeat sales.

Strengthen customer retention, repeat sales, and referrals

Customer retention has a direct impact on your profitability. Successful customer retention starts with first contact and continues throughout the lifetime of the relationship that your organization has with each customer. Your ability to attract and retain new customers depends upon effective EIM in a broad sense and CEM specifically. If you exceed your customer's expectations, your customer lifetime value increases incrementally, as a satisfied customer is more likely to be a loyal customer. A good customer experience nurtures brand loyalty and advocates for your brand(s) and presents an increased likelihood of repeat sales and even referrals to other prospective customers.

An enterprise-wide EIM strategy integrates both your front-office (or public-facing products and services) with your back office (internal-only systems) to maximize your opportunities to innovate, understand, and improve this value cycle. In short, EIM is a key driver of marketing value.

> *EIM can increase revenue, efficiency, quality, and throughput, while minimizing operating costs and risks. A strong EIM strategy can be the touchstone of an enterprise growth strategy.*

EIM increases operating margins

A healthy operating margin is a requisite for success. Operating margin is an overall measure of your management's efficiency. It compares the quality of your activity to the quality of your competitors' activity in the context of your industry or industries. A low-cost operating model results in high-operating margins. This means that your organization can deliver products or services to customers at cheaper cost than your competitors and still be profitable.

EIM improves throughput and quality of delivery—and increases your operating margins— by improving team productivity through collaboration, streamlining the information flow between departments and teams, and optimizing processes. Small increases, when amplified throughout the organization, help to create a highly functional, highly capable organization with high-operating margins.

There are additional ways that EIM can reduce costs and increase margins. Asset management, from physical assets to human resources and information assets, ensures that assets that are owned are tracked, maintained, supported, and used to their fullest potential. In other words, asset management preserves investments and minimizes waste. Do you have significant sources of waste in your business? In many organizations, just understanding what assets exist, where they are located, and their current condition is extremely complex. Whatever your highest volume and value assets are, whether it is your workforce, your media library, your inventory, or your machinery, EIM asset management capabilities can simplify operations, increase margins, and optimize the value of investments.

EIM maximizes efficiency

As a combination of optimized information, processes, experiences, exchanges, and insights, EIM gives organizations the ability to make optimal use of their resources for great efficiency gains.

Adopting an integrated and holistic EIM strategy can drastically increase the effectiveness of manual and silo-based systems, which often create limitations that inhibit the ability to leverage and reuse information effectively. Managing information securely across multiple programs, processes, and departments empowers your organization to align product development, marketing, sales, and customer support based on insight into how decisions can impact other parts of your organization.

Information drives competitive advantage, but it also presents great risk. In order to capitalize on opportunity and enable innovation, information must be managed.

EIM addresses the challenge of managing and securing growing volumes of information used to support mission-critical processes. EIM can arm your executives and management team by giving them actionable insights and improved decision-making. Better collaboration helps to build agility, along with processes that are extended across departments and functions to generate business value. Finally, a streamlined customer experience helps to create exceptional brand experiences for your customers. With EIM, there is potential to increase efficiency so that your business can reach more customers, accelerate the buying cycle, generate more revenue, and grow in a changing environment.

EIM supports governance and risk management

An EIM strategy based on a platform that has information governance and security at its core ensures that the activity of the enterprise—as expressed by information—can be governed more efficiently.

While productivity and efficiency demand that people share and collaborate with business information, organizations must protect critical information from threats both inside and outside the firewall. A comprehensive EIM Enterprise Content Management (ECM) solution is designed for high-security environments, with the flexibility that allows organizations to configure and set appropriate security levels.

Governance is about leveraging information to conduct business. EIM unites corporate information for a single source of the truth, giving the right people access to the right information at the right time. EIM helps organizations to govern information in accordance with government legislation and regulations, industry standards, and internal policies and procedures.

EIM in action: information creates value

The following OpenText customers are transforming their organizations with a sound EIM strategy, which has enabled them to increase revenue, efficiency, and quality, while decreasing operating costs and risks.

As an illustration, consider **Nationwide Building Society** in the UK. The UK government was concerned that the UK savings banks were taking too long to process asset transfers between certain kinds of banks, with unacceptable consequences for consumers. The industry was told that it would have to meet a 15-day standard for these kinds of transfers within six months. Nationwide had a 23-day process. Investing in EIM BPM not only helped them meet this goal to comply; their customer satisfaction ratings increased, along with their market share and their ability to make fundamental changes and improvements in the future.

Barrick Gold is another shining example of how smart EIM investments bring value to the entire organization. Barrick is a gold mining company that depends on highly technical skills and problem solving while dealing with multiple government regulations. Its business complexity is high, as are its compliance risks. A solid EIM strategy has helped them build their knowledge base, get more value out of it, and ensure that their organization is maintaining good corporate governance and citizenship.

Perhaps our favorite case study, however, is our own. Last year **OpenText** launched its own internal social community as a part of its EIM CEM system. The community serves as a hub to connect our own employees with one another, as well as with our content management and process solutions. We launched to 5,000 users simultaneously on day one. From that day on, we witnessed the solution's remarkable adoption rate, a steady growth in engagement, and impressive improvements to our company culture as people began to gain better visibility into executive priorities, along with the performance and skill sets of their colleagues. People became familiar with their co-workers, engagements deepened as conversations progressed, and gradually we found we had a stronger, more capable, more efficient global team.

> Debra Lavoy

Twitter: @deb_lavoy

Debra Lavoy, Director, Product Management, OpenText

…On the strategic CIO

We've seen the role of information shift dramatically within the enterprise. Information now represents a critical strategic element. Our CIO customers recognize this and are looking for opportunities to become more strategic. They want to provide more strategic, forward-thinking vision to help build value for the organization.

In order for their IT strategy and enterprise information strategy to really meld together and become one, CIOs know they need to create more dynamic capabilities for their organization. This can be difficult because CIOs live at the intersection of the past, present, and future. They have inherited the legacy of the past: vast quantities of information stored in every conceivable place, which must somehow be managed. This information is siloed, disconnected, too important to discard, and too expensive to migrate. In the present, CIOs are facing a dramatic increase of expectations on the part of the user in terms of what they want, how they want it, and when they want it and on the part of the business in terms of what IT needs to deliver and how quickly they need to deliver it. They also face security challenges and basic information challenges (volume, variety, and velocity). Looking toward the future, these CIOs understand that anything they build now will need to change 6, 12, or 24 months from now. They must design for change and evolution. They must build an agile information infrastructure.

Strategic CIOs are building new relationships with the rest of the C-suite. There is a diminishing difference between information strategy and business strategy, and these partnerships are essential to the success of every line of business. CIOs are starting to look at their information enterprise not as a bunch of systems that are sewn together, but as a whole to understand how information flows through their organization, where it's initiated, and where it goes to deliver the most value. The frame of thinking for strategic CIOs must shift from "system to system" to the "whole" that supports the strategic agenda for innovation and growth.

EIM capability drives value

Innovation is built on information. As the set of technologies and practices that maximize the value of information while minimizing its risks, EIM provides control for the enterprise, creating the opportunity for unlimited growth and responsiveness.

As we have just explored, EIM helps to more effectively manage five key value drivers: revenue, customer relationships, operating margin, efficiency, and governance and risk management. As a holistic strategy, the drivers are fundamentally inter-related, and value is compounded by their mutual dependencies. EIM gives you the ability to do more than manage information challenges effectively. You can use it to create significant business value by directing the flow of information throughout your ecosystem—your workforce, markets, customers, and partners.

EIM delivers control and the capacity to create value by optimizing the power of information. What you do with that information is limited only by your imagination.

C H A P T E R **12**

INFORMATION FLOWS AND THE JOURNEY

CHAPTER 12

Information Flows and the Journey: Optimizing Value Chains with EIM

"The market is undergoing a shift to more integrated systems and ecosystems and away from loosely coupled heterogeneous approaches." [92]

Your enterprise is saturated with information, and it's moving at the speed of light. It flows through each process and supports every value chain from beginning to end. And that's a wonderful thing because when those information flows are managed, controlled, connected, and optimized to surface the right information as needed, they ultimately drive your bottom line and your shareholder value. While most companies struggle with optimizing information flows, Enterprise Information Management (EIM) gives you the ability to connect the dots.

But now the question becomes how do you get there? How do you start on "the EIM journey"? The world is evolving around us, and the information world is doing so ten times as fast. Your organization must adapt to that change. This requires new processes, new tools and platforms, and new methodologies, but first and foremost it requires new ways of thinking. Let's look at some of the challenges enterprises are facing today and what concepts to consider when embarking on their EIM journey.

Identify value chains

Information is meant to be shared. It's meant to flow with intended direction from one person or group to another and improve as it moves along. Often, however, information spreads without direction or logic and ends changing uncontrollably with each version until its original source is barely recognizable.

Within an enterprise—where it is imperative that information remain accurate to drive decision-making and where some data, such as design plans or employees' personal details, should not be shared with the public or even with certain internal groups—information should flow seamlessly and securely along the appropriate value chain among departments, teams, and individuals. These value chains and associated information flows are some of the concepts that should be understood and mapped out as part of an EIM strategy.

---

[92] Gartner Inc., *"Gartner Identifies the Top 10 Strategic Technology Trends for 2013"*, Newsroom, Gartner.com, *http://www.gartner.com/it/page.jsp?i d=2209615&sourceid=1-2973570319* (accessed 12 Nov 2012).

Twitter: @neowilson

Neil Wilson, Director of Technical Marketing, OpenText

...on the importance of managing the flow of information

If you look at many recently emerging technology companies, you'll find that the majority of what they do is manage information. Every business is now an information business. We are moving into an age of aggressive change where intellectual property, brand assets, and knowledge of a process is all wrapped up in the value of a company. And the most important aspect to managing all of this information is to understand how the information flows within the business. This means figuring out how to use information to be more successful, more efficient, and more ready to tackle any business challenge that may arise.

Let's say I am creating a new installation, and I want to dig a hole in the ground. I need to know if there are any pipes down there, any electrical work I could run into, any legal or environmental reasons I cannot dig my hole, and I need to know that all of that information is up-to-date and accurate for my situation. I need this information readily available to me so I can make the best decisions possible for the success of my installation. If I don't have the correct information ready when I need it, I am going in blind and any number of disasters could happen.

Another trend in information management is the new generation of enterprise apps that connect to one another and mine information from each other. These apps enable information flow because they connect pieces of related information together in a way that makes sense, allowing you to skip steps that you would normally do manually. For example, there's a note-taking app that automatically creates a notification in your calendar to remind you to review your notes. Or a customer service app that pulls together a customer's history of transactions with that company, any complaints or problems they had, how frequently they shop there, which items they purchased in the past, etc. Having that information at your fingertips ensures more successful transactions with that customer in the future.

The value chain was originally described by Michael Porter in his 1985 book, *Competitive Advantage: Creating and Sustaining Superior Performance*.[93] Once it is determined that an organization can sell products and/or services for more than production costs, value chains can be used to increase competitive advantage.

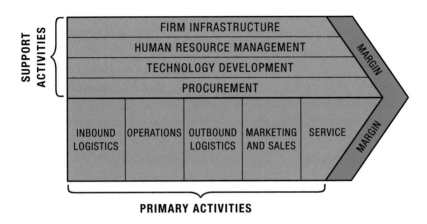

Porter's value chain[94]

A value chain can be described as a series of activities. A product or service moves through all of the activities in the series in order, and at each step, the product or service gains some value. The more value produced, the stronger the organization's competitive advantage.

Value chains exist in any organization. They are the inherent building blocks that drive productivity. In most cases, however, they are not as efficient as they can be and should be optimized. To identify potential areas for improvement, value chains need to be first mapped and analyzed. To do so, a team within an organization will review the activities their products or services move through and lay out all the steps of each activity. They then identify the links and define new or more efficient ways in which products or services gain value as they move through the activity.

Value chain mapping and analysis can quickly help an organization identify "touch points" with customers, recognize pain points, and discover opportunities to improve processes. Once the business functions are broken down into activities, each part of the value chain and how it creates value for the customer is much clearer. It becomes much more obvious what consumers are expecting at each step and whether enough value is being created for them. This is especially important today with a personalized social experience being at the forefront of each customer interaction.

---

[93] Michael E. Porter, *"Competitive Advantage: Creating and Sustaining Superior Performance"* (New York: The Free Press, 1985).
[94] *Ibid.*

In terms of creating value, let's consider a marketing campaign. It may include activities such as the creation of promotional content, publishing this on the organization's website and across social media, measuring the responses, adjusting for a more successful campaign, and delivering the focus for customer consumption. Breaking down and examining the process in this way enables the teams involved to focus on the details of the process and maximize value.

The quicker, more accurate, more integrated a process is, the better the results. For example, a source of revenue growth is retaining and growing current customers. Key factors that impact current customers no matter where they reside are enhanced sales, quality, delivery, billing, and exception resolution. The processes that enable improvement to these impacts are customer relationship management, customer satisfaction, quality, pricing, and new product development. And the more efficient these processes are, the more efficient the margin will be—and that results in revenue growth.

Porter called the interconnected web of value chains the "value system."[95] A value system includes your organization's value chains, your suppliers' value chains, your distribution channels' value chains, and your buyers' value chains. With all of the interrelated material, it's important to ensure the activities are followed in the right order and that a holistic approach is applied.

Information flows at the heart of value chains

Value chain mapping and analysis are vital for identifying potential optimization opportunities. These are necessary and much needed steps to gain a holistic view of where optimization opportunities lie. The second step is to identify and analyze the information flows that support that value chain.

Data lies at the heart of each value chain. And as we move through each step of the value chain, new data and information are created and added to improve the end result. Incrementally, each step depends on data previously created. High quality data produces more comprehensive and informed insights. The easier it is to access this information, the better the outcome of that process step and the higher the productivity and overall value of the value chain. Any supporting IT investment is only as good as the understanding of the existing value chains and their associated information flows.

For example, consider the information flow for "Discover to Analyze" within a value chain step. The activities might include discovering unstructured as well as structured information, capturing both types of information, managing and assigning access rights, exchanging the information with the appropriate individuals and/or teams, and analyzing the data in order to make the best business decisions.

---

[95] Michael E. Porter, *"Competitive Advantage: Creating and Sustaining Superior Performance"* (New York: The Free Press, 1985), 34. "A firm's value chain is embedded in a larger stream of activities that I term the value system..."

DISCOVER   CAPTURE   MANAGE   EXCHANGE   ANALYZE

Discover to analyze information flow

Those familiar with ERP-based value chain enablement will feel at home with the concepts presented so far as they pertain to structured data. Value chain enablement drives the ERP industry, but our understanding of supporting information flows must adjust with the arrival of the social era.

Add unstructured data to the flow

A few years ago, 121 billion minutes were spent on social media each month, and that rate has been growing by approximately 37 percent each year.[96] Ideas are exchanged, news is shared, and opinions are expressed on everything from foods to governments to autotronics.

And it's not just the general public using social media. Organizations create most of the world's data—96 percent—and lock it behind organizational firewalls. You may recall our brief look at "the deep web" (and the illustration) from chapter one. And you may remember we noted of that 96 percent secured data, about 80 percent is unstructured.[97] New frameworks and solutions based on unstructured information flows enable organizations to derive value from this previously unchartered territory—the untapped 80 percent. Ignoring—or worse, dismissing—all of that information leaves an organization open to miscommunication, errors, and possible legal action.

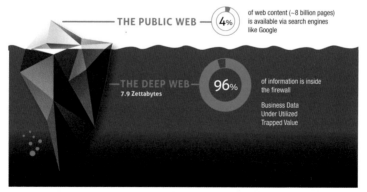

THE PUBLIC WEB — 4% of web content (~8 billion pages) is available via search engines like Google

THE DEEP WEB 96% of information is inside the firewall
7.9 Zettabytes
Business Data Under Utilized Trapped Value

The deep web[98]

[96] Wikipedia, *"Social Media"*, Wikipedia.com, *http://en.wikipedia.org/wiki/Social_media* (accessed 16 Apr. 2013) "44 million-plus tweets per day in 2009".
[97] Stephen Pritchard, *"How to manage unstructured data for business benefit"*, ComputerWeekly.com, *http://www.computerweekly.com/feature/How-to-manage-unstructured-data-for-business-benefit*, Dec 2012 (accessed 5 Jan. 2013).
[98] Invention Machine, *"The Deep Web: Semantic Search Takes Innovation to New Depths"*, Goldfire Blog, *InventionMachine.com, http://inventionmachine. com/the-Invention-Machine-Blog/bid/79363/The-Deep-Web-Semantic-Search-Takes-Innovation-to-New-Depths* (accessed 5 Oct. 2012).

Today's ultimate business challenge is to capture, manage, and analyze this unstructured information because the data derived from that is what will enable your organization to achieve two things. Your organization will be able to understand and truly delve into (1) what customers expect and what gives your organization competitive advantage and (2) what is going on within your organization's own walls. Having up-to-date internal information that can be trusted is paramount to maximizing ROI.

The social era

Since Porter conceived of the value chain in 1985, things have changed with the introduction of social media, the deep web, and big data. But none of these have shifted Porter's model or what consumers buy: the unique and the bargain. In 1985, being big and having scale were key contributors to competitive advantage and profitability. Now, almost any organization can offer online "aisles" of products or services and deliver the cost-savings approach, where consumers are at the end of the value chain.

> *"While social media doesn't shift Porter's model, the social era surely does."*[99]

However, one thing has significantly impacted Porter's model: the social era. In today's market, selling the unique is the key to profitability. The customer experience is everything. Consumers today expect to provide feedback, and this feedback is what can make an item unique. Every organization has the ability to get direct and virtually free feedback from consumers by taking part in a social media conversation. It also makes that item less expensive to create as it is essentially "made to order" according to social feedback.

Organizations can also take control of their image and protect their reputation much quicker in this social era. While it's true that a negative comment or event regarding an organization can go viral in a matter of minutes, destroying years of customer trust (and shareholder value), negative feedback can also be managed much more expediently and effectively than before to transform bad press into good press to the organization's advantage.

For example, when someone complained to a major fast food chain that their foot-long sandwiches were not actually 12 inches long, the company quickly apologized using social outlets and explained that the dough for each bun is weighed exactly the same, but due to the variations in kneading, rising, proofing, etc., some buns end up being slightly longer or shorter. They even promised that their foot-long sandwiches would never again be shorter than 12 inches and put on a special promotion for the "footlong". Overall, the result was a positive one because the company tapped into social media, used it to their advantage, and reacted quickly and honestly.

[99] Nilofer Merchant, *"Why Porter's Model No Longer Works"*, HBR Blog Network, Harvard Business Review, *http://blogs.hbr.org/cs/2012/02/why_porters_ model_no_longer_wo.html Feb 2012* (accessed 12 Mar. 2013).

In another example, when an airline company broke a passenger's guitar and did nothing to rectify this, it damaged their brand.[100] After nine months of calls and emails, the company ended all communications with the disgruntled customer, ignoring his promise to write, perform, and post three songs about the experience on YouTube. The first song received more than 1.5 million views within four days of posting (and views continue to skyrocket). Despite their attempts to right the situation, the complaint had gone public and their brand reputation was impacted as a result.

The social era, or to be more specific, the social experience, has given organizations more control and consumers more power by putting them at the center of the process. Placing customers at the center of the value chain requires support for new types of information flows, ones that allow for adjustments. And change is always on the horizon, so your organization must be flexible, prepared, and willing to adjust.

New information flows for new types of information

From an information technology perspective, this is a huge opportunity and a big challenge. IT departments and CIOs have an unparalleled opportunity to address that challenge and turn it around to drive value for the business. But they must first grasp how value gets created in the organization, how information flows, and then provide the tools, systems, policies, and governance structures that will support that flow. They also must embrace new thinking toward information flows:

1. Different data means a different information flow

Information flows are adapting to the challenges and opportunities of unstructured data. The way organizations search for, process, and transfer information will change the role of managers, the way businesses market and sell products and services, how organizations buy, and ultimately how they are managed and led. The disruptive natures of social networks and the resulting information-flow adaptations are merely the beginning of this vast evolution. Information flows could even be viewed as one of the most transformative forces in modern society.

Graeme Codrington, futurist and founder of *TomorrowToday*, states that the technology behind information flows will completely change business in the next decade.[101] Improved information flows and social media are already changing the way customers buy. Increasingly, buying decisions are based on trust or the relationship the customer has with an organization (the customer's experience). And as the way that customers buy changes, the way that organizations sell must also evolve.

---

[100] Ravi Sawhney, *"Broken Guitar Has United Playing the Blues to the Tune of $180 Million"*, FastCompany, *http://www.fastcompany.com/1320152/broken-guitar-has-united-playing-blues-tune-180-million*, 30 Jul. 2009 (accessed 5 Apr. 2013).
[101] James Kirk, *"New Opportunities In New Information Flows"*, Digital Transformation, *http://digital-transformation.yourbusinesschannel.com/2012/08/new-opportunities-in-new-information-flows/* (accessed 30 Mar. 2013).

2. Bigger opportunity and bigger risk

Organizations now have the ability to combine internal data with external information flows. Although this provides an exciting opportunity to push brand awareness and source big data at the same time, dealing with unstructured data affects risk management. It's important to maintain security and minimize risk while still promoting the organization's brand wherever conversations occur. Failing to grasp unstructured data sources leaves organizations vulnerable to greater risk, missed opportunities, and lost customers.

3. Data analytics optimize decisions

Smart business decisions come from smart data analytics. Effective information flows must include internal data as well as external information from all sources because, as Sir Francis Bacon and Alexander Pope surmised, "a little learning is a dangerous thing".[102] If certain pieces of information are missing, even the best business decisions suddenly become a gamble.

4. Social era impacts and directs change

There are many examples of social media impacting social change, such as the Tunisian and Egyptian revolutions. The unstructured conversations that took place within social media had a direct impact on the action that took place on the ground. The opinions and voices expressed were amplified in a way that had never before been possible, and this power can be channeled through information flows to advocate or improve products, services, or events. Even negative conversations can result in positive experiences.

Information flows in action

New frameworks and solutions based on unstructured data lead to new information flows within a value chain. For organizations trying to determine how their IT investments can support the organization in deriving maximum value from its value chains, streamlining information flows where such support would generate the most benefit to the company should be a priority.

Consider a value chain in an organization that brings new products to market. Such a value chain is made up of multiple activities and supports multiple information flows. A potential activity is the creation of a web-based campaign as part of a product launch. This activity includes a step to measure consumer responses and another one to adjust to these responses for a more successful campaign. This type of framework allows enterprises to tap into previously unchartered territory by deriving value from unstructured information and creating a more unique or valuable item or service—thereby creating competitive advantage and realizing ROI.

---

[102] *"a little learning"* is widely attributed to Alexander Pope (1688 - 1744). It is found in An Essay on Criticism (1709), but it was Sir Francis Bacon's idea, *http://www.phrases.org.uk/meanings/a-little-knowledge-is-a-dangerous-thing.html* (accessed 6 Apr. 2013).

Ideally, an information flow should use a holistic software suite, with each component able to complete its tasks independently while at the same time working seamlessly with other components as part of the bigger vision of EIM. This is the way to derive maximum ROI.

To clearly illustrate both a holistic approach and just one way that information can flow through an organization, let's examine the steps that a fictitious corporation called Innovate Corporation might take to ensure the good governance of information.

Introducing Innovate Corporation

Innovate Corporation is a fictitious manufacturer of consumer electronics, such as smart phones, laptop computers, printers, and tablets. They have just received a request for information as part of a legal investigation. This activity generates an information flow that they call "Capture to Archive." This information flow is shown in the following five simple steps: capture, classify, manage, discover, and archive.

innovate | Capture to Archive

Capture to Archive

Capture to archive information flow

1. Capture

The legal department at Innovate receives notice of a legal investigation into the quality of goods sold over the Internet. They are asked to provide information in response to an investigation into Expedite, the shipping company they use. Fortunately, Innovate has a defensible disposition policy, and as part of it, they use OpenText Records Management to classify all Innovate business records to respond to investigations of this nature.

Using OpenText Enterprise Content Management (ECM) to capture and classify content for records management is not difficult. One member of the Innovate legal team creates a new folder to capture data relating to the investigation. The folder is based on a template, which is comprised of required metadata and sub-folders for content.

One user has received a number of emails in Microsoft Outlook relating to the investigation. To add these to the matter folder, he simply drags and drops the emails into the right folder—directly in the Outlook interface. He can also add a record classification to the messages or, as we'll see later, he could simply let the system automatically classify the emails. The uploaded messages can still be accessed and viewed from the Outlook user interface.

Back in the content repository, a records manager can quickly find all records for a given classification using facetted browsing, and then further filter the results by file type, author, or any other metadata.

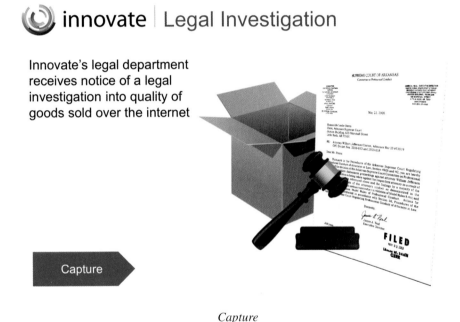

Capture

2. Classify
OpenText Auto-Classification can ensure that all Innovate records, including web pages, emails, paper documents, and office documents, are properly classified.

First, the records manager is going to select a collection of incoming content for processing. Next, she asks the system to classify the content in the collection—the progress is shown as the collection is analyzed. For most records, the system can determine the right classification to add, but for some records, the system needs a little help. Results indicate that the tool has made a judgment call on a classification but seeks confirmation from a human operator. As the records manager works her way through the confirmations (allowing or denying), the system "learns" how to tag future records.

innovate | Auto-Classification

OpenText's **Auto-Classification** can ensure that all Innovate records, including web pages, emails, paper documents, and office documents, are properly classified and archived through defensible disposition

| Capture | Classify |

Classify

3. Manage

Innovate has received a number of complaints about damaged shipments in the care of Expedite, their shipping agent. The compliance officer at Innovate uses OpenText Content Server to find any content relating to the company's dealings with the Expedite Shipping Co. and applies a legal hold. To create the hold, he simply chooses to add a new hold and completes the required fields in the form.

 **innovate** | Investigation

Innovate receives a number of disputes about damaged shipments. They package the devices themselves and then use a company called **Expedite** to ship them.

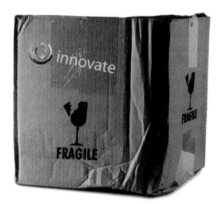

Manage

4. Discover

OpenText Content Server has built-in search capabilities to enable the end user to establish the criteria for holding a business record. Once a search-enabled hold is in place, any newly added content that meets the hold criteria can also be managed.

The compliance officer sets up a search-enabled hold for the Expedite investigation. From the function menu, he chooses the option to select the hold criteria. Then he sets up the search query for the hold. The query may include full-text search, system defined or custom metadata, or classification fields, but in this case, it's just a simple list of required keywords. To finish, he simply saves the query for the hold.

Having prepared the archived materials, the Innovate compliance officer prepares to export the content "on hold" to support the legal investigation. The search query will find and hold all of the records related to the case, so Innovate's compliance officer can now prepare to export the content as evidence to respond to the legal investigation. He simply selects the command to export the hold contents—here he can choose to export all document versions or just the most current version. The system works it's magic as a background task, and lets him know when it's complete.

innovate | Search Enabled Holds

Search Enabled Holds, use OpenText Content Server's built in search capabilities to establish the criteria for holding a business record. Once a search enabled hold is in place, any newly added content that meets the hold criteria will also be managed

| Capture | Classify | Manage | Discover |

Discover

5. Archive

All of the business information at Innovate is securely retained within OpenText Enterprise Archive, where it is de-duplicated, compressed, and stored according to the company's retention policies.

The Innovate IT department configures OpenText Content Server to automatically archive content from the repository. As part of the setup process, the systems administrator at Innovate defines a number of different storage providers, including fast Serial ATA (SATA) storage for rapid access to content and less expensive tape backup for content that is only needed once in a while. She then defines the rules that will determine where each type of content is stored. In this case, she creates a new rule to store any "Closed Legal Cases" on the compliance data archive. The rule is triggered whenever content is classified with the LEG-CL file number. She also creates a rule that sets the archiving job to run at 2:20 pm every Thursday. And when the process is complete, a full audit is created.

OpenText Enterprise Archiving can be configured to use different types of data storage— even Cloud—so Innovate can choose the right storage solution for their needs without being tied to a single vendor. They have decided to set up OpenText Enterprise Archive to store selected content in the Cloud using Windows Azure®.

To optimize storage and security, Innovate also activates encryption and data compression on all their archives. And to optimize storage and security, the system can be configured to automatically encrypt and de-duplicate the archive.

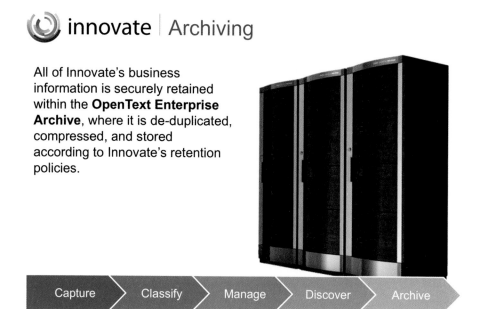

innovate | Archiving

All of Innovate's business information is securely retained within the **OpenText Enterprise Archive**, where it is de-duplicated, compressed, and stored according to Innovate's retention policies.

Capture ⟩ Classify ⟩ Manage ⟩ Discover ⟩ Archive

Archive

Innovate uses this information flow to capture important business records that they are required to present in a legal investigation. They use auto-classification to prepare records for archiving and disposition, their compliance officer uses the system to discover and hold records relating to the investigation, and finally they use OpenText archiving technology for cost-effective and long-term storage of their records.

Although the organization used here is fictitious, the information flow is not. Many organizations can relate to the described activities on a daily basis. It's clear to see the fusion of the individual components of the information flow as a holistic value proposition that is part of an EIM vision that offers competitive advantage and increases ROI.

Achieving compliance through optimized information flows

A major communications giant has integrated several OpenText products into its information flows. Using OpenText ECM, the organization has built automatic classification behind their processes so that users aren't burdened with manual classification. In fact, a few years ago, they indicated that many of their users didn't even know classification was taking place. Everyone at the company files enterprise content according to organizational policies, thereby ensuring regulatory compliance and reducing the risks associated with audit and litigation. And they have had tremendous results: they have classified more than 14 million documents—all because the user-friendly solutions from OpenText allow the records management process to integrate seamlessly into the way people work.

Enterprises must evolve

The Capture-to-Archive information-flow example illustrated above shows how value chain activities within an enterprise can be streamlined for maximum value. By considering all such value activities in their organizations and by supporting them through a holistic and integrated EIM platform, organizations are well positioned to leverage information and not only derive competitive advantage but also quickly react and respond to change.

Organizations that are slow to react to change are the most vulnerable to dynamic, stressful, and volatile market conditions. These organizations are hampered by a critical component: timely (or no) access to information. Organizations that leverage information as well as data enriched with heuristics or trial-and-error experimentation to both mitigate the turbulence in their respective ecosystems and profit from the entropy that acts as a disruptive force are referred to as "anti-fragile" organizations. EIM, effectively employed by a strategic CIO, can rapidly put an organization on a trajectory toward achieving anti-fragile characteristics.

EIM and the strategic CIO are key catalysts in the new economy where business is becoming social; the lines between work, home, and play are blurring; and both ideas and information are free flowing. The CIO should take advantage of the emerging EIM doctrine and leverage it to transform their business into one that is information driven and thusly anti-fragile—one that thrives in volatility.

The tenets of the EIM doctrine are not revolutionary: they are the result of an evolving, volatile market where new threats and business models appear and expeditiously harvest market share from traditional players that are slow to react and adapt. Fundamentally, EIM strives to improve business performance and agility by
- increasing business insight;
- catalyzing operational efficiency;
- increasing transparency between organizational silos, departments, and divisions; and
- most importantly, being information centric, i.e., putting information to work by making it accessible and operational.

In certain contexts, EIM could be seen as breathing life into the static modalities of Enterprise Architecture (EA) as well as Information Architecture (IA). EA and IA disciplines have existed for over 30 years, and yet the very core tenets of these frameworks are haphazardly implemented because they lend themselves to brittleness. EA and IA promote the framework (architecture) itself, whereas EIM promotes the asset (information) and accessibility to it. Because of this very principle, EIM acts as a key catalyst for building anti-fragile organizations.

To undertake this transformative journey toward becoming an anti-fragile organization, the enterprise must begin by examining two areas:

1. The role of the CIO must be revisited. In a way, it has moved from boardroom strategy to datacenter tactics, and the time has come for CIOs to re-invent their role and usher in the age of information. Strategic CIOs and their departments are the ultimate internal consultants. The only reason they exist is to provide business insights and constantly explore avenues to make efficient use of technologies in support of business agility.

2. The organization must look for its information. Information in today's enterprises is housed in a data warehouse, filed in an Enterprise Resource Planning (ERP) system, or scattered throughout disparate systems and repositories. Structured data, tabular in nature, resides within the data warehouse or ERP system. Unstructured data, representing more than 80 percent of the information behind an organization's firewall— the untapped 80 percent, as noted earlier—resides on many other systems, including on mobile devices and in the cloud. How does the CIO leverage the principles behind EIM to catalog, organize, integrate, share, and describe unstructured data?

Optimizing value chains with EIM

There is a formula to managing the chaos of unstructured data. The formula begins at the very source, with capturing unstructured data, digitizing it (if needed), managing it in a consistent way (by leveraging Information Governance), operationalizing it by integrating it with core business processes, making it universally accessible by creating ways to seamlessly search for it, and finally, archiving it for both regulatory compliance and corporate memory purposes.

While this framework might seem simple, it's in fact quite complex as the information must interface with and permeate the organization in a secure fashion. Knowledge workers must be able to create and collaborate within their enterprise and with their partners and suppliers beyond the corporate firewall. This is exacerbated by the blurring of lines between the technologies used in the office for work and those used at home for both work and play. Today's workforce wants access to their data on their own terms, and this extends the value chain well beyond the firewall. This also applies to partners, suppliers, and customers.

Twitter: @kevinc2003

Kevin Cochrane, CMO, OpenText

...On the relationship between the CIO and the CMO

Historically, the CMO and the CIO have competed with each other. A new trend that I would like to see is for these individuals to start teaming up instead. Both are essential to ensuring growth, evolution, and ultimately customer satisfaction within a company, and a strong CMO-CIO alliance would be a powerful innovative force indeed.

The CMO is responsible for delivering a superb customer experience. He/she needs to understand which strategies are working, and where customers respond. The CIO's role, on the other hand, is to ensure employees have the tools they need to be successful and to create an information infrastructure that is responsive. Can you imagine what would happen if these two heavyweights sat down in a room and brainstormed ways to combine excellent customer experience with responsive infrastructure? Magic! Unfortunately, this is often easier said than done as there can be a lot of tension between CMOs and CIOs.

So how can these two learn to work together? The first step is to align. Gather your respective teams to agree on a set of goals and expectations. Discuss key performance indicators and ensure that each teams' KPIs relate to one another and make sense together. It doesn't help anyone to put in place two different strategies that don't build on each other. As well, time frames and budgets for the agreed-upon KPIs should align. But perhaps the most important thing is to partner on new initiatives and bring them to the CEO and the board together. By joining forces, you are much more likely to get support from the rest of the C-suite.

One thing we are working towards at OpenText is an adaptive information platform for our customers centered around our ability to reach the omni-channel definition. We are doing this while no one else in the market is looking at the synergy between the CMO and CIO and the ability to move across departments. The race to create a more responsive customer experience and responsive enterprise is relentless. Working together, the CMO and CIO can help each other be more successful than ever before!

Creating seamless, smart applications on top of this platform to accomplish the free flow of information at the most opportune moments (managing the chaos) is the very goal of EIM. Once your CIO implements the tenets behind the EIM framework, your organization can begin the journey toward becoming an antifragile organization.

There are many ways to leverage a multitude of technologies to achieve the seamless flow of information within and beyond the corporate firewall. There are entire platforms dedicated to achieving this outcome as well as point solutions and niche offerings that provide a facet or two of the holistic EIM capability. Organizations that leverage a cohesive portfolio that provides for the greatest coverage of EIM capability will arguably be the most successful as their implementations will be the most structured.

AFTERWORD

Through this book, we've come to learn that information is the lifeblood of today's organization. Information drives strategy, information is at the core of all business processes, and the information an organization has at its fingertips drives all business transformations. Whether transformation is based in manufacturing efficiency, the better management of intellectual property, the protection of trade secrets, optimization of business processes and business process architecture, or other factors, information guides your decisions, informs your business, and often is the trade asset of your industry.

Today's organizations are also highly driven by government and industrial compliance and regulation: effectively adhering to standards and regulations is the price of admission for contemporary organizations in many markets.

Effective, secure Enterprise Information Management (EIM) is about controlling and optimizing the information flows within your company and making effective decisions about how data is handled from individual contributors right up to your board of directors and how this same information can be used to drive business transformation.

Bringing it all together

EIM should be thought of as business information handled in the context of your processes. As we discussed, we call these information-driven processes "information flows", and they represent the origin and destination of your data and the transformations that happen with that data as your business processes are executed. Information flows are what brings an organization together and enables effective, secure, compliant, and robust management of your data at all stages of its lifecycle, which might include

- Capture to Archive
- Task to Result
- Objective to Outcome
- Value to Customer
- Acquisition to Disposition

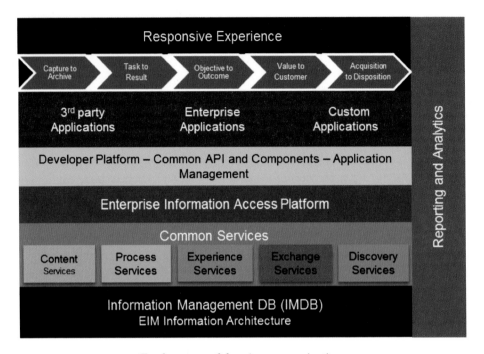

Total amount of data in an organization

Embarking on your EIM journey means understanding the information flows of your organization and aligning efficient EIM practices and technologies around them to deliver measurable and repeatable results.

The future of EIM

EIM is a relatively new market, defined by analysts and visionaries like OpenText to encompass several practices including Enterprise Content Management, Business Process Management, Customer Experience Management, Information Exchange, and Discovery capabilities.

Today, EIM provides the capabilities necessary to understand, measure, and optimize your business processes, while ensuring your content is secure, auditable, mobile, and leveraged effectively within the organization. The volumes of information captured and managed in EIM systems also provide the corpus of data necessary for deep analysis and big data initiatives. Information is the fuel for the big data engine. Further, EIM solutions act as a social catalyst within organizations and drive collaboration and the effective and secure sharing of information between employees, management, and external stakeholders alike.

In the future, EIM platforms will evolve to provide recommendations and deep semantic analysis of content, delivering the data and procedural support employees seek before they're aware they need it. Today's capacities for information management, collection, and storage are unprecedented. The challenge in the coming years will be to advance the technology sufficiently as to make it predictive, proactive, and interactive, rendering suggestions, support, and coaching for end users who seek to accomplish a business objective. Predictive and semantic or "learning" systems can also provide insight into functions such as product pricing, social throughput, and common tasks within an organization and opportunities for gained efficiency and myriad other capabilities that are labor intensive and require highly specialized human skillsets to accomplish today.

The future of EIM is also responsive. With the evolution of client and consumer interfaces in the past five years—from smartphones to tablets, laptop and desktop computers and "clientless" web browser access—today's information workers expect a user experience that adapts to the platform they prefer. No longer are employees shackled to the desk with a single mechanism, usually a desktop computer, as their means of interfacing with and contributing to the organizations collective corporate memory.

With responsive design also comes the concept of Enterprise Applications. This is an emergent theme, but it draws from the compelling and simple user experiences most information workers have come to expect from consumer analogs such as App Stores and mobile providers. The ability for organizations to quickly, cost-effectively build enterprise applications, which leverage secure, robust back-end systems while providing a simple, compelling, and responsive consumer-style user experience, will be the status quo in the years to come. This concept of Enterprise Applications means that organizations can deploy pointed, specific applications to employees who are trying to complete an information flow. Examples of Enterprise Apps could include the following:

• Insurance Claims Adjustment

• Environmental Health & Safety Inspection

• Human Resources and Employee Onboarding

• Sales Enablement and Reference

• Commercial Lending

• Anti-Money Laundering

• Employee Engagement and Secure Social Networking

• Expert Identification and Skills Exchange

The key differentiator between consumer and Enterprise Apps is that Enterprise Apps appear ubiquitously on desktop, laptop, web, mobile phone, and tablet devices for users. They are in fact coupled securely with your enterprise infrastructure, while providing the simple, purpose-driven, and compelling user experience that users expect from their involvement with consumer apps.

This concept of simple, pervasive, and responsive app design, coupled with robust and encompassing information management, leveraging learning systems, semantic analysis, and predictive engines, represents the future of EIM. In the past 30 years, we have seen a massive evolution in the ERP world; so too shall we see EIM evolve. However, unlike ERP, CRM, and other structured data management practices, EIM is unbounded in its opportunity for technological advancement by virtue of the data types it supports, namely, unstructured data.

EIM deals with information the way people deal with information, through written word, spreadsheets, office documents, images, video, media, and business processes. This means the capacity for innovation is limited only to our capacity and hunger for innovation as a society: there is no limit.

The strategic CIO

The strategic CIO is all about transformational leadership. Change doesn't really happen at a company; it happens with people. Understanding how your people execute the processes of your business and what information is critical to their success are the underpinning tenants of successful strategic, transformative information leadership.

Kevin Ford, co-author of *The Leadership Triangle*[103] and CIO of Tag Consulting, references three leadership styles seen in today's modern CIO:

1. **Tactical:** These leaders are solving straight-forward problems. "Tactical issues are solved by expertise. Tactical challenges are the daily bread of the operations-oriented manager," writes Ford in *The Leadership Triangle*.

2. **Strategic:** These leaders are working toward the future with a vision. "Visionaries are different in that they tend to be creative or generative in their approach. They have the ability to see the future and predict specific trends," says Ford.

3. **Transformational:** This leader is a facilitator who doesn't make decisions or establish strategic plans but, instead, facilitates a series of conversations among key stakeholders. "Transformational leaders are driven by a strong set of values and a sense of mission. Oftentimes, the strategic leader will have a vision but can't execute it because they can't deal with the transformative issues. A transformational leader has a more generalized vision—one for the common good or what's in the best interests of the stakeholders.

---

[103] Rich Hein, *"How to apply Transformational Leadership at Your Company"* (Jun. 2013), CIO.com, *http://www.cio.com/article/735121/How_to_ Apply_Transformational_Leadership_at_Your_Company?page=2&taxonomyId=3171* (accessed 22 Jun. 2013).

Combining a Transformational leadership style with the capabilities of a robust EIM platform gives today's Strategic/Transformational CIO the tools they need to facilitate organization-wide discussions and to deliver on vision. EIM is where the rubber hits the road in today's business strategy and transformation initiatives, especially in heavily information-driven industries.

Most CIOs face an 80/20 problem, where 80 percent of their budget is pre-disposed to the operations of the business and "keeping the lights on". This theme means most CIOs have 20 percent or less of their resources available for innovation, strategic implementation, and transformation. EIM platforms allow CIOs to capitalize opportunity for years to come by providing the capacity for growth with respect to information and business process optimization, innovation, and capacity. With EIM, CIOs can leverage a platform, which will grow with their business and accommodate the continually shifting landscape of strategic CIO objectives.

EIM and the strategic CIO are inextricably linked to enable organizations to unleash their company's intelligence, lead a social revolution, simplify IT, and embrace the engagement economy by teaming the back office, front office, and customer office.

The OpenText EIM suite makes this all possible by providing integrated, compelling, and responsive apps and capabilities spanning the EIM spectrum and composed of Enterprise Content Management, Business Process Management, Customer Experience Management, Information Exchange, and Discovery services. OpenText EIM can help you unleash the power of your information.

GLOSSARY, BIBLIOGRAPHY, AND INDEX

GLOSSARY

Advanced Search- A variety of software tools that allow users to get more relevant search results. These tools include Boolean Operators, Stemming, Adjacency and Proximity Searches, Thesauri, and Synonyms.

API- See Application Programming Interface.

Application- Software or programs used to execute tasks on computers.

Application Programming Interface (API)- An interface implemented by a software program to enable interaction with other software, much in the same way that a user interface facilitates interaction between humans and computers.

App Store- A digital distribution platform for iPhone® mobile apps developed and maintained by Apple Inc. Users can visit the App Store® for example, to browse and download apps developed by Apple.

Archive (verb)- Systematic transfer to alternate storage media of digital data of continuing value that is no longer required to be immediately accessible. Often stored on Computer Output to Laser Disk (COLD) systems.

Archives (noun)- Records and digital assets that have been identified as being needed for future legal, evidentiary, or historical value. These are permanently preserved in the context of their creation as evidence of action, decision, and transaction. "Archives" also refers to the department or institution entrusted with this task.

Bandwidth- The volume of information per unit time that a computer, person, or transmission medium can handle.

Big Data- Information assets that exist in high-volume, -variety, and –velocity and require innovative analytics to extract intelligent information that result in improved decision-making.

Blog (also Web Log)- A chronological and topic-oriented collection of entries posted on a web page. Typically, blogs communicate an author's point of view and solicit feedback in the form of comments which can be posted with the blog.

BPM- See Business Process Management.

Bring Your Own Device (BYOD)- A policy that enables employees to use their personal devices at home or in the office for work purposes.

Browser- See Internet Browser.

Business Applications- Software programs used to solve business needs such as word processing, accounting, or customer relationship management.

Business Intelligence (BI)- A technology for analysis of information contained in structured data. It is the structured counter-part to content analytics.

Business Process Management (BPM)- Refers to aligning processes with an organization's strategic objectives, designing, and implementing process-centric tools or architectures, and determining measurement systems for effective process management.

CEM- See Customer Experience Management

Channel- A communication medium to output content. It could be via the web, printed materials, video, CD-ROM, etc.

Chat (also Instant Messaging or IM)- Real-time instant messaging and other forms of chat within the context of an overall topic, website, or meeting space.

Cloud Computing ("The Cloud")- A metaphor inspired by the cloud symbol used to represent the Internet in flow charts and diagrams, Cloud computing describes the disruptive transformation of IT toward a service-based economy, driven by economic, technological, and cultural conditions.

Collaboration Software- Programs that link processes and individuals across different locations and time zones to create an environment where team members work together to share ideas, experiences, and knowledge.

Collaborative Workspace (or "Conference")- A shared workspace in a connected environment where users can collaborate and work together even when separated by geography. Users can both store content in the workspace, as well as hold discussions.

Commenting- Adding online comments to social media to add value, including commenting on online documents, blogs, wikis, and more.

Compliance- Adherence to a body of regulations, government legislation, or standards (for example, ISO 9000).

Composite Applications- Model-driven development environments that rely on graphical process modeling tools to support direct interpretation of the models into executable code. The technical concept can be compared to mashups, however, composite applications use business sources of information, while mashups typically rely on web-based sources.

Conferencing- Real-time meetings between groups over the web. In organizations, these meetings facilitate the exchange of information as if all the users were in one room together, such as collaboration around presentations or spreadsheets, on white boards, and shared screens.

Connectors- In database management, a link or pointer between two data structures.

Content Analytics- A technology for analysis of information contained in content. It allows customers to optimize user experience by dynamically serving up content based on automatically created content relevance.

Content Lifecycle Management (CLM)- The combination of document management, records management, workflow, archiving, and imaging into a fully integrated solution to effectively manage the lifecycle of content, from creation through to archiving and eventual deletion.

Content Management- Storage, maintenance, and retrieval of HTML and XML documents and all related elements. Content management systems may be built on top of a native XML database and typically provide publishing capabilities to export content not only to the website, but to physical media and print.

Content Syndication (also Web Syndication)- A form of syndication that makes website content available to multiple sites, often in the form of web feeds delivering summaries of recently added or updated content.

Contextual Information (Collaboration)- Smaller services/objects that can be embedded in business applications.

Contextual Searching- Contextual search goes beyond searching on file name or key fields. It looks at the data within documents and records and supplies results based on the context of content.

Control- A program module or routine that enhances program functionality. A control can be as small as a button on a user interface or as large as a complicated forecasting algorithm. The term is often used with regard to user interface functions such as buttons, menus, and dialog boxes.

Converters- An application that converts data from one code to another.

Cross-Platform- Refers to developing for and/or running on more than one type of hardware platform. It implies two different processes. The first is programming source code that is compiled into different machine environments, each of which has to be supported separately. The second method is with the use of an interpreter such as the Java Virtual Machine.

Customer Experience Management (CEM)- A set of technologies that helps your organization offer the customer more than expected, reach new markets, and provide outstanding experiences across all digital touch-points. It includes the presentation, assembly, and interaction of your organization's information with your customer.

Customer Relationship Management (CRM)- Enterprise-wide software applications that allow companies to manage every aspect of their relationship with customers. The goal of these systems is to assist in building lasting customer relationships and to turn customer satisfaction into customer loyalty.

DAM- See Media Management.

Data Archiving- Data archiving offloads historic data from the online database and archives it for future access on a secure media.

Database- A collection of data arranged for ease and speed of search and retrieval.

Database Management Systems- Software packages that control the creation, maintenance, and use of a database.

Data Capture- A method of data input that requires no data entry. Specific devices are designed to capture data such as barcode readers or magnetic stripe readers (like on a credit card).

Data Center (also called Server Farm)- A collection of computer servers usually maintained by an enterprise to accomplish server needs far beyond the capability of one machine. Server farms often have backup servers, which can take over the function of primary servers in the event of a primary server failure.

Data Warehouse- A database designed to support decision making in an organization. Data from the production databases are copied to the data warehouse so that queries and analysis can be performed without disturbing the performance or the stability of the production systems.

Deep Web- Refers to World Wide Web content that is not part of the surface web, which is indexed by standard search engines. The Deep Web consists of content within organizations, behind firewalls and other security processes.

Desktop- The area of the monitor screen in a graphical user interface (GU I) against which icons and windows used to run applications appear.

Digital Asset- Describes any subdivision or collection of content g social collaboration tools within the enterprise.

Digital Media- The term encompasses a wide variety of content types: photos, graphics, audio files, video clips, Flash® animations, PDFs, PowerPoint files, and design layouts.

Discovery- A category of EIM offerings that helps organizations capture, combine, and transform data across information silos into formats that can be analyzed for deeper business insight.

Disposition- Final deletion of content when it reaches the end of its lifecycle. Disruptive Innovation or Technology— Used in business and technology, a disruptive technology or disruptive innovation is an innovation that creates a new market and value network, and eventually disrupts an existing market to displace an earlier technology there.

Document- A piece of work created with an application, such as by word processor. A computer file that is not an executable file and contains data for use by applications.

Document Management (DM)- Involves the capture and management of documents within an organization. The term traditionally implied the management of documents after they were scanned into the computer. Today, the term has become an umbrella under which document imaging, workflow and information retrieval fall.

Document Repository- A database that includes author, data elements, inputs, processes, outputs, and interrelationships.

ECM- See Enterprise Content Management.

ECM Applications- Applications usually tailored to address line-of-business problems or customized for specific vertical markets.

EDI– See Electronic Data Interchange.

EIM– See Enterprise Information Management.

Electronic Data Interchange (EDI) - A document standard that acts as common interface between two or more computer applications to better understand the document transmitted. EDI is commonly used by large organizations in e-commerce processes.

Electronic Digital Management System- In order to manage digital documents, systems created to allow users on a network to view, markup, and edit documents.

Email- One of the first and most popular uses for the Internet, email (electronic mail) is the exchange of computer-stored messages by telecommunication.

Email Management- The application of content lifecycle management to emails to manage the creation, archiving, storage, and disposition of email messages.

Enterprise Application- A computer program designed to perform specific functions, such as inventory control, accounting, payroll, material management, etc.

Enterprise Application Management (EAM)- As IT departments increasingly develop and maintain a variety of very personalized apps unique to each organization, EAM describes the management of a new set of tools that will be required to manage content inside the firewall within the web operating system environment.

Enterprise App Store- The enterprise equivalent to the Apple App Store® as a distribution platform, only maintained behind the firewall (or in a private Cloud).

Enterprise Content Management (ECM)- Systems that capture, store, retrieve, print, and disseminate digital content for use by the enterprise. Digital content includes pictures/ images, text, reports, video, audio, transactional data, catalog, and code.

Enterprise Information Management (EIM)- Enterprise Information Management can deliver a comprehensive software suite that encompasses the capture of information; the management of structure, unstructured, and application data; the exchange and presentation of information on both sides of the firewall; intelligent business processes and solutions; information applications that parallel ERP data and process; enterprise information architecture that enables enterprise applications as well as mobile, social, and Cloud; and Business Intelligence and analytics. Complete EIM consists of Enterprise Content Management (ECM), Business Process Management (BPM), Customer Experience Management (CEM), Information Exchange, and Discovery.

Enterprise Resource Planning (ERP)- Any software system designed to support and automate the business processes of medium and large businesses. This may include manufacturing, distribution, personnel, project management, payroll, and financials. ERP systems are accounting-oriented information systems for identifying and planning the enterprise-wide resources needed to take, make, distribute, and account for customer orders.

Entity Extraction- An entity extractor locates and extracts places, people, organizations, and more. Controlled vocabularies and linguistic rules are used to identify and extract all occurrences of an entity type. Entity types can include product names, company names, proper names, geographic locations, dates, times, and more.

Exabyte (EB)- The exabyte is a multiple of the unit byte for digital information storage. 1 exabyte is 1,000 PB. The unit symbol for the terabyte is EB.

Firewall- A firewall is a part of a computer system or network that is designed to block unauthorized access while permitting authorized communications.

Forums- Online discussion forums in which users post "articles" to forums organized around a topic, typically in question and answer format resembling an offline discussion

Gigabyte (GB)- The gigabyte is a multiple of the unit byte for digital information storage. One gigabyte is 1,000 MB or one thousand million bytes. The unit symbol for the gigabyte is GB or Gbyte.GPS or Global Positioning System—A satellite-based navigation system maintained by the US government that provides location and time information anywhere on the Earth, which is freely accessible by anyone with a GPS receiver.

Hosting- Maintaining a computer system and its applications at a third-party site.

Hypertext Markup Language (HTML)- A structured document format in which elements (commonly referred to as "tags") are embedded in the text. Tags are used for presentation formatting to delimit text which is to appear in a special place or style. HTML is an extension of SGML.

Hypertext Transfer Protocol (HTTP)- The networking protocol that serves as the foundation of data communication for the World Wide Web.

Index- In data management, the most common method for keeping track of data on a disk. Indexes are directory listings maintained by the operating system, RDBMS, or the application. An index of files contains an entry for each file name and the location of the file. An index of records has an entry for each key field (for example, account number, or name) and the location of the record.

Information Exchange- A set of solutions that allows people inside and outside an organization to efficiently and securely exchange conversational data while the actual organization maintains compliancy. This data includes anything from electronic faxes and cloud services to Electronic Data Interchange (EDI) and large managed-file transfers.

Information Governance- The set of multi-disciplinary structures, policies, procedures, processes, and controls implemented to manage information on all media in such a way that it supports the enterprise's immediate and long-term regulatory, legal, risk, environmental, and operational requirements.

Instant Messaging (IM)- See Chat.

Integrated Development Environment (IDE)- A software application consisting of a source code editor, compiler and/or an interpreter, build automation tools, and a debugger for computer programmers.

Internet- An interconnected system of networks that connects computers around the world via the TCP/IP protocol.

Internet Browser- The program that serves as the client front end to the World Wide Web.

Intranet- An "internal Internet" configured behind a firewall to connect individuals and departments. A privately maintained computer network that can be accessed only by authorized persons, especially members or employees of the organization that owns it.

Java- A programming language that originated at Sun Microsystems (has merged into Oracle®) with the purpose of allowing application developers "write once, run anywhere". It is currently one of the most popular programming languages in use for client/server web applications.

Keyword- A term used as a keyword to retrieve documents in an information system such as a catalog or a search engine.

Knowledge Management (KM)- An umbrella term for making more efficient use of the human knowledge that exists within an organization. The major focus is to identify and gather content from documents, reports, and other sources and to be able to search that content for meaningful relationships. Knowledge Management also concerns the ability to identify high-value individuals within an organization.

Knowledge Worker- One who works primarily with information or one who develops and uses knowledge in the workplace.

Learning Management Systems- A software application to administer, document, track, and report training programs, classroom, and online events, e-learning programs, and the associated content.

Mainframes- Computers used mainly by large organizations for critical applications, typically bulk data processing such as census, industry and consumer statistics, enterprise resource planning (ERP), and financial transaction processing. Media Management (also known as Digital Asset Management, Brand Asset Management or Media Asset

Management- Media Management consists of the ingestion, storage, management, retrieval, production, and distribution of digital assets.

Metadata- Sometimes known as data about the data, metadata describes and provides context for content.

Mobile App- Mobile apps, also called mobile applications, are software applications that run on smartphones and tablet computers. Mobile apps are discreet programs designed to solve a specific purpose with a tether to back-office servers or new types of ultra availability via "app content servers". They are designed to perform at the touch of a smart screen, enabling users to do things that begin to exceed what is possible with a conventional PC connected to the Internet.

Mobile Device- Includes personal digital assistants, smartphones, and tablet computers. A mobile device is a small hand-held computing device typically operated with a touch screen or miniature keyboard.

Multimedia- Integration of text, voice, video, images, or some combination of these types of information. Also called Rich Media.
Online—Connected to or accessible via a computer or computer network. Typically refers to being connected to the Internet or other remote service.

Operating System- A computer's master control program that manages its internal functions controls its operation. An operating system provides commonly used functions and a uniform, consistent means for all software applications to access the computer's resources. Windows® and UNIX® are operating systems.

Optical Character Recognition (OCR)- Recognition of printed or written characters by computer. Each page of text is converted to a digital image using a scanner and OCR is then applied to the image to produce a text file.

Permissions- Management of who can access a computer or network. The Access Control List (ACL) is the set of data associated with a file, directory, or other resource that defines the permissions that users, groups, processes, or devices have for accessing it.

Petabyte (PB)- The petabyte is a multiple of the unit byte for digital information storage. 1 petabyte is 1,000 TB. The unit symbol for the terabyte is PB.

Platform- The term originally concerned only CPU or computer hardware, but it also refers to software-only environments. A messaging or groupware platform implies one or more programming interfaces that email, calendaring, and other client programs are written to in order to communicate with the services provided by the server.

Portal- Within the enterprise, software that provides access via a web browser into all of an organization's information assets and applications. Portals provide a variety of services including web searching, news, white and yellow pages directories, free email, discussion groups, online shopping, and links to other sites.

Process Management- The automation of business processes using a rule-based expert system that invokes the appropriate tools and supplies necessary information, checklists, examples, and status reports to the user.

Records Management (RM)- Refers to the creation, retention, and scheduled destruction of an organization's paper and film documents. Email and computer-generated content also fall into the RM domain.

Redundancy- The duplication of critical components of a system with the intention of increasing reliability of the system, usually in the case of a backup or fail-safe.

Relational Database- A database in which all the data and relations between them are organized in tables. A relational database allows the definition of data structures, storage and retrieval operations, and integrity constraints.

Reporting- Metrics-focused analysis of user behavior (unlike web analytics, which is experience driven).

Repository- Think of this as the enterprise library—it is a location for storage, often for safety or preservation within the enterprise. It is a trusted source of content that can be searched and retrieved.

Rich Content or Media- See Digital Media.

Rights and Permissions- Identifies the circumstances under which a particular asset may be used. For instance, indicates who legally owns the asset, in what mediums it may be used (web, print, TV) and the financial liabilities incurred to include the asset.

Scalability- Ability to reach high-performance levels.

Search- A technology focused on user-driven information retrieval based on statistical occurrence of search keywords in text-based content.

Secure Socket Layer (SSL)- A protocol that encrypts information over the Internet. Many payment websites use SSL to protect users' personal information.

Semantics- A term used often in the context of the Semantic Web, which typically refers to RDF-based modeling of online user experience. In the context of content analytics, the term semantics is sometimes used to refer to the connotation of information contained in content or what is the information about.

Semantic Search- Searches data beyond just word recognition but seeks to understand the intent of the user and the contextual meaning of words as it searches.

Sentiment Analysis- Sentiment analysis detects the tones in content, identifying and displaying opinions that are expressed in clusters of sentences, phrases, or entities.

Server- A server computer, sometimes called an enterprise server, is a computer system that provides essential services across a network, to private users inside a large organization or to public users in the Internet. Enterprise servers are known to be very fault tolerant, for even a short-term failure can cost more than purchasing and installing the system.

Short Message Service (SMS)—Text messaging sent using this service, which allows a short alphanumeric message (160 alphanumeric characters) to be sent for display on a mobile or cell phone.

Smartphone- A mobile phone that offers advanced, PC-like functionality such as email, Internet access, calendaring, and viewing capabilities, along with a built-in full keyboard or external USB keyboard and VGA connector.

Smart Process Applications- Application software that supports people-intensive business activities that are very changeful, highly flexible, and loosely structured. These packaged apps incorporate current best practices and can easily be updated to reflect continuous collaborative business process improvements.

Social Media- Media designed to be disseminated through social interaction, created using highly accessible and scalable publishing techniques. Social media uses Internet and Web-based technologies to transform broadcast media monologues (one-to-many) into social media dialogues (many-to-many).

Social Networks- Websites that facilitate connections of people based on self-generated user profiles. Facebook.com and LinkedIn.com are examples of social networking sites.

Social Workplace- The social workplace uses Web 2.0 technologies to connect people with their peers and with critical content and information. Also referred to as Enterprise 2.0.

Social Software- Describes software programs that lets users leverage the Internet to interact, collaborate, and communicate. Examples include social sites like Facebook®, Flickr®, and YouTube®, along with ecommerce sites Amazon.com and eBay®. The terms Enterprise 2.0 (E2.0) and Web 2.0 are also used to describe this style of software inside the enterprise (for organizations) and outside of the enterprise (for individual consumers), respectively.

Software- The programs, routines, and symbolic languages that control the functioning of a computer and direct its operation. Software as a Service (SaaS)—This type of computing delivers a single application through the browser to a large number of customers using a multi-tenant architecture.

Structured Data- Data that resides in fixed fields within a record or file. Relational databases and spreadsheets are examples of structured data.

Tablet- A tablet computer, or tablet, is a mobile computer that is larger than a mobile phone or personal digital assistant (PDA) but smaller than a laptop, with a flat screen that is operated through touch and an onscreen virtual keyboard.

Tagging- Enables users to assign keywords to content such as blogs, documents, forums, and video files without following predefined terms.

Taxonomies- The classification of data into groups or categories. Terabyte (TB)—A unit of computer memory or data storage capacity equal to one trillion bytes or 1,000 gigabytes (GB).

Touchscreen- A visual display that can detect the presence and location of a touch within the display area.

Transaction- Synonymous with a specific business application, such as order entry, invoice information capture, etc. To create, change, or display business information in an enterprise application, users have to call certain transactions in the system. See also—Transactional Data.

Transactional Data- Orders, purchases, changes, additions, and deletions are typical business transactions stored in the computer. Transactions update one or more master files and serve as both an audit trail and history for future analyses. Ad hoc queries are also a type of transaction but are usually not saved.

Transport Layer Security (TLS)- TLS and its predecessor, Secure Sockets Layer (SSL), are cryptographic protocols which are designed to provide communication security over the Internet.

Tweet- See Micro-blogging.Unstructured Data—Data that does not reside in fixed locations. Free-form text in a word processing document is a typical example.

User-Generated Content (UGC)- Refers to different types of content or digital media produced by end-users and made publicly available. Also known as consumer-generated media (CGM) or user-created content (UCC).

User Interface (UI)- A user interface is the system people use to interact with a computer or other device. Typically, a system may expose several user interfaces to serve different kinds of users.

User Profiles- A collection of personal data associated to a specific user typically within an online community or corporate intranet. Profiles often contain a picture, relevant personal and professional information including knowledge, skills, abilities, department, projects, roles, other contacts and links.

Video- The technology of electronically capturing, recording, processing, storing, transmitting, and reconstructing a sequence of still images representing scenes in motion. Virtualization—An umbrella term that describes software technologies that improve portability, manageability, and compatibility of applications by encapsulating them from the underlying operating system on which they are executed.

Virtual Private Networks (VPNs)- Allows remote users of a network to access a central organizational network and its data through an authentication process like a login.

Web- A shorthand way to refer to the World Wide Web and possibly its complementing technologies. For example, a web authoring tool might be used to create documents that contain HyperText Markup Language (HTML).

Web 1.0- Began with the release of the World Wide Web to the public in 1991, and is the general term that has been created to describe the web before the web 2.0 phenomenon.

Web 2.0- Refers to web-based applications that enable new and emergent ways of searching, presenting and consuming information using the internet. Web 2.0 is characterized by predominantly by technologies that use the web as a platform for collaboration and communications. The term also covers applications that are participatory in nature, lightweight, and easy to deploy (APIs and mashups, for example) and are available online as a service.

Web Analytics- A technology for user behavior analysis (click-stream analysis). It allows customers to generate reports on user behavior on the site and to optimize user experience by dynamically serving up relevant content based on metadata (=recommendations).

Web Browser- See Internet Browser.

Web Content- The content featured as part of the user experience on websites, including text, video, images, sounds, and animations.

Web Content Management (WCM)- Systems designed to drive websites by separating content from presentation and providing the following capabilities—capacity planning, site design/layout, look/feel navigation, content development, production, delivery, session tracking, and site evolution.

Web Services- Web Services refer to the web-based provision of services via open interfaces. This enables the integration of "third-party" applications with a website, giving rise to new sites or mashups.

Website- A collection of related web pages with supporting images, videos, or other digital assets that share a common domain name or IP address in an Internet Protocol-based network.

Widget- Highly portable web applications that allow non-technical users to add dynamic content or functionality to web pages. User-friendly Webweb sites are increasing their use of widgets to simplify and enhance the Internet user's experience.

Wi-Fi- A very high bandwidth connection. A Wi-Fi-enabled device such as a personal computer, video game console, mobile phone, MP3 player, or PDA can connect to the Internet within range of a wireless network connected to the Internet.

Wiki- A collection of articles that can be entered, edited, linked, and expanded by any authorized user. Wikis facilitate the open sharing of knowledge on a designated web page. Workflow—Using applications and technology to automate the execution ofeach phase in a business process.

World Wide Web (WWW)- An HTML-based Internet system developed at the European Center for Nuclear Research (CERN) in Geneva. Also relates to the complete set of documents residing on all Internet servers that use the HTTP protocol. The web is accessible to users via a simple point-and-click system.

Zettabyte (ZB)- A multiple of the unit byte for digital information storage. One zettabyte is 1,000 EB (exabytes) or 1000 bytes.

BIBLIOGRAPHY

Aberdeen Group, *"Customer Experience Management: Using the Power of Analytics to Optimize Customer Delight"*, Research Preview, Aberdeen Group, *http://www. brandchannel.com/images/papers/531_aberdeen_group_wp_customer_experience_ management_0911.pdf* (accessed 15 Feb. 2013).

Alexander Pope, *An Essay on Criticism,* W. Lewis, London, 1711.

Andrea Coombes, *"Don't You Dare Email this Story"*, MarketWatch, The Wall Street Journal (17 May 2009), *http://online.wsj.com/article/SB124252211780027326.html* (accessed 3 Dec. 2012).

Andrew Bartels and Connie Moore, *"Smart Process Applications Fill A Big Business Gap"*, Forrester, November 5, 2012 *http://bps.opentext.com/resources/Smart_Process_ Application.pdf* (accessed 2 Sep. 2013).

Andrew Bartels and Connie Moore, et al., *"Smart Process Applications Fill A Big Business Gap"*, Forrester Research, *http://www.forrester.com/Smart+Process+Applications+Fill+A+ Big+Business+Gap/fulltext/-/E-RES77442* (accessed 2 Apr. 2013)

Andrew Bartels and Connie Moore, *"The next frontier for software: Smart process appli-cations fill a big gap"*, KMWorld, 30 Oct. 2012, *http://www.kmworld.com/Articles/Editorial/ Features/The-next-frontier-for-software-Smart-process-applications-fill-a-big-gap-85806. aspx* (accessed 15 Mar. 2013).

Andrew Conry Murray, *"Ease the Pain of E-Discovery"*, Global CIO, Information Week (30 May 2009), *http://www.informationweek.com/global-cio/legal/ease-the-pain-of-e-discov- ery/217700666* (accessed 30 Jan. 2013)

Andrew McAfee and Erik Brynjolfsson, *"Big Data: The Management Revolution"*, Harvard Business Review (2012), *http://hbr.org/2012/10/big-data-the-management-revolution/ar/ pr* (accessed 5 Nov. 2012).

Andrew McAfee, *"Big Data, Bright Future"*, on24.com (2012), *http://event.on24.com/view/ presentation/flash/EventConsoleNG.html* (accessed 5 Nov. 2012).

Alan Weintraub and Craig Le Clair et al., *"The Forrester Wave™: Multichannel Capture, Q3, 2012: Vendors Move Toward Mature Service Offerings"*, Forrester Research, *http:// www.forrester.com/The+Forrester+Wave+Multichannel+Capture+Q3+2012/fulltext/-/E- RES78702* (accessed 14 Jan. 2013).

AIIM White Paper, *"Making the Most of Mobile – Content on the Move 2011"* *http:// campaigns.opentext.com/forms/FY12-Q3-AM-ALL-ECMC-IG-Mobility* (accessed 19 Nov. 2012).

Ben Hicks, *"Increase sales by integrating social media and email marketing"*, Signal, *http://blog.signalhq.com/2013/07/08/increase-sales-by-integrating-social-media-and- email-marketing/* (accessed 10 Jul. 2013).

Bill Guptill and Alex Bakker et al., Saugatuck Technology, *"2012 Cloud Business Solution Survey Global N=228"* (February 2012) *http://saugatucktechnology.com/research/browse-research-library-by-category/1041ssr-2012-cloud-business-solution-survey-summary-data-report.html* (accessed 3 Mar. 2012).

Bill O'Kane and Andrew White, et al., *"Predicts 2012: Information Governance and MDM Programs Gain Traction"*, Gartner Inc., *http://www.gartner.com/id=1856616* (accessed 12 Jul. 2013).

Bob Hayes, *"Is the Importance of Customer Experience Overinflated?"*, CustomerThink.com, *http://www.customerthink.com/blog/is_the_importance_of_customer_experience_overinflated* (accessed 30 Sep. 2012).

Chetan Sharma, *"2013 Mobile Industry Predictions Survey"*, Chetan Sharma Consulting (Jan. 2013), *http://www.chetansharma.com/MobilePredictions2013.htm* (accessed 7 May 2013).

Chetan Sharma, *"Competition and the Evolution of Mobile Markets – A Study of Competition in Global Mobile Markets, A Working Paper"*, Chetan Sharma Consulting (2011), *http://chetansharma.com/mobilecompetition.htm* (accessed 7 Feb. 2012).

CNME, *"Big Data Deserves IT's Attention"*, CNME Online (Aug. 2012), *http://www.cnmeonline.com/insight/big-data-deserves-its-attention/* (accessed 18 Jan. 2012).

Dale Carnegie, *"Dale Carnegie Quotes"*, Thinkexist.com, *http://thinkexist.com/quotation/when_dealing_with_people-remember_you_are_not/171139.html* (accessed 30 Apr. 2013).

David Roe, *"State of the ECM Industry 2010: Enterprises Still Battling Content Chaos"*, CMS Wire (May 2010), *http://www.cmswire.com/cms/enterprise-cms/state-of-the-ecm-industry-2010-enterprises-still-battling-content-chaos-007576.php* (accessed 6 Nov. 2012)

Debra Lavoy, *"Steve Jobs Did NOT Predict the Future. He Invented It"*, CMSWire, *http://www.cmswire.com/cms/social-business/steve-jobs-did-not-predict-the-future-he-invented-it-018192.php* (accessed 5 Apr. 2013).

Doculabs, *"Quantifying Return on Investment for ECM: A Methodology"*, Doculabs.com (2009), *http://www.doculabs.com/wp-content/uploads/downloads/2011/12/A-Doculabs-White-Paper-Quantifying-ROI-for-ECM1.pdf* (accessed 10 Oct. 2012).

Doug Miles, *"Information Governance: records, risks, and retention in the litigation age"*, AIIM, *http://www.aiim.org/Research-and-Publications/Research/Industry-Watch/InfoGov-2013* (accessed 20 Mar. 2013).

Fabrizio Biscotti and Paolo Malinverno et al., *"Market Trends: Multi-enterprise/B2B Infrastructure Market, Worldwide, 2010-2015, 1Q11 Update"*, Gartner Inc., February 2011, *http://www.gartner.com/id=1545115* (accessed 23 Mar. 2011).

Fabrizio Biscotti and Yefim V. Natis et al., *"Gartner Forecast: Platform as a Service, Worldwide, 2010-2015, 3Q11 Update"*,14 September 2011, Gartner Inc., *http://www. gartner.com/id=1792219* (accessed 29 Oct. 2011).

Forbes Insights, *"Managing Information in the Enterprise: Perspectives for Business Leaders"*, Forbes Insight (2009), *http://fm.sap.com/data/UPLOAD/files/Managing%20 Information%20in%20the%20Enterprise%20Perspectives%20for%20Business%20 Leaders.pdf* (accessed 24 Oct. 2012).

Gartner Inc., *"Gartner Says Solving 'Big Data' Challenge Involves More than Just Managing Volumes of Data"*, Newsroom, Gartner.com (Jun. 2011), *http://www.gartner. com/newsroom/id/1731916* (accessed 15 Nov. 2012).

Gartner Inc., *"Enterprise Resource Planning (ERP)"*, IT Glossary, Gartner.com, *http:// www.gartner.com/it-glossary/enterprise-resource-planning-erp/* (accessed 2 Dec. 2012).

Gartner Inc., *"Enterprise Content Management (ECM)"*, IT Glossary, Gartner.com, *http:// www.gartner.com/it-glossary/enterprise-content-management-ecm/* (accessed 2 Oct. 2012).

Gartner Inc., *"Business Process Management"*, IT Glossary, Gartner.com, *http://www. gartner.com/it-glossary/business-process-management-bpm/* (2 Oct. 2012).

Gartner Inc., *"Gartner Identifies the Top 10 Strategic Technology Trends for 2013"*, Newsroom, Gartner.com, *http://www.gartner.com/it/page.jsp?id=2209615&source id=1-2973570319* (accessed 12 Nov 2012).

Gartner Inc., *"Customer Experience Management"*, IT Glossary, *http://www.gartner.com/ it-glossary/customer-experience-management-cem/* (2 Oct. 2012).

Geoffrey Moore, *"Systems of Engagement and the Future of Enterprise IT: A Sea Change in Enterprise IT"*, AIIM, *http://www.aiim.org/futurehistory* (accessed 10 Jan. 2012).

Go-Globe, *"60 Seconds - Things that Happen on Internet Every Sixty Seconds [Infographic]"* (1 Jun. 2011), Blog, Go-Gulf.com, *http://www.go-gulf.com/blog/60- seconds/* (accessed 7 Oct. 2013).

Goldfire Blog, InventionMachine.com, *http://inventionmachine.com/the-Invention- Machine-Blog/bid/79363/The-Deep-Web-Semantic-Search-Takes-Innovation-to-New- Depths* (accessed 5 Oct. 2012).

Hackmageddon.com, *"Cyber Attacks Timelines and Statistics"*, *http://hackmageddon. com/* (accessed 10 May 2013).

Health Data Management Staff, *"The Four Horsemen of Cyber Security Threats in 2013"*, Information Management, *http://www.information-management.com/news/the- four-horsemen-of-cyber-security-threats-in-2013-10023736-1.html* (accessed 17 Jan, 2013).

Help Net Security, *"Cybergangs embracing crimeware over social engineering"*, *http:// www.net-security.org/secworld.php?id=14343* (accessed 24 Feb. 2013).

Hendrikse, Rene, *"How to Introduce Bring-Your-Own-Device Schemes in the Enterprise Computer Weekly UK, 2013"*, *http://www.computerweekly.com/opinion/Bring-Your-Own-Device-in-the-Enterprise* (accessed 14 Jun. 2013).

IBM, *"Big Data at the Speed of Business"*, Big Data Hub, *http://www.ibmbigdatahub.com/video/big-data-speed-business* (accessed 8 Jul. 2013).

IBM, *"How SOA can ease your move to Cloud Computing"*, IBM.com, *http://www-01.ibm.com/software/solutions/soa/newsletter/nov09/article_soaandcloud.html* (accessed 14 Apr. 2013).

Information Management, *"The Four Horsemen of Cyber Security Threats in 2013"*, Forecast, Information Management.com, 27 Dec. 2012, http://www.information-management.com/news/the-four-horsemen-of-cyber-security-threats-in-2013-10023736-1.html (accessed 6 Jan. 2013).

Invention Machine, *"The Deep Web: Semantic Search Takes Innovation to New Depths"*, Goldfire Blog, InventionMachine.com, *http://inventionmachine.com/the-Invention-Machine-Blog/bid/79363/The-Deep-Web-Semantic-Search-Takes-Innovation-to-New-Depths* (accessed 5 Oct. 2012).

Invention Machine, *"The Deep Web: Semantic Search Takes Innovation to New Depths"*, Ravi Sawhney, *"Broken Guitar Has United Playing the Blues to the Tune of $180 Million"*, FastCompany, *http://www.fastcompany.com/1320152/broken-guitar-has-united-playing-blues-tune-180-million*, 30 Jul. 2009 (accessed 5 Apr. 2013).

invodo, *"ComScore"*, invodo.com, *http://www.invodo.com/resources/statistics/* (accessed 21 Mar. 2013).

James Kirk, *"New Opportunities In New Information Flows"*, Digital Transformation, *http://digital-transformation.yourbusinesschannel.com/2012/08/new-opportunities-in-new-information-flows/* (accessed 30 Mar. 2013).

Johnny Tam and Joshua But, *"It's tough to trace hackers, says internet security expert"*, South China Morning Post, (28 Jun. 2013), *http://www.scmp.com/news/hong-kong/article/1269775/its-tough-trace-hackers-says-internet-security-expert* (accessed 5 Jul. 2013).

KPMG, *Business Implication of Cloud*, KPMG.com, *http://www.kpmg.com/global/en/topics/cloud-computing/pages/default.aspx* (accessed 16 May 2013).

Larry A. Bettino, *"Transforming Big Data Challenges Into Opportunities"*, Information Management, April 18, 2012, *http://www.information-management.com/newsletters/big-data-ROI-IBM-Walmart-USPS-10022342-1.html* (accessed 22 Apr. 2013)

Les Rechan, *"Big data' could help solve Canada's productivity problem"*, The Financial Post, *http://business.financialpost.com/2012/08/13/big-data-could-help-solve-canadas-productivity-problem/* (accessed 4 Feb. 2013).

Leslie Owens, *"Semantic Technology in the Enterprise"*, Forrester Research, *http://blogs.forrester.com/leslie_owens/12-04-18-semantic_technology_in_the_enterprise* (April 2012).

Lorrie Luellig, *"A Modern Governance Strategy for Data Disposal"*, CIO Insight, *http://www.cioinsight.com/it-management/inside-the-c-suite/a-modern-governance-strategy-for-data-disposal.html/* (accessed 12 Jul 2013).

Mann, Stephanie, *"Mobile App Development Trends in 2012 and beyond"*, *http://searchsoa.techtarget.com/feature/Mobile-app-development-trends-in-2012-and-beyond* (accessed 8 Feb. 2013)..

Mark P. McDonald and Dave Aron, *"Amplifying the Enterprise: The 2012 CIO Agenda"*, Gartner Inc., *http://www.gartner.com/id=1901814* (accessed 5 Apr. 2013).

Mark McDonald, *"2012 CIO Agenda"*, Gartner Inc., *http://www.gartner.com/technology/cio/cioagenda.jsp* (accessed 8 Oct. 2012).

Mark Raskino and Jorge Lopez, *"CEO Survey 2012: The Year of Living Hesitantly"*, Gartner Inc., *http://www.gartner.com/id=1957515, 21 Mar. 2012* (accessed 4 Apr. 2013).

Matthew J. Schwartz, *"Cybercrime Attacks, Costs Escalate"*, Information Week, (8 Oct. 2012), *http://www.informationweek.com/security/attacks/cybercrime-attacks-costs-escalating/240008658* (accessed 5 Mar 2013).

Michael Biddick, *"Research: The Big Data Management Challenge"*, Information Week, *http://reports.informationweek.com/abstract/81/8766/business-intelligence-and-information-management/research-the-big-data-management-challenge.html* (accessed 2 Mar. 2013).

Michael E. Porter, *"Competitive Advantage: Creating and Sustaining Superior Performance"* (New York: The Free Press, 1985).

Michele Goetz and Henry Peyret, et al., *"Data Governance Equals Business Opportunity. No, Really"*, Forrester Research, *http://www.forrester.com/Data+Governance+Equals+Business+Opportunity+No+Really/fulltext/-/E-RES83342* (accessed 20 May 2013).

Mikako Kitagawa, *Principal Analyst Gartner, Gartner Inc.*, *http://www.gartner.com/AnalystBiography?authorId=17156* (accessed 14 Jun. 2013).

Mike Lynch, *"Data Wars: Unlocking the Information Goldmine"*, Business, BBC News, *http://www.bbc.co.uk/news/business-17682304* (accessed 4 Oct. 2012).

Mike Miliard, *"Vampire data and 3 other cyber security threats for 2013"*, (31 Dec. 2012), Government Health IT, *http://www.govhealthit.com/news/vampire-data-and-3-other-cyber-security-threats-2013* (accessed 12 Oct. 2012).

Mobile Marketing Watch, *"Major Mobile Trends Show Global Mobile Industry Is Now the Fastest Growing Market in the World"*, MobileMarketingWatch.com, *http://www.mobilemarketingwatch.com/major-mobile-trends-show-global-mobile-industry-is-now-the-fastest-growing-market-in-the-world-16840/* (accessed 3 Jun. 2013).

OpenText and IDG Research, *"Unleashing the Power of Information"*, IDG Research, *http://resources.idgenterprise.com/original/AST-0079214_OpenText_li_0115_FINAL.pdf* (accessed 1 Mar. 2013).

Osterman Research, *"File Archiving: The Next Big Thing or Just Big?"*, An Osterman Research White Paper (Dec. 2012), SlideShare.com, http://www.slideshare.net/ emcacademics/analyst-report-osterman-research-file-archiving-the-next-big-thing-or-just-big (accessed 6 Jan. 2013).

Paul Krill, *"The Cloud-SOA Connection"*, InfoWorld *http://www.infoworld.com/d/cloud-computing/cloud-soa-connection-724* (accessed 8 Jul. 2013).

Ray Paquet, *"Technology Trends You Can't Afford to Ignore"*, Gartner Inc., http://www. gartner.com/it/content/1503500/1503515/january_19_tech_trends_you_cant_afford_to_ ignore_rpaquet.pdf (accessed 10 Nov. 2012).

Rick Burnes, *"Study Shows Business Blogging Leads to 55% More Website Visitors"*, Hubspot, *http://blog.hubspot.com/blog/tabid/6307/bid/5014/Study-Shows-Business-Blogging-Leads-to-55-More-Website-Visitors.aspx* (accessed 15 Apr. 2013). Definition and image courtesy of Wikipedia.

Sam Shead, *"Cloud decisions are no lon* SEJ, *"The Growth of Social Media: An Infographic"*, Search Engine Journal, Infographic Series, Social Media, Infographics, Spotlight (30 Aug. 2011), *http://www.searchenginejournal.com/the-growth-of-social-media-an-infographic/32788/* (accessed 10 Dec. 2012).

Stephen Pritchard, *"How to manage unstructured data for business benefit"*, ComputerWeekly.com, *http://www.computerweekly.com/feature/How-to-manage-unstructured-data-for-business-benefit*, Dec 2012 (accessed 5 Jan. 2013).

Temkin Group Research, *"The ROI of Customer Experience"*, Temkin Group (Mar. 2012).

The Marketing Bit, *"Online for One Minute"*, TheMarketingBit.com, *http://www. themarketingbit.com/infographics/online-for-one-minute/* (accessed 13 Oct. 2012).

William Bruce Cameron, *"Informal Sociology: A Casual Introduction to Sociological Thinking"* (New York: Random House,1966).

Wikipedia, *"Social Media"*, Wikipedia.com, *http://en.wikipedia.org/wiki/Social_media* (accessed 16 Apr. 2013) "44 million-plus tweets per day in 2009".

INDEX

V

Variety, 12

Velocity, 9, 11, 13, 107, 113, 144, 193, 224

Video, 3, 23, 44, 78, 81, 83, 90, 96, 108, 117, 134, 193

Volume, 11, 12, 18, 19, 26, 149

Virtual Private Network (VPN), 163

W

Web 2.0, 96

Web Content Management (WCM), 18, 19, 187

Web Services, 74, 205

Widget, 133, 136

Wiki, 13, 87, 140, 144, 183, 232

Workflow, 51, 57, 59, 60, 62, 64, 67, 70, 71, 74, 90, 107, 171, 180, 207

Y

YouTube, 42, 43, 78, 79, 234

Z

Zettabyte, 4, 232